... Now They Don't

I have written this personal account of what it was like to live and operate in a nuclear submarine in the Cold War [against the Soviet Union] and in a hot one [the Falklands War 1982]. I wrote it specifically for my family so that they would understand what I did and what life was like as a Commanding Officer in a submarine.

"Of all the branches of men in the forces there is none which shows more devotion and faces grimmer perils than the submariners"

Sir Winston Churchill

About the Author

Rear Admiral Roger Charles Lane-Nott CB is a former Royal Navy officer who served as Commander Operations and Flag Officer Submarines (FOSM).

He was educated at Pangbourne College and Britannia Royal Naval College. Lane-Nott joined the Royal Navy in 1963 and was appointed Commanding Officer the submarine HMS WALRUS in 1974, of the submarine HMS SWIFTSURE in 1976 and of the submarine HMS SPLENDID in 1979. As Commander of HMS SPLENDID he saw action during the Falklands War and was Mentioned in Despatches. He went on to be Commander of the 3rd Submarine Squadron in 1983, Assistant Director of Defence Concepts at the Ministry of Defence in 1986 and Commanding Officer of the frigate HMS COVENTY in 1989. After that he became Commander 1st Frigate Squadron in 1990, Chief of Staff, Submarines in 1992 and Commander Operations and Flag Officer Submarines (FOSM) in 1993 before retiring in 1996.

In retirement he became the FIA Formula One Race Director running all F1 races worldwide and then Secretary of the British Racing Drivers' Club.

Rear Admiral Roger Lane-Nott CB

First published in the United Kingdom
by Roger Lane-Nott 2021

Copyright © Roger Lane-Nott 2015

Roger Lane-Nott has asserted his moral
right to be identified as the author of this
work in accordance with the Copyright,
Designs and Patents Act, 1988.
All Rights Reserved. No part of this publication
may be reproduced in any form or by any means
without the written permission of the author.

A catalogue record for this book is
available from the British Library.

ISBN: 978-1-7398283-0-1

Typeset in Minion Variable by Toby Vintcent

Dedicated to the amazing, thoroughly professional submariners I served with and those in the wider Submarine Service. They are the best of the best.

To my wife, Roisin, to whom I owe so much.

To my children, Antonia, Patrick and Olivia and grandchildren, Jake, Eleanor, Buzz, Lara, Bibi, Henry, Orla, Elliot, Wolfie, Nuala, Imogen, Jemima and Ted – the apples of my eye!

NOW YOU SEE US...

ROGER LANE-NOTT

FORENDS

Contents

PROLOGUE	Is this the start of World War III?	13

PART 1

Introduction	The Cold War Background	23
Chapter One	What is a nuclear submarine?	33
Chapter Two	Living in a nuclear submarine	43
Chapter Three	Time to go	59
Chapter Four	Time to dive	82
Chapter Five	A close shave – HMS CONQUEROR	94
Chapter Six	Casing Rattle	117
Chapter Seven	Getting in Close	127
Chapter Eight	Underwater Look	141
Chapter Nine	Missile Firing	150
Chapter Ten	Soviet Shotgun Submarine	159
Chapter Eleven	Is this the start of World War III?	170

PART 2

Chapter Twelve	Proceed with all Dispatch	189
Chapter Thirteen	Transit to the South Atlantic	195
Chapter Fourteen	On Station	210
Chapter Fifteen	Torpedo Evasion	213
Chapter Sixteen	Do we go inside the Falkland Sound?	218
Chapter Seventeen	Is this the Argentine Carrier Group?	222
Chapter Eighteen	Can we get the Carrier?	229
Chapter Nineteen	Break Contact or Nelsonian blind eye?	237
Chapter Twenty	False contacts and Belgrano sunk	240
Chapter Twenty One	Is it our turn now?	244
Chapter Twenty Two	Defects and their rectification	250
Chapter Twenty Three	Back to the fray	261
Chapter Twenty Four	Re-invasion starts	266
Chapter Twenty Five	Being bombed	270
Chapter Twenty Six	Withdrawing	278
Chapter Twenty Seven	Reflections from me and MEA Jim Knight	294
Epilogue	Visit to Russia in 1992	300
Appendix I	Naval career summary	315
Appendix II	History of HMS SPLENDID	339
Appendix III	HMS SPLENDID – Ship's Company 1982	343

PROLOGUE

IS THIS THE START OF WORLD WAR III?

'He's turning to starboard,' said leading sonar operator, Nick Slide. I looked at my watch. Soviet ballistic nuclear submarines [SSBN] often changed course according to a series of random numbers generated on the boat, not some pre-ordained plan. This was to retain an element of unpredictability and frustrate the likes of me [and HMS SPLENDID] who might be following him.

I had had several hours to get to know this Delta-class submarine and, perhaps, something of the man driving it. Perhaps he thought he was manoeuvring at random. He wasn't. There was a pattern and we had been working it out for a while. Patience provides its own rewards.

'Delta turning to starboard,' said the report from the sonar sound room at the noise in the Control Room.

'Quiet,' I said a little irritated.

According to our assessment of the pattern, a sort of long-phase zigzag, he should be turning to port.

We waited. Down on my left, the target analysis operators battered their keyboards, plotting the Delta's range and bearing.

'Target bearing 031°,' Course 211°. Range 5900 yards,' came the report. This meant he was heading straight towards us!

'Where is the Victor? 'I said impatient for an answer, asking about the second submarine – a Victor III-class Soviet attack boat [SSN] – that was escorting the ballistic Delta.

'Target remaining out to starboard. Bearing 085°. Range 9500 yards. Still on a course of 010°. Speed 7 knots,' came the reply.

'Keep a close eye on him and tell me if anything changes,' I replied.

Target analysis will give you a range and a bearing, but it cannot tell you the depth of the target. Soviets like to be at round numbers of metres. Therefore I always preferred a depth in feet that did not translate into a round number of metres – for example 100, 150 or 200 metres and the sort of depth a Russian commander would order. By doing this I minimised the chances of an underwater collision.

There was sweat on my palms. Deciding what depth to keep was always tinged with risk.

This manoeuvre could be leading to evasive action by the Delta. It could even be that he had detected us and wished to play silly buggers, though this was not normal SSBN behaviour. Not this SSBN anyway, from what I knew of him. Or, it could be that he was breaking off from his accompanying Victor riding shotgun for him. Or, it could be that there was another shotgun as well as the Victor. A shotgun that had perhaps been there all along, following us (the sweat now turned cold and my stomach turned over) and we had not realised this. The Delta could be trying to draw us off towards the other shotgun SSN, who would then play much sillier buggers with us while the SSBN faded into one of the underwater so called 'safe areas' where the Soviet submarines can retreat to if they need to do so.

We do not know whether they have special protection provisions in these areas, but they do like going under the ice and, in later years, there was a great deal of evidence that they were using these areas more often. We are always trying to establish where these potential safe havens are and how they are used.

'Turning to starboard,' came from sonar. 'Target bearing 049°. Course 039°. Range 3500 yards.'

He had been clearing his stern arcs – to check if anyone is hiding in his wake, a potential blind spot – looking for any followers and that was probably all. He was not reacting as though he had detected us.

I decided that I needed to have a good look around, just in case there was a third submarine in the area. Three Soviet boats and one Brit could make for a very lively encounter, but I was hoping to avoid that.

We cleared our own stern arcs carefully – very carefully – and returned to the trail. Instinct told me that I need to get another navigational fix and read the communication broadcast from Northwood HQ as I may be down here for a while.

With the Delta and Victor both moving to the northeast at 6 knots now, and both being held well at a range of around 8000 yards, we could safely go to periscope depth and return as quickly as we could.

We came up to periscope depth slowly, got the fix and the latest single signal for us on the broadcast. This was not a good place to be if you did not know where you were accurately. How glad I was that I did not have to rely on an old Loran C radio aid for navigational fixes and how glad was I that satellite navigation had made so much difference.

We were about to go deep again when there was another report from the sound room. 'He's altering course,' followed by, 'to port.'

I sat in my Captain's chair and let that one sink in. Turning to port was not part of his pattern, either. I was about to order the submarine deep again when there came an unexpected report 'Traffic for the target,' from the team listening to all the communications we could from their miniscule office on the next deck down under my feet. There was traffic all the time, but there was something in his voice that made me think this might be different.

Alexander Peters is a specialist communications technician and was in the sound room with a pair of headphones on. He was listening, rewinding and re-listening to the tape. All the sonar sets are recorded continuously.

Alex was a fluent Russian speaker. He had come to the United Kingdom as a young boy when his parents had defected and would not talk of what happened to make his father Mikhail Petrov defect. Mikhail changed his surname to Peters when he arrived in the UK. Alex did not like Soviets. Eavesdropping on Soviet Naval communications was a job that suited Alex fine. In some way he was getting his own back – at least that is the way he saw it. This form of tactical guidance is vital to the Commanding Officer and acts as a significant addition to the boat's sensors.

Just then Alex Peters came into the control room in a rush and came straight to me. 'I stumbled across this frequency by chance,' he said. 'I am pretty certain that these signals are for this Delta. I think he is up to something – he's just received twelve groups.'

That meant he'd just received a signal that may indicate some form of drill or tactical instruction for the Delta but I wondered what it really meant. The Delta was either at periscope depth, and we had not realised that, or he was receiving this message by some other means – a trailing wire?

'He's slowing down,' came from the sound room. 'Three knots. I can hear his planes,' said Nick Slide.

'He's going up. He's using his upward-looking echo sounder.' So the Delta was returning to periscope depth and had either been alerted by this signal or he had a pre-arranged rendezvous to receive it. I looked at the clock – it was almost exactly 1558 – two minutes to 1600. What did this mean? What should I do? Have I missed any clues here?

I ordered the submarine back to a deep anti-metric depth and took stock of the situation. Ian Richards [HMS SPLENDID's Executive Officer (XO), a command-qualified officer in his own right] and I reviewed the situation carefully and mulled over what we knew and what we did not.

We still held both the Delta and the Victor at 10000 yards and I was very confident that if there was somebody else around I would have heard them and hold them on sonar.

Twelve groups was clearly a significant signal – but what did it mean? Had the Delta received it already or was he on his way up to receive it at a pre-arranged time – like 1600? And what would he do when, and if, it was for him? I suddenly had a strong feeling of foreboding and was struggling to make sense of what was really happening here. Why would a Delta SSBN and a Victor SSN, acting as a shotgun escort, be doing this and was it just routine – or something else.

My knowledge of a twelve group signal was that this was a probably part, or all, of a firing signal and could either be an exercise or – God forbid – a tactical launch. But I had no idea which one it was. I was really worried! – What was going on here?

Ian Richards and I went to the chart table and started to review all the options on a piece of paper. He had the national rules of engagement with him and reminded me of the new clauses that we had received about 3 weeks ago. I had read them cursorily then but now I was reading them intently. The rules directed that in the event of a Soviet SSBN preparing to fire its nuclear missiles, I was ordered to open fire when I heard him open his second pair of missile doors. The first set of doors could be a test, but the second could only mean he was going to launch.

Oh dear! This was very serious stuff and as the words on the page starting to sink in I had a real feeling of apprehension and physical tension. I could feel the same from Ian and he started to speak quietly saying, 'You know what this means don't you?'

'I do,' I replied downheartedly, 'we may have to fire here,' and picked up the intercom.

'Wireless Office, this is the Captain. Was there anything startling on the last BBC World Service news?'

'No sir. Only the football results. Dumbarton lost. Again.'

It is at times like this that training helps. The training meant that I did not have a picture in my mind of that great steel slug drifting upwards towards the white screen of the ice pack; the training meant I was not thinking of a signalman taking the Soviet captain the message which, although in code, was looking awfully like a firing signal. Or envisage the captain fetching the first lieutenant or the political officer. The two men following protocol and using their keys to open the safe with the firing codes, walking quickly to the panel in the missile control centre, taking out the keys on the chains round their necks, turning them, starting the sequence that would burn the US eastern seaboard, the UK, Faslane or wherever together with its men and women and children. It did not bear thinking about.

Instead, I was thinking about what came next. What I might have to do and what might happen.

'He's settled,' said the report from sonar.

'He's slowed right down,' said the tactical displays operator.

'Sound room? Is the Delta at periscope depth? Ian asked.

'Could be going into the hover at 120 feet,' came the reply.

Oh My God! He was going into a launch sequence. Of course it could just be an exercise, I convinced myself. Ian came over and said 'I am not sure whether this is an exercise or not. I will talk to Alex again and see if he is sticking to his story and what he intercepted.'

'Good idea,' I replied rather unconvincingly. Bracing myself, I said,' 'Officer of the Watch. Go to the Search Quiet State and Action Stations. Slow down to 4 knots.'

Having the Victor as shotgun was now beginning to hold more credence and, if this Soviet SSBN was getting ready to fire his missiles, he would be relying on the shotgun Victor to keep anyone away.

But the Victor had not done anything alarming and had only slowed down to keep in station on the Delta's starboard beam. It was a strange place to be, but then I did not know the reason.

We had been watching carefully, tensed to react to any unforeseen movement that could indicate that he knew we were there. But we had been staying outside the Delta's counter detection range so we could hear him, but he had not been able to hear us – we hoped!

We had been concentrating on the ballistic boat. Perhaps too hard!

What was the Victor going to do? If he was doing his job properly he would have got a sniff of us and would know we would be readying our torpedoes if we suspected a missile firing. And he would be readying torpedoes of his own. Was he preparing to fire at us without us knowing it?

'Officer of the Watch – systematic all round sonar search; Sonar – have a really good listen. I need to know exactly what is going on and if there is another shotgun with us,' I said.

'Keep reporting the Delta and the Victor as well,' I said, perhaps a little too tersely. I must not show my tension to the control room team. If I am calm, they will be calm. But I was not calm inside. Ian was repeating what we knew, and my mind was racing with all the possibilities and how I should react to each. Dismissing some options and favouring others and at the same time trying not to kid myself into thinking what I wanted to believe.

The reports came in. 'Delta. Bearing 015°. Range 7600 yards. Course North. Speed 3 knots.'

'Victor. Bearing 034°. Range 8200 yards. Course North. Speed 4 knots.'

I looked at the tactical display and took that in. Ian, over my shoulder, said reassuringly that we were well positioned on the Delta's port quarter at 7600 yards and there were no torpedoes coming at us. That was comforting – of sorts.

After 7 minutes we had completed the sonar search and resumed our position. I had not dwelled on the clearing course for long – just enough to get a decent sonar picture, but it was enough to get the all clear from sonar.

No other submarine was a good sign. Normally, we thought that the Soviet ballistic subs had shotgun nuclear subs glued to their tails but we did not really know that this was their modus operandi. Particularly if there was going to be a live firing – or worse a tactical launch!

I knew where the Victor was and I felt we were in control of the situation. I prayed that I was right. Action Stations were closed up and Ian made a brief pipe on the turned-down main broadcast to tell the Ship's Company what was going on and how important that we remained alert and quiet.

It takes around ten minutes for any NATO ballistic submarine to move from orders received to missile launch. It would take a Soviet boat about the same. There were a long series of actions to come, each of them easily audible. We would follow the sequence and we knew what it was likely to be. Intelligence, while always very useful, is no substitute for having heard the real thing. And US and UK submarines had heard the Soviets firing their missiles often enough to know what to listen for.

That meant the opening of his missile hatches could be eight minutes away. Was this a non-firing drill, a test firing or tactical launch? We needed to be ready for anything and be prepared to fire if we thought it was the latter.

I rushed to my cabin and opened my safe and pulled out the latest procedure from intelligence to read again. Eight minutes was as good as a lifetime. The preliminaries would be in full swing. The Soviet missile ratings would be in what we called "Sherwood Forest" – among the missile tubes. Pairs of men would be taking the firing keys to the tubes. They would be sorting out the electronics. They would be hitting the switches that ran up the gyros that worked the missiles' inertial navigators.

'Sounds like a gyro running up,' said Nick Slide from the sound room.

I acknowledged, indicating my understanding, 'Roger.'

Out there, in the dark, that huge tin can would be taking measures to make itself a stable platform for launch. If a ballistic missile does not know where exactly it started from, it can have absolutely no idea where it is going to end up.

Then, 'Going into the hover,' said Nick Slide.

To keep 13,000 tons of submarine dead still in the water there is a big tank and a big valve and a huge, high-revving pump. These are computer controlled by sensitive sensors that measure and anticipate the movement of the submarine up and down and bow down or bow up. In essence, they allow the boat to hover in the water, the same way as a helicopter does in air. This provides the perfect stable platform from which to launch ballistic missiles.

This was not looking good. Not good at all.

I whispered to Ian, 'Do you think he is going to launch?' This was more in hope that he would say no. Ian replied, 'All the signs are there but it could be a drill. We are ready for both.'

The training is still there, though. Our torpedoes were loaded and the tubes were flooded.

I was looking intently at the picture in front of me on the DCB tactical display – we were in the centre and the Delta and Victor were clearly there but nothing else. I watched as the new bearings kept coming in and continued to confirm what were now very good course, speed and range solutions on both boats. I was transfixed and totally focused, waiting for the next thing to happen.

I had asked for the latest fire control solutions and had them in front of me and my mouth was certainly a lot drier than it ought to be. Because the 'what-ifs' were running through my mind again and again and I was rehearsing my reaction. The biggest ones were: 'Is he going to conduct a tactical launch?' and, 'Is the Victor going to move and, if so, where?' Towards me, I wondered. I must be prepared for that. And had the Victor actually detected us, and was he waiting to fire at us, lulling us into a false sense of security? Was there a torpedo running, racing towards us right now, and we had not heard it?

I dismissed all that because I wanted to, but there was no real evidence either way. Ian had been to the sound room and came back into the control room and whispered that Alex was certain of what he heard so that was that. Ian and I went over the possibilities again quickly and how we could or should react.

'Nitrogen,' said Nick Slide from the sound room. This was the one certainty that the missile tubes were being readied. This was bad news and had my mind working overtime.

Before a ballistic submarine opens its missile hatches, it is necessary to equalise the pressure in the tube with the pressure of the water outside. Nitrogen is pumped into the tube to do this. As the submarine hovers, it makes tiny movements in the water. The nitrogen pumps compensate for each one, to keep the pressure in the tube and in the water outside equal. The sound is distinctive: a random series of hisses, like a big animal sniffing.

I look to Ian. 'Let's refine these fire control solutions again. Are we ready to shoot?' I asked.

'Re-computing target parameter again, and affirmative. Ready to fire,' replies Ian.

'Missile hatches opening,' said Nick Slide. 'One ... two.'

We were now two minutes away from ... something.

PART ONE

A CAREER IN SUBMARINES

INTRODUCTION

THE COLD WAR BACKGROUND

In 1948 the journalist Walter Lippman first used the term Cold War borrowing from a French phrase cordon sanitaire to refer to a "constant war of nerves" between the Soviet Union and the United States who had emerged from World War II with incompatible ideologies and national interests. The wartime alliance against Nazi Germany had begun to unravel even before the fighting ceased.

There was no doubt that the United States and its Western European allies considered the expansion of Communism a threat to their national interests and security and wanted to stop it spreading. In an attempt to contain that potential spread a number of alliances were formed in various parts of the world, countries becoming either allied or aligned with the United States or the Soviet Union. Those that did not became known as the "nonaligned" countries, and their support was courted by both sides.

The armed forces of the United States and the Soviet Union did not confront one another directly in battle during the Cold War period. However, both sides were drawn in as supporters, suppliers or participants in so called "brushfire" wars, or larger conflicts like the Korean and Vietnam wars, which were viewed as part of the worldwide struggle between Communist and non-Communist powers. And there is no doubt that the formation of the North Atlantic Treaty Organisation (NATO) was seen in the Soviet Union as a major threat against them.

The phrase, Cold War, caught on in the UK too and came to describe nearly four decades of enduring hostility between the United States and the Soviet Union with weapons of mass destruction serving as a frightening backdrop. That Cold War period only came to an end with the fall of The Berlin Wall in 1989 and what we then assumed was the defeat of the Soviet Union.

And that old, cold, war is where we, the Royal Navy, came in.

There have been many attempts to write about the activities of both US and UK nuclear submarines during the long and uncertain years of the Cold War. Much of this is, by necessity and in the interests of national security, clouded in secrecy and it is only now that some of the stories are coming out into the open. After all, the equipment we used has now been superseded and most of the tactics we used no longer either practical or secret.

In 1977, the BBC broadcast a programme called the "Deep Cold War" when the BBC journalist, Tom Mangold, spent time in a Nimrod Anti-Submarine Warfare aircraft and revealed facts and conclusions that many of us, serving in the Royal Navy at the time, thought were too close to the bone. This was followed up by Tom Clancy's books, "The Hunt for Red October" and "Red Storm Rising", which revealed more inside information and described for the first time the Sound Surveillance System [SOSUS].

I remember these well. I was a Lieutenant Commander, serving as the Deputy Submarine Operations Officer in Northwood, where all the Navy's operations were controlled and both the Commander-in-Chief and Flag Officer Submarines had their Headquarters. We were shocked and furious that this type of highly sensitive information – information that directly affected our current operations - was permitted to be released into the public domain. The Soviet Union, our enemy, might well suspect that we had these systems, but confirming it like this in the interests of mass entertainment just gave them one less secret on which to spend their time and resources. And, any edge we gave the other side, however slight, could have had dangerous, perhaps fatal consequences under the sea, where we plied our trade, because the Royal Navy were in the middle of a very deadly 'game' as we referred to it. But the Cold War was not a game. It was all too serious. In the Submarine Service we were obsessed with the Soviets and tried everything in our power to keep ahead of them in equipment, tactics, quality of training and most of all, intelligence.

The Soviets were equally as keen as we were to find out everything they could about our capabilities. After all, we had, since 1968, a UK nuclear deterrent in the form of Polaris (the forerunner of today's Trident system). These were nuclear missile carrying, nuclear powered submarines, of which one at least was always at sea engaged in 'Continuous at Sea' deterrence. Put bluntly, that meant we always had a nuclear missile submarine, hopefully hidden, at sea, ready and able to retaliate to a Soviet nuclear first strike on the West with a devastating riposte. That was détente: the ability to respond to an attack with our own nuclear Armageddon. A deterrent that was so terrifying that it was designed to stop the Soviets pressing their trigger first.

This single TV programme would have confirmed to our enemies everything they suspected. In particular that the US had laid underwater sonar arrays that listened for and detected the passage of submarines in choke points like the Greenland-Iceland-Faeroes-UK gaps. Although, and to be fair to him, Tom Mangold was careful not to give more than cursory possibilities as to where these arrays were actually positioned.

But, damage us, I for one believe, this perhaps even well intentioned BBC programme did. The very fact it confirmed we were tracking Soviet submarines in this manner led to the Soviets putting even more effort into noise quietening, as we were to see over the next few years as their boats grew ever more silent and more difficult to find and track.

Today there is a plethora of information available on the internet about SOSUS, although I believe that the exact details and locations are still a secret. SOSUS was gradually reduced during the 1970s and 1980s, but it remained important to both the US and the UK. The nature of the listening arrays meant that updating them was both complex and expensive, and technology was moving on at a pace. By the time the Cold War effectively ended, with the demise of the Soviet Union in 1989, the intrinsic need for SOSUS decreased. It was declassified by the US in 1991.

Whilst SOSUS tipped us off to where enemy submarines were, the nuclear submarine was the perfect Cold War intelligence collecting vehicle for establishing the strengths and weaknesses of the Soviet

Navy. It could operate covertly with almost unlimited endurance, both at periscope depth and deep, and use all its sensors to collect intelligence. Whether it was the acoustic intelligence [ACINT] of all the sounds a vessel of any sort makes; Communications Intelligence [COMINT] that could be received on aerials or masts; Electronic Intelligence: both Electronic Countermeasures [ECM] or Signal Intelligence [SIGINT] and the ability to collect all forms of electronic intelligence from enemy missile firings and any other transmission. A nuclear submarine could go where it wanted, collect what it wanted and return without anyone knowing it had even been there. No other platform could do that, and sustain it for 90 days, without being detected.

But, for submarine commanding officers in the Cold War there were a host of other things to consider. There were always lots of balls thrown in the air as priorities changed and we found out more about our adversaries. There was always danger: from the sea itself; the submarine and its systems and the ever present possibility of equipment failure deep under the ocean; the risk of close confrontation with the Soviets and close quarters situations. Collisions on one level. Enemy attack when we were doing what we should not, on another. That meant there was always excitement, but an excitement closely allied with apprehension and, at times, fear.

When things go wrong! The Russian submarine Kursk

First I suppose was my own position. I loved the Royal Navy and what it offered. I felt immensely privileged to be not only in the submarine service but also to be in command of my own boat [submarines are referred to as "boats" and never subs] in my early 30s. Like most of my contemporaries I was ambitious and wanted to go further in the Navy, but this meant that I had to perform. I had to run an efficient boat and I had to bring back the goods, or the "take" as it was referred to in the submarine service. Fail to do so and my masters – greedy for information about our enemies – would give the boat to someone who did. But, first and foremost, I had to be safe and ensure I brought the boat and its people back in one piece. This was a huge responsibility, but one I revelled in.

Submarine Commanding officers in World Wars One and Two were names of legend for their nerve, courage and achievements, and I was very aware of what I needed to live up to. Names like Norman Holbrook, Martin Dunbar-Nasmith, Max Horton, John Linton, Malcolm Wanklyn, Basil Place, Ian Fraser and Ian McGeoch were etched in my mind.

My immediate Cold War predecessors and contemporaries were outstanding too and men such as Sandy Woodward, Richard Sharpe, John Speller, Geoffrey Biggs, Barry Carr, Mike Boyce, James Perowne, Martin MacPherson, Chris Roddis, James Taylor and Doug Littlejohns were men I served alongside – and set the example for me. I had to deliver, and keep delivering, if I wanted to be as good as them.

The Ship's Company were, of course, also in on this. They wanted to be in an efficient, happy and successful boat and they needed confidence in their Commanding Officer. While they wanted to be safe and come home in one piece too, they were a competitive lot and wanted to be proud of what they had achieved on their latest patrol and, whenever possible, have the bragging rights in the Squadron and the Submarine Flotilla as a whole. Life for a successful submarine captain was a constant balance between risk and reward, the lives of my men and the very existence of my boat at risk if I were to get it wrong. Then again, this is what I had trained for. This is what I wanted.

This was a good time for the Royal Navy as we had taken the feet from under the Royal Air Force when the responsibility for the nuclear deterrent had been transferred from the V bombers to Polaris. And they did not like it. The Royal Navy was now the front line and SSBNs [nuclear missile boats] and SSNs [nuclear hunter killers] were getting the lion's share of the money in the procurement area. So the pressure was on from the naval hierarchy to maintain our position in the Ministry of Defence and with government ministers.

This was not just the MOD we were dealing with, but also the

Foreign Office. The operations we were tasked with presented political risk if they went wrong but, if we could show that it was worthwhile, then our political masters would continue to support us and ask for more.

And our successes reflected well on the country as a whole. Although we remained the Silent Service it was not lost on the politicians that our credibility with the US Navy and the US government was an important part of the so called "special relationship." Therefore, the stakes for the nation were high every time a nuclear submarine went to sea: what if you were fired at a Soviet submarine or they fired on you? What if you bumped into one underwater? Or had a confrontation with a surface unit or helicopters?

The potential for a sensitive, and perhaps embarrassing, diplomatic incident at least, and possible nuclear war and inevitable global destruction at worst, was not a good thought. Neville Shute's book "On the Beach", when a US submarine returns to San Francisco to find it annihilated, is a scenario that is too awful to imagine. But it was one entirely foreseeable outcome if we got it 'wrong' and one we were all too aware of back then.

Royal Navy submarine Commanding Officers are not trained or appointed without the relevance of these potential outcomes being considered, and I have never been in any doubt as to the responsibility, and some may say burden, that I carried when I commanded a nuclear SSN.

The picture of life under the sea would not be complete without strong reference to the Soviet Submarine Service too and some of the characteristics of both the submarines and their commanders – our enemies. I always made a point of having a picture of a Soviet submarine Commanding Officer stuck to the bulkhead next to my chair in the control room. This was to remind me that I was opposing the man not the machine. I sometimes did not know his name, but I knew he was the Captain of a Victor submarine and I had a good appreciation of his background, likely training and probable capabilities. I knew that I was his enemy, just as he was mine.

And then, shortly before I was due to give up command and head for the surface breezes of Newport Rhode Island, USA and a senior international command course, the 'cold war' turned very hot indeed when the Argentineans invaded The Falkland Islands in 1982. I was told to remain in command of my boat as, once again, we slipped beneath the waves: destination, the South Atlantic. Only this time our orders were to engage an enemy determined on our destruction.

And this is where my story might have ended. Incredible memories of an extraordinary time 'not fighting' a Cold War that ostensibly ended in victory for the West and defeat for the Soviet Union; a victory that my men and I had played a significant part.

Because, in 1993, as a Commodore and Chief of Staff to Vice Admiral Sir Toby Frere KCB I had the privilege of leading the first NATO visit to our old enemies of the Northern Fleet at Murmansk and Severomorsk. The last time I had visited here I had been Captain of HMS SPLENDID and I had been sneaking up the main channel as I trailed and photographed the latest class of Russian hunter killer submarine: something that certainly gave us bragging rights in the fleet for many months afterwards. And, here I was now, inspecting their fleet from topsides and in a spirit of mutual, albeit guarded, friendship, rather from underneath the waves and with our hearts nearly literally in our mouths lest we were detected. A scenario I would have thought you quite mad had you told me it would come to pass in the early 1980's when I commanded that nuclear hunter killer submarine.

Sadly we now know that this period of glasnost was but a brief glimmering of what might have been if western politicians had been more magnanimous and constructive in their moment of 'victory', instead of revelling in the defeat of our old enemy.

Because, as I write this today, it looks to this submariner's eye as if we are back where we were in the 1980's, with Russian surface ships now taunting us as they sail down the English Channel; Bear Fs flying very close and ever more frequently to UK airspace and, in so doing, constantly testing our capabilities and response times.

Put bluntly, this is not something a friendly country does to another. It is something a country does to another country if they think there is a possibility of a future conflict.

And, they are sending submarines into our British backyard. This reminds me very much of the 70s and 80s. With one huge exception. With politicians all too eager to trouser the 'defence dividend' – in other words cut back on defence spending as we have ostensibly 'defeated' our enemy - we no longer have any maritime air capability. That means that Russian submarines can creep undetected into our territorial waters and spy on us. The now decommissioned SOSUS used to pick them up as they came through the various gaps and our hunter killers then used to follow them. If we lost them, as happened of course, our maritime aircraft laid sonar buoys and we picked them up again. Now, without maritime aircraft, we have lost that key ability to track enemy submarines and the Russians can now do to us exactly what we used to be able to do to them. In fact, when in 2015 a Russian submarine was supposed to have been spotted close to UK waters, we had to ask the Germans for help.

A triumph of NATO co-operation the politicians would trumpet. But, as any military man will tell you from any age in history, a nation that cannot look after itself, by itself, has no one to blame but itself when it all goes horribly wrong.

And then, finally, there is the submarine service itself. Trident apart, the SSN hunter killer force, although of high quality, is very small compared with my time.

HMS ASTUTE – Latest class of Royal Navy SSN

Submarines cannot live at sea all the time. They need to dock and be serviced. If we do not have enough submarines to counter the Russians in our own waters, then do not be surprised that the Russians will treat us with ever greater contempt.

Because, even if the politicians decide today that they have cut too far and too fast, it takes years to build and commission a new submarine. And, with every submariner who leaves and is not replaced, there is a strong risk that skills – often learned and handed down over generations – are lost. My men and I did not just come into being on those boats, we were the sum total of all that carefully built up knowledge and experience which was so expertly handed down to us and on which the submarine service so prides itself. Lose the experience and you lose the skills. That simple.

The submarine service is now trying to bring back engineers that they made redundant!

This book is therefore a tale of a lifetime of adventure under the high seas. But it should also serve as a timely warning. The Soviet sailors and ships we 'fought' in that Cold War are back again and in increasing force. They are again probing our defences. They call themselves Russians now, but the boats, the men and the mission have not changed under this increasingly belligerent Russian President and his supporters.

So this is why I feel this book had to be written: not only as my account for my children and grandchildren but also as a reminder that we cannot ignore what is going on. Along with the Royal Air Force the Royal Navy and the submarine service in particular need to be boosted in numbers as a matter of urgency. This takes time and we do not have it.

This then is the story of my submarine time. Whether 'hot' or 'cold', when my boat slipped its mooring and headed out to sea, it was exciting and demanding. We were on the front line and knew it. We certainly understood the seriousness of the situation and were all the more vigilant as a result.

Today, the debate is as hot as ever whether the UK should replace the Trident submarines or not. Despite the wild assertions in the press that it will cost 100 million pounds this is way off the mark. And it is not the Trident system we need to replace but the submarines hulls which are now in their 20s. We also have to consider the ramifications of NOT building new submarines. The Submarine Service has delivered Continuous At Sea Deterrence since May 1968 which is an incredible achievement. Trident IS our ultimate deterrent and we should not underestimate that. Add the fact that if we did not replace these submarines we would lose our independence to use Trident, be chucked out of the UN Security Council, would reduce NATO's effectiveness and severely dent our relationship with the United States and the reasons for replacement are compelling. We should not doubt either the fact that Submarine Commanding Officers would not hesitate to fire if directed. We MUST replace them and soon!

Make a mistake deep under the sea and sailors – whether British, Soviet or Argentinean – would die. Nothing has changed…

CHAPTER ONE

WHAT IS A NUCLEAR SUBMARINE?

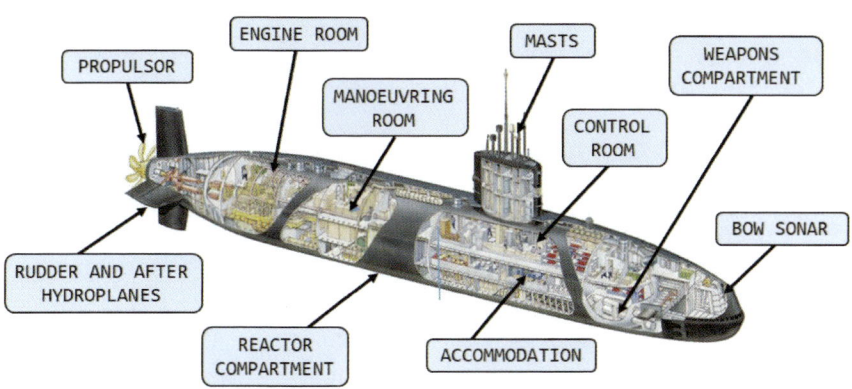

The old WW II diesel submarine was based on agricultural engineering. It was all about mechanical and electrical systems that controlled water, air, hydraulics and movement. But as fantastic as they were, and submarines did make a massive impression in both WW I and WW II on both sides of the conflicts, their basic Achilles heel was endurance.

When I was the Captain of HMS WALRUS – a Porpoise class diesel submarine, which was launched in 1952 by Princess Alice Duchess of Gloucester and the first Captain of which was Lieutenant (later Admiral Sir) John Fieldhouse – if I selected to propel on a single shaft with a full battery and kept at 4 knots, I could last for around 45 hours underwater without needing to charge the battery by snorting at periscope depth or on the surface. But if I selected 'full speed ahead', even starting with a full battery, WALRUS could last for only 17 minutes!

Nuclear power solved the endurance problem. Although the principles of submarining were very much the same, the ability to propel without refueling or charging your power source was a significant element of being able to operate in a completely different manner. In a diesel submarine you probably only had one chance to conduct your attack as surface ships were able to move very much faster than you could. The key advantage of nuclear propulsion is that you can choose your time and position to suit the best conditions for your submarine. You can run fast and deep and overtake a surface ship and thus get in a better position. Or simply come back another time when conditions are more in your favour.

Diesel submarines had to either snort or surface to charge their batteries and were thus vulnerable at that time. But a nuclear submarine does not even have to consider that option as you will see as you read further into this book. That made a huge difference to a Commanding Officer's attitude as to how he operated the submarine, but it did not stop you wanting to do your attack at the first attempt.

Nuclear power though gives you many more options.

The power generation system is the main difference between conventional submarines and nuclear submarines. Nuclear submarines use nuclear reactors as a heat source to heat water in a steam generator (or kettle) that produces steam that can power steam turbines for both electrical, through turbo generators, and propulsion power through steam turbines to a gearbox, shaft and propellor or propulsor.

Pressurized-water Naval Nuclear Propulsion System

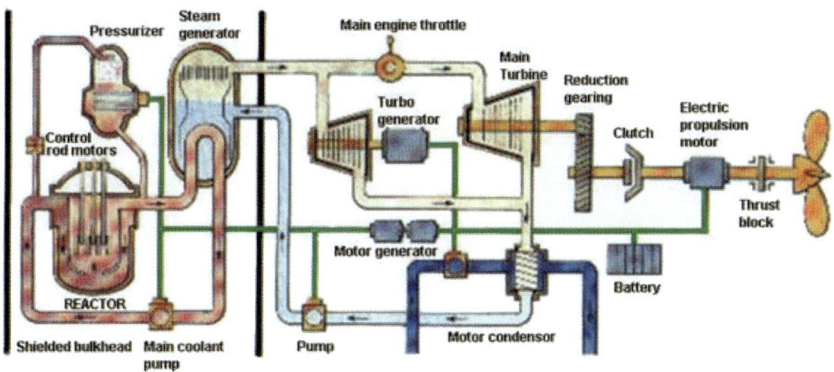

Submarine reactors usually use highly enriched uranium fuel which means they can produce a large amount of power from a smaller reactor and operate for longer periods before refuelling the reactor is required.

The capacity of a reactor is measured in Effective Full Power Hours [EFPH], which means for every hour that a reactor is run at 100% capacity this is defined as one EFPH. The capacity is so good today that a nuclear submarine, with careful management, will not need to refuel in a 25 year life span. If that is not astonishing, I don't know what is!

In addition, the Paxman diesel generator fitted in each nuclear submarine is there to allow charging of the battery, either if the reactor is shut down at sea for some reason or requires electricity to an electric motor for emergency propulsion.

Some of the old salts, or "diesel dinosaurs", struggled to make the change, but many became extremely valuable nuclear submariners. One well known character is Chief Petty Officer "diesel" Jones, with whom I had the privilege of serving. He embraced everything that was new, although he had spent years as a Chief Stoker in diesel boats: hence his nickname.

A nuclear submarine looks menacing on the surface, even though you can only see about one third of the hull above the waterline. Even that third looks big from the outside, but is actually quite small and cramped on the inside. That is only because it is a machine of war. Man has had to give way to the priorities of the machine and a nuclear submarine is simply stuffed full of machines, electrical and electronic boxes and all manner of pipes and valves. That leaves surprisingly little room for men.

The hull is cigar shaped, tapering from bow to stern, with the fin (the large superstructure that sticks out of the top of the boat) that acts as a shroud and support for all the masts and also provides a bridge for ship handling and navigation on the surface.

A submarine can float because the weight of water that it displaces is equal to the weight of the submarine. This displacement of water creates an upward force called the buoyant force and acts opposite to gravity, which wants to pull the ship down.

Unlike a ship, a submarine can control its buoyancy, thus allowing it to sink and surface at will. To control its buoyancy, the submarine has ballast tanks and auxiliary, or trim, tanks that can be alternately filled with water or air. When the submarine is on the surface, the ballast tanks are filled with air from external high pressure air bottles that can be charged by air compressors inside the submarine. The result is that the submarine's overall density is less than that of the surrounding water. This means that it floats (positive buoyancy).

As the submarine dives, the ballast tanks are flooded with water and the air in the ballast tanks is vented from the submarine until its overall density is greater than the surrounding water and the submarine begins to sink (negative buoyancy).

In addition, the submarine has two sets of hydroplanes (like the ailerons on aircraft), one set on the bow and one set on the stern. These, like an aircraft, are designed to control the depth and angle (attitude) of the submarine as it moves up and down in the water.

A Royal Navy nuclear hunter killer submarine like HMS SPLENDID has a crew of 13 officers and around 103 ratings, depending how many trainees are on board.

Maximum capacity is around 125 but that is very cramped. Polaris and Trident submarines have more room and can carry around 145 Ship's Company in total.

The submarine is divided into five main compartments. The first compartment can be isolated at what is termed 29 bulkhead door. Included in the first compartment is the forward escape compartment on 1 deck and some of the sleeping areas.

At the very front – or the bows – and external to the pressure hull, is the hull mounted sonar. It is placed right up front for obvious reasons – to look forward as the submarine moves forward, and to be as far away as possible from any interference from the propulsion systems, mechanical and electrical noise, which mainly comes from the stern or rear of the submarine.

The sonar actually looks from right ahead to 120 degrees on either side of the bow, leaving only a small window of 60 degrees either side, at the stern which is not properly covered by the main sonar and from where it may be possible to be caught napping!

On 1 deck, at the front, is the Forward Escape Compartment. This consists of the forward escape tower, which is replicated at the back end of the submarine too. The principle is that the whole of the Ships Company, plus about 15%, can escape from either end of the submarine if that was necessary.

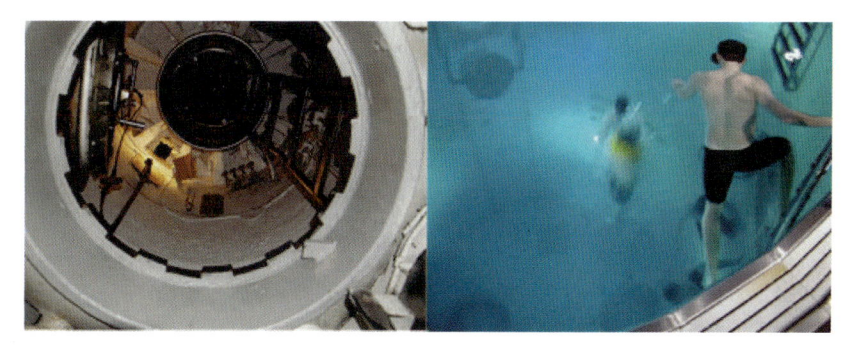

Submarine Escape Tower and training tank at Gosport

All submariners have to be schooled in escape training and complete refresher training courses every 3 years. This is done at HMS DOLPHIN in Gosport (in the Royal Navy every naval establishment, even if it is ashore like DOLPHIN, is still called HMS.) In the finest British tradition this, of course, not only confuses the enemy, but also our own side!)

The Submarine Escape Training Tank at HMS DOLPHIN in Gosport

The SETT or Submarine Escape Training Tank is a tall building which had a cylindrical tank with 100 feet of water in it. It is still physically there today, but modern training does not include time on the tank. In my day the training was done in steps, starting at 30 feet and wearing just bathing trunks and a nose clip. From a chamber at the side, at the required depth, you took a breath and ducked under the doorway and into the tank of water as warm as a bath! Divers are all around you just in case of emergency.

All being well you then rose to the surface having remembered to blow out all the time to release the pressure in your lungs. Fail to do so and you would be punched in the stomach by one of the divers to make sure you did expel the air from your lungs. It was amazing how much air was still in there as it expanded as you ascended in the tank. This was repeated at 60 feet and then 100 feet.

The first time I did this from 100 feet I was fine at first and rocketed out of the chamber at the bottom and I started to exhale. I felt good for the first 30 metres and I was blowing out well. But then I started to get panicky as I felt myself running out of air. I was still going up at 11 feet per second, but I was now certain I was going to run out of air. I was struggling and I thought I was not going to get to the top. I was trying to decide when to stop blowing and gulp instead, also knowing that would be it and at the same time putting it off. There was nothing left – I felt quite clearly that there was nothing left.

I was just about to give up and accept my fate when I received another punch in the stomach, which doubled me up and caused a mass of bubbles around me! Out of nowhere I was able to breathe out again and I was now passing 60 feet. Where was this air coming from? I didn't care as I continued to fly up and then – I bobbed right out of the water to my waist at the top of the tank. I gasped for air before settling on the surface. I was exhausted, but it had been exhilarating in a peculiar sort of way. If you managed that lot you were qualified for another three years underwater.

There are two methods of escape. First is the 'compartment escape', where the compartment (either the forward or aft one) is partially flooded to a level just about the lowered canvas trunk under the escape hatch. Your head is above the waterline but you breathe through the Built in Breathing System [or BIBS]. This uses mouth pieces which are fed air from special compressed air bottles carried within the submarine connected to a ring main with nozzles on the deck-head of the escape compartment – enough for the whole Ship's

Company plus 20%. When it is your turn to escape you take a deep breath and duck under the skirt and that leads out of the boat through the escape hatch. Once clear of the boat you once again need to blow out the air in your lungs all the way to the surface.

There are times when you think you are really going to run out of air but, as the air expands in your lungs, there is always plenty more to come and you reach the surface breathless but alive.

The other alternative is to use the one man escape tower. Here you go from a dry compartment and transit individually in an all in one rubber immersion suit which includes a plastic hood so you can see. Each person takes it in turn to enter the one man chamber and those below shut the lower lid.

It is a very tight fit and claustrophobic, but you are not in there long. You plug in your suit to an air supply, flood the chamber yourself and breathe normally – a strange feeling particularly as you see the water passing your face. Before you know it the pressure in the chamber is equalized. The upper lid opens as the pressure equalizes and you are on your way. The buoyancy of the suit just takes you out of the chamber and up you go like a rocket, remembering to breathe normally this time as you go up. You are travelling so fast that, as you hit the surface, you come out of the water by some distance. The advantage of this system is that you have a personalized lifejacket and preservation system to assist survival if you are on the surface in cold weather. There are the usual lights and whistles attached.

This was never practiced at sea, although everyone trained in getting into and familiar with the immersion suits. There were annual trials conducted, usually in the Mediterranean, to prove the system from 600 feet and try out new changes to equipment. These trials and their success were promulgated to the whole Submarine Flotilla.

Control Room

Further aft consists of, on the top or 1 deck, the control room, sound room, the Officers' Wardroom and cabins and bathrooms, and Captain's cabin. On 2 deck there is the galley, separate messes for senior and junior rates plus bathrooms (ratings or rates are general expressions for non-officer sailors).

Submarine Galley and Sailors Mess

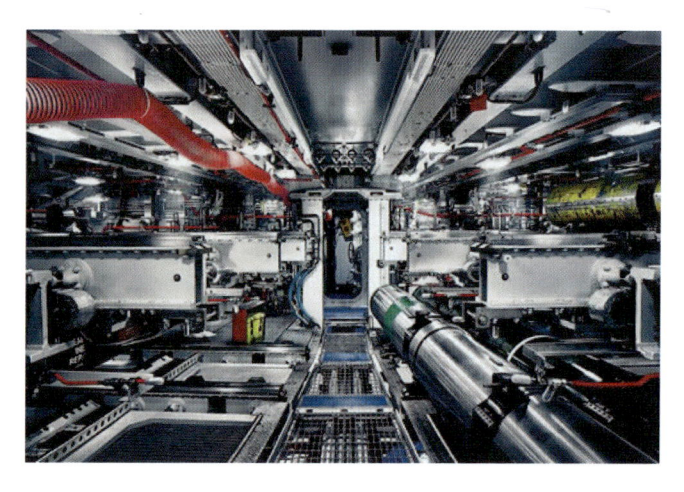

Weapons Compartment

Below that, on 3 deck, is the Weapons Compartment [often called the Torpedo Compartment or Bomb Shop], which not only has the inboard end of the 5 torpedo tubes and all their associated water ram discharge systems, but also a mass of racks and winches to move weapons backward and forward into the tubes and laterally across the compartment. This was also the place where extra pallets could be put in a spare torpedo rack to serve as additional bunks for extra personnel. These could be 'Part Three' trainees and/or "riders" – specialist personnel extra to the Ship's Company taken on board for a specific purpose or mission. There is room for 35 weapons of various types. It is in the control room area, on 1 deck, that the ship is fought. The Sonar and Tactical Systems ratings are the people that operate the sonar systems. They take the sonar output and use their skill to try to turn sonar bearings and noise analysis information into a geographical picture of everything going on around the submarine on the various tactical screens.

Also, here are the two periscopes. One is binocular – called the search periscope – and one monocular, called the attack periscope. The Wireless mast runs through the control room. The navigation is also conducted in the control room together with access to the various electronic aids readouts (Global Positioning System [GPS], log speed date, Ships Inertial Navigation System [SINS] information and, of course, charts. These days these have all gone electronic and modern IT techniques have resulted in huge progress, although there are still some that prefer to use proper old- fashioned charts to electronic ones, preferring not to rely entirely on technology when it comes to the safety of the boat and their men's' lives.

The next compartment going aft is the reactor compartment, which has a passage over the top, called the "tunnel." The reactor itself is about the size of a dustbin, but it is heavily shielded and the compartment also includes the two steam generators and the pressurising system.

The Manoeuvring Room

Behind that is a compartment with three levels. On 1 deck is the manoeuvring room where the Engineer Officer of the Watch [EOOW] and the Chief of the Watch [COW] oversees the three panel operators – one on the nuclear reactor panel, one on the electrical panel and one on the propulsion panel.

On 2 deck is the switchboard room and on 3 deck is the diesel generator. The fifth compartment contains the main engines, turbo generators, gearbox and main propulsion shaft, together with a mass of ancillary and associated equipment.

Everything behind that or 'aft' of the control room is known as "back aft."

CHAPTER TWO

LIVING IN A NUCLEAR SUBMARINE

HG Wells said "I must confess that my imagination refuses to see any sort of submarine do anything but suffocate its crew and floundering at sea"

The great, if long winded sea writer Joseph Conrad once said that "the true peace of God is found a thousand miles from the nearest land." He is entitled to his own opinion but my own view is that the closest a submarine captain gets to this happy state is outside the 100 fathom line, on passage to his patrol area.

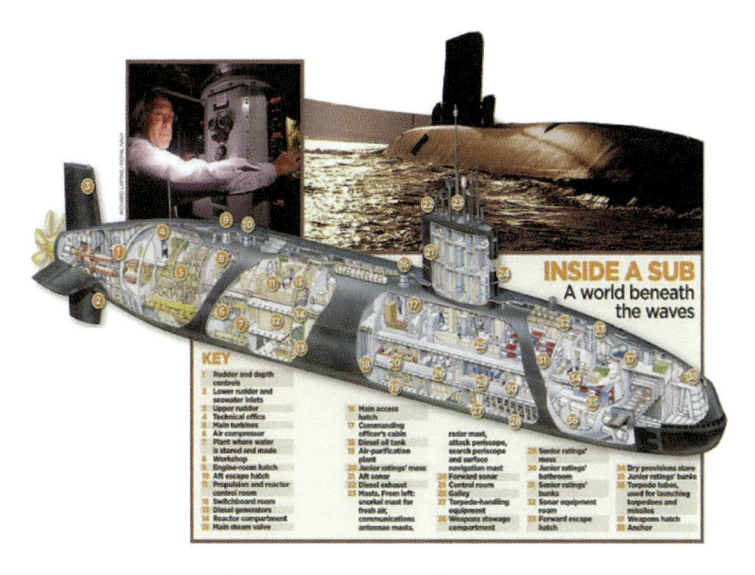

Royal Navy Swiftsure Class Cut away

Life aboard a nuclear submarine is not naturally suited for everyone – first of all the Royal Navy Submarine Service is voluntary. While there is screening to an extent, the initial selection from the volunteers is decided on his physical and mental abilities as well as his psychological and emotional well-being. Although I don't remember being psychologically tested as such. It soon becomes clear whether someone is suited or not and if they want to leave then they do. I have never come across anyone trying to open a hatch when dived. Most settle down very quickly and find the informal discipline and team ethos to their liking. Submarine pay helps of course and it is absolutely qualification pay not danger money. In my day it used to pay the mortgage but I doubt if it does today!

From Left to Right: Able Seaman (Sonar) Jumper Collins, Able Seaman (Sonar) Elliot, Able Seaman (Tactical Systems) Scott, Able Seaman (Tactical Systems) Phil Padgett, Leading Seaman (Tactical Systems) Cox, Leading Seaman (Sonar) Nick Slide - with 'Splendid' moustache, and a bin bag (unknown rating!)

A submariner receives formal training for about three months. He learns about the history of submarines, the different classes and types of submarines, systems and engineering instruction, standard and emergency operating procedures, submarine weaponry, details of damage control measures and escape systems and how to adapt to the dynamics of working together as a Ship's Company.

Submarine deployments can vary in length, depending on the type of submarine. Overall appointments (for officers) and drafts (for ratings) last around two to three years but some ratings may well stay longer. On a Polaris or Trident submarine the two full crews (Port and Starboard) rotate every 4 months shifts to allow the submarine to be at sea for as much time as possible thus maximizing its capability. This programming continues and allows the Ship's Company and their families an opportunity to plan to a certain extent. Even children are planned to be born in off crew periods.

On SSNs it is much more haphazard. A sea period or mission may last a few weeks -- or six months. Today, sailors can use email (with some restrictions), but in times past, sailors were not allowed to communicate with the outside world while aboard their boat at all.

New ratings are known as "Part Threes" as the first few months on board is to allow them to continue their training on the job. Apart from getting help from their colleagues they are also assisted by Training Aid Books. These are loose leaf books on waterproof paper with detailed drawings and mimics of every system on board.

To make things more manageable there are books for hydraulics and air systems, electrical systems, escape systems, reactor systems, steam systems and many more – probably around 20 volumes but they have proved to be vital in the training field and in damage control. Established sailors know the boat inside and out and have already become qualified submariners, and have earned their "dolphins."

Submarine Qualification "Dolphins"

This insignia is a badge of responsibility, qualification and togetherness. A Part Three must constantly continue to learn the ship's systems and operating procedures and pass a test on each one. Although a torpedo man or supply rating won't need to know how to operate the nuclear reactor or the navigational systems, both will be trained to understand the systems, their safeguards and emergency procedures. A Part Three has to undertake an oral examination, taken usually by the Executive Officer while walking round the submarine and when and if he passes he earns his dolphins in a special ceremony with the Captain where his dolphins are in a glass of rum. Then and only then is he accepted as a member of the submarine family.

However, this is not the end of training as this goes on all the time. There are regular training exercises, some planned and some not, to deal with the host of possible emergency procedures from fighting all sorts of fires to floods electrical failures and hydraulic or air bursts.

There is not much space for privacy and each bunk in blocks of three is about all you get. Some submariners may have to hot-bunk- that is get into a bunk that has just been vacated by someone else starting his watch. A curtain provides privacy, and a small locker or drop-down shelf is all each submariner has for storage.

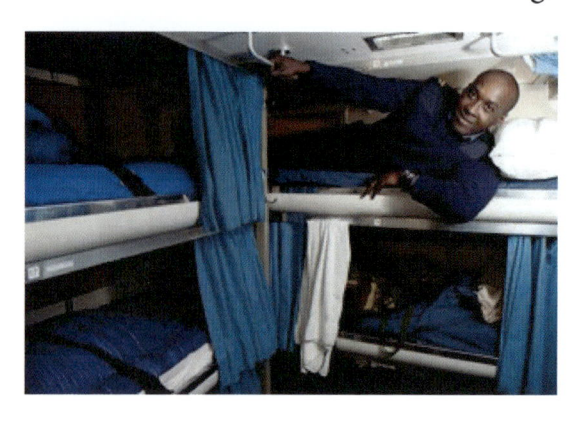

In the submarine's mid-section, people were living and eating and sleeping. Some were on watch like those in the control room and the sound room. The sonar operators were the boat's ears slicing up sea sounds with a mass of specialist analysis equipment designed to break down every last sound the hydrophones on the sonar sets could detect.

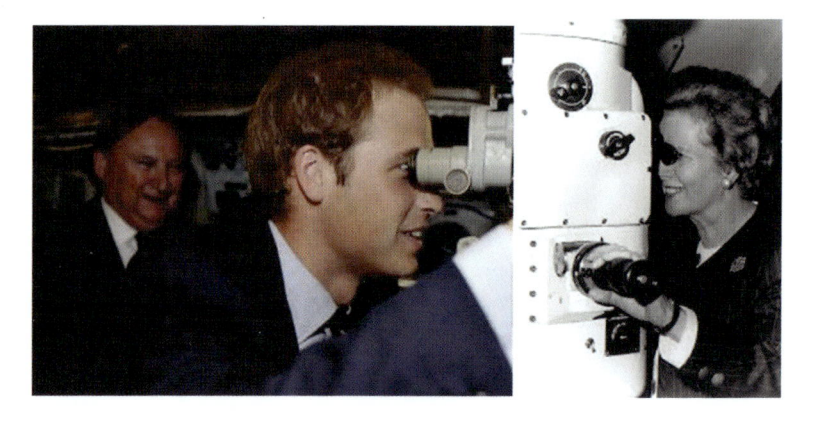

HRH Prince William Commodore in Chief of the Submarine Service on HMS ALLIANCE periscope in Gosport during visit to the Royal Navy Submarine Museum and Lady Thatcher during one of her many visits to Royal Navy nuclear submarines

Submarine sound room is all technology

Navigation Area

Attack and search periscopes in HMS WALRUS. Note search periscope has a seat and roundabout for prolonged periods at periscope depth

Tactical Systems (DCB) Displays in the Control Room

Tactical Systems (DCB) Displays in the Control Room

Control Room HMS VICTORIOUS today

Submarine masts: From left to right Attack periscope, Search periscope, radar mast, telescopic wireless mast

Galley in HMS SPLENDID

In the galley – cooks cooking lunch for the men who wanted it - not many did. After a few days all the salad gear is gone and the fresh vegetables and potatoes start to diminish and for most the four meals a day had shrunk to two, and people were moving precisely, but quietly and with no excess of energy. The port watch were in their bunks, reading or dozing, preparing themselves mentally for the showing of the movie on the boat's VHS – no internet downhere!

Junior Rates Mess in HMS SPLENDID

Senior Rates Mess HMS SPLENDID

Up in the nose, the weapons men were maintaining equipment, fussing around their weapons as though they were thoroughbreds being readied for the Derby.

SPLENDID was a small town moving through the pitch-black sea, as close to peaceful as she could be. Which, in reality, was not very peaceful at all.

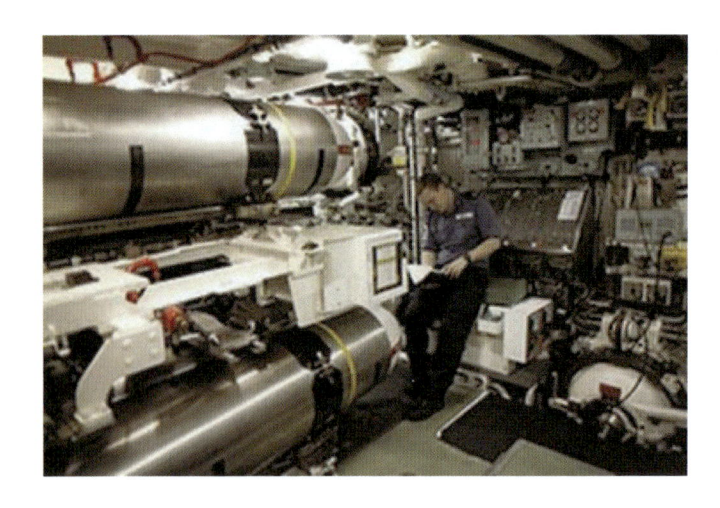

Weapons Compartment in HMS SPLENDID

Inside a torpedo tube

Loading a Tomahawk Cruise Missile

Ship Control Officer of the Watch and Planesman in the Control Room

Control Room

Working out in the machinery spaces

Some of HMS SPLENDID Ships Company
Back row left to right: Leading Seaman (Sonar) Mick "chequebook" Chandler, Able Seaman (Sonar) Jumper Collins, Captain Geoff Jacques (Captain SM2), Chief Radio Supervisor Pincher Martin, unknown CPO and Chief Petty Officer (Tactical Systems) Ken Douglas.
Front row: Leading Seaman (Sonar) Nick Slide and Leading Cook Pete Preston.

HMS SPLENDID Ships Company Members. Executive Officer Lieutenant Commander Ian Richards in submarine sweater extreme left

For a nuclear attack submarine, the Cold War could turn hot at five minute's notice. SPLENDID's purpose in life was to be aggressive, to track down Soviet SSBNs, stalk them, listen to their activity and noises they made, noting their communications and habits, and recording them for addition to the great library of intelligence that the MOD tries to keep up to date. This all adds up to a better understanding of your potential enemy. "Know your Enemy" is a key element of peace time activity.

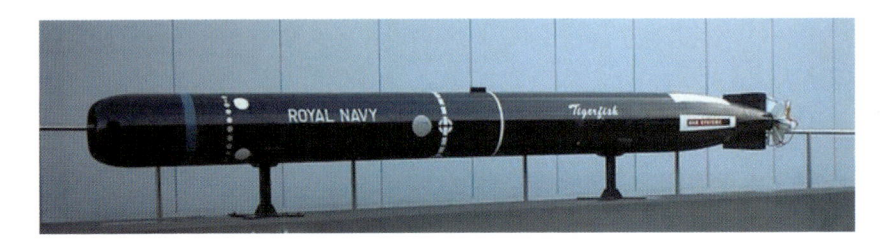

Tigerfish Mk24 Torpedo

In the event of the Soviet boat preparing to fire missiles, SPLENDID'S role was to fire and direct a Tigerfish torpedo to sink the Soviet SSBN before it could launch its missiles and potentially destroy most of the UK, North America, or whatever else they had targeted. Our torpedo tubes were already loaded – just in case. Provided the missile firing was not just an exercise. And provided SPLENDID was not herself sunk by the Soviet SSN that would almost certainly be riding 'shotgun' on the Soviet SSBN. Usually a Soviet SSN [attack submarine] would be in close proximity to the SSBN [missile submarine], its mission to protect the Soviet SSBN from our torpedo attack for long enough for the SSBN to fire its nuclear missiles.

And provided our Tigerfish torpedoes worked, which was by no means certain! We normally had the tubes loaded but not flooded. However as the environment in which we were operating became more potentially hostile we flooded at least two tubes and made them ready. Flooding torpedo tubes made a noise and we made sure that this was done well away from prying ears. The world of submarine warfare in the age of deterrence contained far too many provisos ever to be peaceful.

Men explained things that needed explaining. This was useful. But what we were really looking for was noise. We are very, very fussy about noise. Active sonar, the kind that goes 'ping,' is something you hear in war films, or when things have gone so far someone is about to shoot at you or you are about to shoot at them. Passive sonar on a quiet boat means that we can hear a Soviet boat before he hears us and follow him at a distance. To do this, it is crucial that we can hear him, but he cannot hear us. We call this the sonar advantage. UK submarines do have an active sonar capability and in the early 1970's it was very much in our favour but the passive sonar advantage is key.

CHAPTER THREE
TIME TO GO

The second-hand silver Volvo 245 car heater is too hot, but it needs to be in the dull, cold, almost always wet, West of Scotland weather. Roisin, my wife, brakes and comes to a halt in front of the barber-pole striped barrier. We kiss and hug each other and say our goodbyes. We are used to this and there is little to say at this stage. One of the wiper blades is squeaking.

I get out. The car makes a U-turn and hisses back down the wet, black road, past the concrete boxes of Faslane and we wave as the car moves away. We should have bought a Volvo Estate, but neither of us likes estate cars. Roisin will get the wiper fixed. During the next three months she will do everything that is required: pay the bills nurture the children, and get something done about the slipped tile on the roof.

She is used to this and will stoically continue without me or my input into anything domestic. She may go to see other members of the family "down south" and do all the things that any mother would do – but alone and without support from me.

I watch her go, wave again at each other, and then turn away. There is water dripping from the peak of my naval officer's cap and down the collar of my navy-blue Burberry [this is the Royal Navy's word for a raincoat but is not made by the well-known department store!]. I let it drip. Submariners do not get to see much good weather.

'Afternoon, sir,' says the Ministry of Defence [MOD] policeman in the security office, checking my pass. The water is soaking through my shoes as I walk through the various barriers and into the command complex of offices next to the submarine berths. Faslane was first home to depot ships like HMS MAIDSTONE, HMS FORTH and HMS ADAMANT in a time before nuclear submarines, when most of the support services for diesel submarines were provided by the depot ships.

On the left are more concrete buildings. On the right is the Gareloch, a sheet of water like dirty slate. The tugs are out there, the crews drinking tea, waiting.

A rating comes splashing through a puddle and, recognizing my face or maybe the 'scrambled egg' – the gold embroidery – on the peak of my cap – he salutes. I return it with a nod in acknowledgement. I do not recognize him, but his sailor's cap has HM SUBMARINES in gold braid around it. Submariners do not have cap badges to identify the name of their submarine, a tradition that goes back to the First World War.

So here I am – all the time moving away from home and Roisin and my three children: Antonia, Patrick and Olivia. I will miss them, but for the moment my priority is HMS SPLENDID.

Turn a corner, then on through another gate and another pass check. I get a short glimpse of my boat.

There she is!

I take a quick, irresistible pause to admire. A nuclear powered, hunter-killer submarine: SSN to the Royal Navy. Ink-black casing, towering fin [the Americans call it the sail], name boards shipped, gilt gleaming under a coating of rain. HMS SPLENDID, say the boards. My ship – my command – and I walk taller with pride. I never tire of the feeling.

The shore power cables are still on, but in the process of being removed. But in the back end of her black bowels the reactor plant will be self-sustaining, having been cooking superhot steam for three or four hours to provide steam to the electrical generators and the main engines. The ratings making up the upper deck or casing party on the flat section of submarine's casing, forward of the fin, look up, see me, and say something to each other. A professional Navy does not feel tension. But a professional Navy can be curious about where it is going on patrol. If they have brought their sun oil they are going to be disappointed.

Here comes the Petty Officer Steward. 'Afternoon Petty Officer Steward', I say. 'All set?'

'Everything in order, and I've made sure the chef has kept some steak and kidney puddings for you, sir' he replies.

He knows only too well that I have a special addiction to Royal Navy steak and kidney puddings!

'Very good,' I say and he takes my hold-all from me and disappears back down the boat. (Submarines are "Boats" whatever size they are

– a term used in the First World War that has stuck even into the nuclear age and 16,000 ton Trident submarines).

But it is not yet time for me to go down the boat. I turn left into a doorway of the Faslane Command Building, trotting wet foot up the stairs. I go into the Captain (Submarines) of the Third Submarine Squadron, [or Captain (SM) for short] outer office to say farewell. The Third Submarine Squadron is based in Faslane and consists of a mixture of nuclear and diesel submarines. SPLENDID is part of the Second Submarine Squadron which is based in Devonport.

He is a submarine CO too and knows me well – too well! But I trust his judgment and he has always given me good advice. My own Captain (SM) is Captain Mike Ortmans who is in Devonport. I was a junior officer when he was Captain of the Polaris submarine, HMS REVENGE. I learnt a great deal from him when he made it his task to educate the junior officers in the nooks and crannies of operating a nuclear submarine effectively. It is traditional to call on your Squadron Commander before sailing and Captain Andy Buchanan is taking the place of Mike Ortmans in this instance. I did not know at the time of course, but I too would go on to serve as Captain (SM) Three in the mid-1980s.

I am ushered into the wood panelled office overlooking the jetty by a WRNS officer who acts as a Personal Assistant and who, as always, offers me a cup of coffee.

I decline.

'Good afternoon, sir,' I say in greeting to Captain Buchanan. 'Hello, Roger. All ready to go?' he replies.

We discuss the status of the submarine, and I tell him that I have struggled a bit with getting all the stores that I need and will be going without an extra lye pump for the Electrolyser (the machine that turns sea water into oxygen). The supply of these pumps has always been a problem and the manufacturer continues to try to resolve the reliability issues. It should not be a problem but it is a worry.

I update him on the personnel situation and briefly discuss our mission. There is no need for too much detail now as we have been over this before. We have received several briefings over the last two weeks, including a full day with the Command Team at the Flag Officer Submarines HQ at Northwood, just outside London. We discuss the latest intelligence reports and then go into the operations room to look at the large map plot and confirm the latest status.

That visit to Northwood was, as usual, most important. I am used to "The Hole" as it is called. I spent two years in there when the Submarine Service set up centralized operational control (Opcon) in the mid 1970's. This organization goes under the title of Commander Task Force 311 (CTF 311). This is the title under which Flag Officer Submarines – FOSM, a 2 or 3-star Admiral – exercises operational control of his submarines.

Opcon is based on three elements. First is water-space management (the underwater equivalent of air traffic control), which is designed for the mutual avoidance of collision of friendly submarines. This, of course, does not take account of hostile submarines, or those of nations that do not want to tell NATO or the UK or anybody else for that matter where their boats are.

The second element is Intelligence. By centralizing, analysing and disseminating the very best intelligence in one place from numerous sources this allows the Opcon authority to provide the most up to date and best information and guidance to the boats at sea.

All this information is dependent on the third element – Communications. The national deterrent of Polaris missile submarines – known as SSBN, standing for: Submarine (SS) Ballistic (B) Nuclear (N) – is under the command of the Commander-in-Chief Fleet as CTF 345, but in essence is actually run by Flag Officer Submarines and his staff. CTF 311 is adjacent to CTF 345 (where the control of the broadcast of information to the submarines is coordinated). This is done by various methods, but the main one is still Very Low Frequency (VLF) radio signals. These are sent out at fixed intervals so they can be read by submarines at periscope depth, or from the deep, but only if they have a trailing wire aerial that allows them to pick up the VLF broadcast from deep.

The entrance to "The Hole" at Northwood is very unimpressive – just a few doors in the side of the hill, but with large steel reinforced blast doors that can be shut in times of tension or expected attack. The Hole is self-sufficient – food, water, bathrooms, toilets, all crammed into a series of rooms in a labyrinth of faceless and difficult to comprehend corridors. By the time you have gone through the doors, had your pass checked and start down the stairs you soon lose your sense of direction or the depth underground that you have attained. After several minutes of meandering around and going down stairs, you end up at an equally unimpressive door with a small sign saying "CTF 311" on it. There is a cybernetic keypad and a bell by the door and a series of warning notices making you feel very unwelcome.

But, once inside, it feels and smells like a submarine. Fans whirr, there is not much space to work and the lights are bright. Every space is utilized and there are maps, charts, signal logs, screens and people everywhere.

The briefing covers all aspects of the operation and this is the chance for the Command Team to ask all the difficult and nagging questions they have. It is also a bonding time. The officers here have a key role in assisting you in your mission and they are keen to understand you, your likely action in given situations and your worries. They will be trying to second guess your requirements at every turn and it comes as no surprise that there is as much professional satisfaction for the CTF 311 operations team helping you as actually doing the mission themselves. They are all submariners. They have seen much of it before and will again when their time comes to return to sea, just as I know that in a couple of years I might find myself back there and they will be the ones getting briefed before putting to sea. I question the likelihood of Soviet submarines: the latest movements and recent intelligence recovery and which classes I might encounter.

After that day of briefings, questions and answers, my team returns to the submarine to continue the last few days of preparation: fixing defects, storing all the innumerable items you really need and might need. But now all that is complete and we are almost away.

From Captain(SM)'s office we move to the Base Operations Room. HMS SPLENDID is visible in plain view from the outward-tilting glass windows. A fat steel tube covered in black rubber or very expensive acoustic dampening tiles (if only they could find a better glue and get them to stay on properly, I ponder).

The Clyde Submarine Operations Officer, Lieutenant Commander Tony Taylor, hands me a sheaf of papers and starts describing shipping movements. 'Cable laying off Arran and the Brodick ferry running to schedule,' he says. 'Bomber [submariners' affectionate name for Polaris submarines] due in tomorrow morning. Too many fishermen off Campbeltown.'

Tony Taylor knows what I want. He used to be my First Lieutenant when I was in command of the diesel submarine HMS WALRUS a few years ago. Now I exchange pleasantries with him.

'Sandy (his wife), will be in touch with Roisin while you're away,' he says. 'Thanks,' I reply. 'She'll appreciate that.'

At the end of the Gareloch is the River Clyde, which is to Scotland's shipping routes what the M8 is to Scotland's road traffic.

'And,' says Tony. 'You have AGIs north of Rathlin. Certainly one, maybe two by the time you get there, if they are changing over'".

This is no surprise. AGI (Auxiliary Gatherer of Intelligence) are the infamous Warsaw Pact trawlers, converted and equipped to catch electronic intelligence instead of fish. They are driven aggressively by their captains and crews and can be a pain. It is the job of a submarine to be invisible. It is the job of an AGI to detect and harass a submarine any way it can. To collect intelligence and report UK and US submarine movements. They do this on the surface and we, the submarines, do it underwater.

They are particularly dangerous as they are aggressive in their manoeuvring and can get very close. That is all very well but a submarine on the surface is not able to change course or stop very quickly and, although there have not been any collisions over the years, there have been some very close shaves. If they pick you up they can gain intelligence – acoustic, electronic and photographs. They can log your signature on the surface and might be able to find some discreet noise that would allow a Soviet submarine to identify you in the future. The biggest worry is when you have a towed array behind you as the AGI can't see that as it is below the surface but, should he decide to cut across your stern at close quarters, there is every possibility that he will sever your towed array.

We want to make every effort to avoid detection by an AGI. First they will report you and they may well be able to identify you or correlate your movement with other information and we do not want to provide the Soviets with a starting point. That is why we frequently dive in the Clyde Inner areas, off the Isle of Arran, and go out to sea in a dive. But it is difficult with shallow water and using well defined routes that a dived submarine will have to take.

And, you can guarantee that the AGI will be sitting in a position to force you into shallow water, even if he has not detected you. I have put to sea many times and it is a big relief when you are past the AGI and in deeper water.

These are tense times in the wider world and it spreads through the boat. We are at real risk here and we need to ensure that we use all our knowledge, guile and experience to see the AGI off!

The problem is that anything that is discovered about the boat could put our lives at risk in a future and could result in an entirely foreseeable show down. Similarly, anything we can find out about the enemy can give us a critical edge that could be war winning were the cold war to turn hot.

Like the Army in Germany in the late 70's, the submarine service is on the front line and we played it as though we were at war. We certainly thought we were, and we operated the submarine as though we were at war.

There was only one change that I would make in a genuine 'killing' war situation and that was to lock the emergency blow valves and take away from the Officer of the Watch the ability to surface the submarine in an emergency without my say so as the Captain. We were always ready for battle. We had live torpedoes ready and loaded and we went about our business as though we were at war.

The attitude of submariners is different because we have to operate and fight in a hostile environment – not just the opposition but the sea itself – and we were always one step short of a disaster that could kill us, whether it be a flood, fire or plane jam, as well as trying to outwit the enemy. Just think of the disaster that struck the KURSK – this was something we were all aware of whenever we put to sea.

We went through more than just the motions and I think nearly all the Ships' Company was as conscious as I was that there was a real threat. We could see it and we were in the middle of countering it. Submarines and submariners are always at risk from the moment you slip from the wall and there is always a real sense of relief when you are back alongside. I don't think we were living in a permanent state of fright, but we were very wary. That is why we trained so hard and why submarine crews tend to be much more bonded than on any other type of warship. We know the danger and respect it.

At this time the Soviets were building nuclear submarines at a tremendous rate and far quicker than either the USA or the UK. There were different classes emerging with different roles. There were four generations of nuclear attack submarines from the November class through the Victor I, II and III, the Alfa, Sierra I and II and the Mike and then the Akula. All these classes demonstrated improvement in one area or another. In submarine launched guided missile submarines they developed from the Yankee Notch, through the Charlie I and II, to the Oscar I and II, to the Sevorodvinsk. In strategic ballistic missile submarines they moved from the Yankee I and II, through the Delta I, II, III and IV, to the Typhoon to the Borei. These submarines were sometimes very fast (the Alfa) and sometimes very big (Typhoon) and the pace of change was huge.

The Soviets were operating in the Atlantic and the Pacific and the Charlie and Oscar submarines, which were designed to attack Carrier Battle Groups with missiles from behind, resulted in a whole new concept of anti-submarine warfare for any Group of warships working together. Soviet submarines were everywhere and it was vital that we knew as much as we could about them, where they went and how they would operate. The Soviets, of course, were equally determined to keep their secrets just that: secret.

In the middle of all this the geo-political situation in early 1980's was also very tense – with a great deal of uncertainty – and getting worse with each new provocation. There had been a serious deterioration in relations between the Soviet Union and the West as a result of the Soviet invasion of Afghanistan in December 1979.

With the election of Margaret Thatcher as British Prime Minister in 1979, and Ronald Reagan as President of the United States in 1980, the corresponding change in the West's foreign policy approach towards the Soviet Union was marked. Friendliness or détente was thrown away in favour of a more confrontational approach towards the Soviet Union. There was no doubt that the threat of nuclear war had reached a nervous level not apparent since the 1962 Cuban Missile crisis.

After the Soviets invaded Afghanistan in 1979, US President at the time Jimmy Carter announced a US-led boycott of the Moscow 1980 Summer Olympics. [Britain did eventually go to the 1980 Olympics.] Moscow was furious, to put it mildly. In fact, in 1984 the Soviets responded with their own boycott of the 1984 Summer Olympics in Los Angeles, California.

Tensions further increased when the US announced they would deploy Pershing II missiles in West Germany, followed by President Reagan's announcement of the US Strategic Defence Initiative. East and West tensions deteriorated even further in 1983 when Ronald Reagan branded the Soviet Union as an "Evil Empire".

In April 1983 the United States Navy conducted FLEETEX '83, the largest fleet exercise held to that date in the North Pacific. This exercise of over forty ships with 23,000 servicemen and women and 300 aircraft was arguably the most powerful naval armada ever assembled. US aircraft and ships attempted to provoke the Soviets into reacting, allowing US Naval Intelligence to study Soviet radar characteristics, aircraft capabilities, and tactical maneuvers.

On April 4, at least six U.S. Navy aircraft flew over one of the Kurile Islands – held by the Soviets but claimed by Japan – Zeleny

Island, the largest of a set of islets called the Habomai Islands. The Soviets were outraged, and ordered a retaliatory overflight of the US Aleutian Islands. The Soviet Union also issued a formal diplomatic note of protest, which accused the United States of repeated penetrations of Soviet airspace. Also during 1983, a civilian Korean airliner Flight 007 was downed by Soviet fighter jets near Moneron Island. In November 1983, NATO conducted a military exercise known as "ABLE ARCHER '83" to practice the realistic simulation of a nuclear attack by NATO forces and this event caused considerable alarm in the USSR, and is regarded by many historians to be the closest the world came to nuclear war since the Cuban Missile crisis in 1962.

This period of the Cold War continued through resident Reagan's first term (1981- 1985), through the death of Soviet Leader Leonid Brezhnev in 1982, and the brief interim periods of Soviet leadership consisting of Yuri Andropov (1982-1984), and Konstantin Chernenko (1984-1985). Things did not first calm down and then improve until the arrival of Soviet leader Mikhail Gorbachev in 1985, which brought a commitment to reduce tensions between the East and West.

So politically and militarily this was a very testing time in 1982, with tensions between the two superpowers ratcheting up and much uncertainty in the world. There was a real worry at how the East-West situation would pan out. And we in HMS SPLENDID, with the other boats of the Submarine Flotilla, and the US Submarine Command were in the front line. We were "spies in a tin can."

The AGIs are the Soviet front line of the Cold War. They lurk on the 12-mile limit, north of Rathlin Island – in other words on the very edge of British territorial waters which are, of course, supposedly out of bounds to them. Stray into 'our' waters and there will be diplomatic notes, frosty relations between nations and demands for action against the trawler's Captain. But it is notoriously difficult to 'arrest' a ship that does not want to be caught. And all this just four short hours from Roisin's warm kitchen in Helensburgh.

My Graham watch says 1449. Outside the windows of the operations room the casing party is helping two stokers on the casing to disconnect the two large and heavy cables that supply shore power to the boat in harbour. We are on our own power now and the reactor is providing steam to the generators which feed the numerous electrical supplies. The propulsion system and everything else is ready.

I thank Tony, shake his hand, and leave the ops room with Captain(SM). We walk down the stairs and out into the relentless rain for the short walk to the jetty. In Faslane you never go anywhere without your Burberry. If you have it on then it is raining. If you are carrying it then it is about to rain!

We reach the top of the brow and Captain(SM) turns to me and says, 'Good luck Roger. And good hunting!' – This is the traditional send off, given to all submarines going on patrol in World Wars I and II and is still so today.

'Thank you, sir.' I shake his hand and salute him.

I walk down the brow onto the catamaran [a floating, flat-topped metal structure that acts as a fender between the jetty and the submarine to protect the submarine from damage] and revel in the moment.

This is what I look forward to. Leaving behind all the paraphernalia of the submarine base and the prospect of exercising command – at sea!

The quartermaster or sentry on the 'casing' (submarine term for upper deck based on the casing around the pressure hull). He has been on duty since 1200 and is looking like a drowned rat, huddled in a soaking foul weather jacket. Nevertheless, he is watching intently and, as he sees me coming down the brow, he shouts: 'Attention on the Casing,' and lifts his bosun's pipe to his lips. This is one of the few bits of Navy bull that the submarine service observes. But a Royal Navy Commanding Officer is a Commanding Officer, regardless of what type of vessel he commands, and piping the Captain aboard is a mark of respect that even submariners follow. I acknowledge the pipe and salute back before disappearing down the main access hatch from the casing, through the pressure hull, to the accommodation space below. I make my way to the control room (the central hub of the submarine) and then to my cabin to put on foul weather gear – jacket and trousers – and a towel around my neck to try to stop the water running down inside my foul weather jacket.

I go back into the control room and can see that everyone is at Harbour Stations and is ready to go. I exchange pleasantries with Lieutenant Jeff Thomas, the Officer of the Watch and the Coxswain – who is the most senior rating on board and it is him who is traditionally on the helm for going in and out of harbour and coordinates the various compartmental status reports that are then fed up to the First Lieutenant. I climb the ladder to the bridge, up through the conning tower.

The conning tower is a tube that goes up about 12 feet above the pressure hull and has the conning tower hatch at the top. The conning tower is a separate, smaller tower inside the fin, which is the fairing structure that covers all the masts and has the bridge at the very top.

I climb through the tangle of pipework that is hidden in the streamlining of the fin itself.

HMS SPLENDID's bridge is not commodious. It consists of a square opening or dent in the top of the fin forward of the masts. In the dent is just about enough room for two people to stand behind a portable compass repeat showing where the ship's head is pointing and mirrors what is being seen by the helmsman below. There is a rudder repeat to show the position of the rudder, although in a nuclear boat the upper section of the rudder is visible above the waterline when the submarine is surfaced and thus is not essential. But this is belt and braces and we still have a voice pipe to the helmsman in the control room some 30 feet below.

There are a couple of microphones that are connected to watertight sockets on the bridge for speaking to the helm and the plots (navigation) radar for when we are doing Blind Pilotage, which is the term used for using radar assistance if visibility is very poor. These microphones are taken below when diving and blanks are put in the sockets to stop the connectors corroding with the salt water.

Aft of this perch are the masts – attack and search periscopes, side by side, then the radar: Electronic Countermeasures mast (ECM), Wireless Telegraphy mast (WT) (radio), snort induction mast and snort exhaust mast. These latter two are used to suck fresh air in and remove exhaust emissions when running the diesel generator when at periscope depth. These are all covered by shutters, or fairings, made of glass-reinforced plastic (GRP). All the shutters automatically close when the mast is fully down.

The bridge has two manually operated shutters which are shut and clipped as the Officer of the Watch comes below on diving and are the first thing he unclips on surfacing. This provides a fairing or fairness of form to the top of the fin when dived to reduce flow noise. The Navigating Officer is up here, waiting for me. He is in his 20's, ebullient with a shock of dark hair that is on the outer margins of Navy regulations. He has a reputation as a bit of a player who, in the true tradition of the submarine service, works and plays hard. He is looking a little the worse for wear after a massive last night ashore and is hoping that the three Alka Seltzer tablets he took half an hour ago will keep his head clear.

The Outside Engine Room Artificer – or Outside Wrecker in submarine language – is fussing about in the fin, making a final set of checks on the various systems. [An Artificer in the Navy is an artisan who specialises in operating, maintaining and repairing the various systems. The Outside Wrecker is responsible for all the machinery outside the propulsion systems e.g. hydraulics, high pressure air, domestic systems, trim and ballast water systems etc.]

In the radar well, with the radar mast up but not operating, is the Signalman, a quiet but personable young lad of 24. He has just got married to a "Dumbarton Deb" – (a local Scottish girl). They moved into a married quarter on the Churchill Estate Married Quarters in Helensburgh only three days ago. He is wondering how his new bride will cope and whether she will already be back with her mother by the time he returns.

Then there is the First Lieutenant, or Executive Officer, or No.1 in nuclear submarines. Lieutenant Commander Ian Richards is a qualified Commanding Officer in his own right and has captained his own diesel submarine and will go on to Captain his own nuclear boat. He is tall, strong, determined, with an infectious laugh and a great sense of humour. He does not suffer fools gladly and I know him well and respect him very much. Ian and I served on HMS AENEAS when I was given a "pier head jump" – or short notice appointment – as First Lieutenant. Ian was extremely supportive in an old submarine with what I would call were a few 'issues'! I am glad he is my No.1. There are black circles under his eyes, which is not surprising. The days before sailing are a busy time for a First Lieutenant. For the last hour, Ian has been taking reports from the Marine Engineer Officer (MEO), Commander John Davis; the Weapons Engineer Officer (WEO), Lieutenant Commander David Crothers; the various departmental seaman officers (Navigation, Sonar, Torpedo, and Communications) and the Doctor, Lieutenant Commander Chris Kalman (MO) who is responsible for Health Physics as well as the medical side of things. These reports cover more than 400 entries on a checklist. Everything is complete.

The shore power cables are off. Men are moving on the casing, orange lifejackets over their blue foul weather gear. They have singled up the mooring lines. They have been on the casing for about 45 minutes, checking that everything is secure and tightening any bolt they see.

I arrive on the bridge and the First Lieutenant and Navigator both salute as I emerge and wedge myself into the front of the bridge. We are quite a crowd.

Ian Richards reports formally, 'Submarine Ready for sea, Sir. Harbour Stations and Special Sea Duty men closed up. Opened up for diving with the exception of main vents which are cottered (locked) and emergency blow valves which are locked shut. Submarine is in the Patrol Quiet State. All hands onboard. Shore power disconnected, singled up. Both tugs secured and ready to go.'

'Very good No 1,' I reply and turn to the navigator.

'Obey Telegraphs.' I order. This is another old Navy ritual, although we do still have telegraphs between the control room and the manoeuvring room. The Navigator repeats the order through the microphone and I listen as the order is relayed to the manoeuvring room deep in the after end of the boat and repeated back. This is the final order that results in the engaging of the giant clutch, which attaches the gearbox to the main propulsion shaft.

I look at my Graham watch. It is 1457.

The tug's crews have put down their tea and are at their stations, hovering. There is no hurry.

This is the Royal Navy. If the Royal Navy says the boat leaves the wall at 1500, the boat leaves the wall at 1500. Not 1459.55 or 1500.05.

Getting a nuclear submarine off the wall is an old-fashioned process. Nelson would have recognized it without a flicker. A submarine is the shape of a fat pencil. At the back end of the pencil is the propulsor or pump jet, 25 feet in diameter, which is, to all intents and purposes, a multi-bladed propellor in a ring fairing. This is a means of propulsion chosen for silence, not maneuverability.

Below four knots, a nuclear submarine is virtually unsteerable. You try to do your close-quarters maneuvers at a speed of around six to eight knots, which in a 4000- ton boat can be alarming. But it is easier to use tugs to get you off the jetty in the first place. If you hit the jetty with a 4000 ton submarine at even one knot, the forces involved can cause a lot of damage. So you try not to be too cavalier when you are close to land and, although it sticks in a seaman officer's gullet not to be able to do extravagant and flashy maneuvers, common sense dictates that there will be no prizes if you wrap Her Majesty's latest nuclear submarine around some unforgiving jetty. So we use tugs to get the boat cleanly off the wall and into the boat's proper environment.

As usual, in Faslane, it is still raining but it has eased a little. Who was it who chose this place for a submarine base?! Visibility is about ¾ mile. I decide not to use the radar – no transmissions at all if I can help it – that gives you away. Ian is controlling the activity of the casing party with hand signals and occasional shouts to the Casing Officer. He knows what he is doing and I don't interfere.

The reports are coming in: 'Let go forward. Let go aft. All lines clear of the water.' We only use hand signals to the tug. No VHF is allowed, because a Very High Frequency or any other type of radio transmission, will tell the Soviet AGIs (Intelligence gathering vessels disguised as trawlers) that a submarine is coming off the wall and will shortly be in their neighbourhood.

If we allow the AGI to get any suggestion that there is a submarine deploying, he will start working out where to intercept you and prepare for the subsequent chase and harassment. There have been several incidents in the past where the AGI has hit a boat's rudder and also crossed so close ahead that the boat had to go to Emergency Stations and prepare for a collision. We have lost towed arrays as the AGI cut across the stern of the boat without warning but, fortunately, this did not result in the AGI collecting the array. That now resides at the bottom of the North Channel.

Moreover, the AGI will pass on the fact that he has intercepted a submarine and that information could result in other forces, including submarines, being sent to intercept you. This has happened on several occasions, but the UK boat was alert to the situation and was able to detect the Soviet before it detected them. The tugs pull the boat sideways off the dock, nose out. The stern is clear enough of the jetty. I have remembered that I can't see the wide after-hydroplanes that control the angle of the boat when dived. But I can see the upper rudder, which is above the water when the boat is on the surface. Once clear of the jetty by about 30 metres we let go the tugs.

It is time for a small display of British sea power. I say, "Uncotter 4 Main Vent. Open 4 Main Vent."

I listen for the repeated order. This is an essential and fundamental part of submarining. All orders are repeated verbatim to ensure that the right order has been received. It seems clumsy, but experience has proved it to be vital.

'Half Ahead. Revolutions for 8 knots.'

Flooding the rearmost ballast tank takes the stern down a couple of degrees and allows the propulsor to bite better and the rudder to be marginally more responsive. 8 knots provides a good starting push to get the boat moving and brings the wake up. I wait for the rumble deep in the submarine and then feel the vibration as the propulsor bites. HMS SPLENDID starts to move. Slowly at first and then quicker. I watch the huge wash rush towards the jetty and realise I have probably overdone it. The Base Maintenance Officer will not be happy as the catamarans – like barges alongside the jetty to ensure the sensitive parts of the submarine's hull are kept well clear of the jetty – all dance about and thump against the jetty.

'Revolutions for 5 knots,' I say with a guilty conscience, but a smile on my face.

That is a great feeling. Your own command – in control – with all that power at your disposal.

We are doing 6 knots now and I say to the Navigator,' Steer 210°. Are you happy to take the con?'

'I have the con,' repeats the Navigator accepting the immediate responsibility for 'conning' or steering the submarine. But he can only give orders to the helmsman down in the control room who is actually operating the steering controls. Ian can see the ship's heading from the compass repeat and where the rudder is from the rudder repeat and by looking over his shoulder.

This is a formal way of passing the responsibility for navigating the submarine and I will just watch and listen as Ian goes through the motions, giving a commentary as we proceed, checking his head mark and clearing bearings, getting ready for his next wheel over position.

He orders the raising of the search periscope having yelled down into the fin, 'stand clear search,' just in case there is someone in there. There isn't, but you need to always check in submarines.

The Petty Officer of the Watch in the control room, will man the search periscope and take fixes (positions from a selection of bearings of known objects) every six minutes to confirm the submarine's position and progress. He will compare this with both SINS and the GPS system and pass the information back to the Navigator on the bridge.

The casing party is grinning as they know they will soon be down below, away from the freezing wind and rain. They pass the name boards and the ensign staff down through the main access hatch and wind the mooring lines tight on their bollards under the casing and secure them down with heaving lines. Were they to come loose when we are dived they would start knocking on the side of the hull: a potential catastrophe for a submarine, which relies on total silence to remain undetected. It is something that has happened to submarines in the past.

The wake is smooth, now chuckling out astern. There is a black wave overlapping the nose of the casing, breaking into foam in way of the fin. A normal ship would be exchanging thanks and pleasantries with the tugs. Not HMS SPLENDID. The tugs know the form and a wave suffices.

As she surges down the Gareloch, she is sleek, black and silent, without distinguishing marks visible or invisible. There is no engine noise in a nuclear submarine, just the noise of the water as it rushes by.

Rhu Spit arrives just off the port bow, a line of white sand on which little black figures grow. A banner says SEE YOU LATER CHUNKY: black paint on a white sheet.

Leading Marine Engineering Mechanic "Chunky" Evans' children are jumping up and down, waving to their Daddy in his black boat, off to nobody knows where for nobody knows how long. They don't know he can't see them, but we all wave from the bridge – as his proxy.

There are other unidentified wives, girlfriends and children there too as well as rubberneckers and "train spotters." One of the train spotters will no doubt stop off at a callbox in Glasgow and mention to someone with an Eastern European accent that he has seen a Swiftsure class SSN heading for patrol. Or training. Or workup. The families do not know. The crew does not know. The train spotter does not know.

A red buoy slides by to starboard. Then Rhu Spit beacon half a cable's length to port, four knots of ebb tide flow bubbling on its base. The submarine is now travelling at ten knots over the ground, keeping the speed on to assist with steering this black beast through this narrow and dangerous gap. It is still raining and Ian, the navigator, has done this many times before, but he still does not look as if he is enjoying it. Nor am I. This is a tricky piece of manoeuvring and concentration is required – a mistake here could be costly and highly embarrassing!

'Steer 163°,' orders the Navigator.

The Coxswain is on the helm. He is the most experienced at this and has done it more times than the Navigator has had hot dinners. But it is a tricky few minutes with the margins for error slight.

I am listening intently now as bearings from the search periscope are being relayed up to the bridge on the intercom. I know the wheel over position by heart and my own personal visual references. I watch the head mark (the navigation mark on shore that provides a visual reference and guides us) and take in the strength of the ebb tide on the buoys and beacon.

We are close to turning and I am anxious to "warm the bell" – that is to turn a little early to get the boat turning in the right direction. As I am about to speak the Navigator orders, 'Port thirty-five, steer 115°,' to miss Castle Point with its white speckle of caravans.

I instinctively look back aft as the signalman reports, 'rudder moving to port sir,' and wait while it takes effect. It seems to take an age to begin to move, but then the boat starts to turn, slowly at first, and then more quickly.

I listen as the bearings of the clearing marks are reported on the intercom. We turn as planned on to the next head mark and then round onto 191°, heading for the red and green buoys down there in yet another dark rain-shower, off Rosneath Point.

The visibility is getting worse. Under the foul weather jackets – they are not that good at keeping out the water – and blue woolly pullies and white shirts, nervous sweat is mixing with the rain and my towel is failing to stop the water running down my neck. Nuclear submarines are born to whisper through the black deep, not be hurled around on the surface of storm-tossed Scottish sea lochs.

The rain suddenly stops and the casing is empty. The casing party has all disappeared below and we are in more open water. Ian Richards takes a report from the Casing Officer that the casing is secured and all personnel are safely below.

Ian Richards asks, 'Fall out Harbour Stations, please sir. Special Sea Dutymen to remain closed up. Casing secured for sea. Permission to go below, please sir?'

I reply, 'Yes please, No 1. Can we have a HOD's (Heads of Department) meeting in half an hour please? I'd like to brief them before we dive.'

'Aye Aye, sir,' says Ian and disappears below.

As we pass Holy Loch (the US Navy Submarine Base) and Dunoon and turn on to a course of 191° to take us down the Firth of Clyde, it has stopped raining and the visibility has increased to 3 miles. I am cold and wet and need a coffee.

We are now out into the River Clyde approaches. Rothesay Bay opens up to starboard. The town sprawls up the hills. It becomes easier to breathe as the boat moves away from the closeness of the land and into open water and with it the risk of grounding or collision. Round the world sailors say that some of the most dangerous moments in their journeys can be leaving and entering harbour: massive nuclear submarines are little different to small yachts in that respect. Inshore waters are a mixture of sand banks, rocks and all sorts of navigational challenges and it does not matter what type of vessel you are in as you need to concentrate and be very aware of the unexpected.

In front of the town of Rothesay, an orange and grey tug is sliding towards us. There is no swell and there is just a trace of "white horses" on the sea, just a black lop pressed down by the fading rain.

'Stop engines,' says the Navigator, who has the con. 'Open the main access hatch and casing party to the casing.' They have only been down below for about half an hour, but they know the drill and will have had a quick cup of tea or coffee and warmed their extremities a little.

Men spill out of the main access hatch and head for the after part of the casing where the inboard part of the towed array is attached, lashed to a single bollard ready to connect. The towed array is a complex sonar detection system. The principle is to have a sonar array [in essence a long plastic hose with hydrophones inside] trailing behind the submarine, thus removing it from any internal noise from the submarine itself and allowing it to 'hear' better.

In the Royal Navy we used a 'clip-on' system which allows an array with a bigger diameter (and thus better sensors inside it). But, conversely, that also meant that having it on a winch system under the casing or in a ballast tank was a difficult engineering problem to solve as the whole array was effectively cocooned. Getting at if there is a potential defect could mean the submarine going into dock or, at least, needing clearance divers to sort out the problem. Reliability is the key and the Royal Navy at that time preferred a thicker "clip on" array.

The US Navy had reliable arrays that could fit onto winches under the casing or in ballast tanks [and we used some of those systems in our Polaris submarines] but the arrays were by necessity much thinner and thus, in our scientists' view, not so effective.

The tug presents its stern to HMS SPLENDID. We stay put, steady as a rock under the hiss of the rain. There is a big reel on the tug's towing deck. Our towed array guru, is supervising things and watches as one of the casing team takes the heaving line, hauls in the end of what is on the reel and watches as it is connected to the inboard fitting. This process takes about five minutes and involves carefully removing the screwed cover and then 'mating' the inboard end of the giant plug on the casing to the outboard end coming in from the tug. Continuity checks are the done with the sound room (where all the sonar equipment is situated) to make sure everything is working as it should. The connection is checked again and then it is smothered with a thick layer of grease over the whole of the connection to – hopefully – keep out any water trying to leak in. Everything is okay.

The tug slides away; slow ahead, the reel unreeling as it opens the range between HMS SPLENDID and itself. HMS SPLENDID moves forward again, very slow and quiet. The gap between us and the tug widens. What is coming off the reel lies for a moment on the water then sinks slowly. It is a tube, one thousand yards long, with hydrophones at intervals along its length, linked back to the sound room, forward of the base of the conning tower. This is the Towed Array, and it is HMS SPLENDID's ears in the dark sea, which means her eyes as well. I am relieved. The Towed Array is a great bit of kit and vital to our mission, but is notoriously fickle. Sometimes they work like a treat, but there are temperamental ones as well. Getting the connection right is crucial.

The casing team goes below and shuts the hatch. If the damn thing did not work then that would mean a delay and the need to wait for another tug to come out with a new one.

'Are you happy, pilot?' ["Pilot" is an affectionate term used throughout the Royal Navy for the navigating officer of any RN ship.]

'We'll dive in the Arran Trench off the measured mile,' I say to him.

'Happy, Sir,' says the Navigator and I say, 'In which case Fall out Special Sea Duty men. Go to Patrol Routine. [This indicates that the submarine is opened up for diving] Patrol Quiet State.'

The Navigator repeats my orders and I then say, 'Usual shipping reports. Are you happy to take the submarine?'

'Yes, sir. I have the submarine.'

I reply, 'You have the submarine.'

With such words I transfer temporary command of the boat to Ian Mackenzie who, as well as being the navigator, conducting pilotage, is now also the Officer of the Watch (OOW). He will still report to me but, despite his tender years and obvious hangover, he is an experienced seaman and qualified as an OOW.

'Going below,' I say.

The Navigator is on the intercom saying, 'Captain coming below.' Under the bridge is a round hatch in the top of a twenty-four-inch diameter steel tube. This is the submarine's conning tower, and all the rest of the fin is just fairing and support for the masts against the rush of water.

The control room seems crowded after the wide-open Clyde. It has the submarine smell we all know so well – like an air-conditioned hotel room whose windows have been left shut for five years. The sound is like air-conditioning too – a dull roar of fans pushing air round the boat, from the weapons compartment in the bow, the control rooms and crew quarters amidships, to the reactor compartment and turbines in the after section, scrubbing out the CO_2, and replenishing the oxygen.

The control room is in Patrol Routine and the Petty Officer of the Watch is taking a fix through the search periscope, reading off the bearings of familiar points to his assistant.

It is now two and half hours since we left the jetty and I am soaked to the skin and I need that coffee. As if by magic, one of the Stewards appears out of nowhere with a steaming hot coffee.

I thank him and take it to my cabin. I am the only one on board with a room to myself. I say a room, but it is more of a broom cupboard, although very comfortable really. My cabin is at the back of the control room on the port side, next to the wireless mast. It takes the shape of the hull and is strategically placed so that I can hear everything going on in the control room.

It has a bunk with drawers underneath and it faces fore and aft so that I can 'feel' the attitude of the submarine at all times. At the end of the bunk there are dials showing me course, speed and depth and an old fashioned chronometer telling Greenwich Mean Time. We nearly always operate in GMT – regardless of the local time. GMT is a true standard that is still recognized the world over.

There is a small sink with a cupboard underneath and a small wardrobe and desk on the inboard side of the cabin opposite the bunk with an inbuilt radio receiver and stereo with drawers underneath. It is secured for sea with retaining bars to hold things in the shelves and locks on the drawers. The bottom drawer contains a safe in which are stored the most secret documents and "CO's Eyes only" crypto cards and codes that I will need to pull out every now and then.

I pull off my foul weather gear, woolly pully and shirt and dry myself off with a towel. The clothes will dry out in an hour or two as the internal temperature of the submarine is around 72°F.

The Chief Steward has ensured that there is a clean, open necked white shirt, with my gold epaulettes on the shoulder, ready for me. This, with dark blue trousers and black shoes, is all I need to wear when inside the submarine – he really is thoughtful.

I go into the wardroom, forward of the control room, and look at the chart as I go by. I speak to the Petty Officer of the Watch to check all is well and establish that we will be in our diving area in 45 minutes. In the wardroom, the officers who are not on watch are drinking coffee and chatting. The Marine Engineering Officer [MEO], Lieutenant Commander John Davis, comes in wearing white – well off white – overalls and tells me all is as it should be back aft. John is a very professional, experienced and innovative engineer with a penchant for good jokes and singing.

But there are more things to think about at the moment. The Weapons Engineer Officer, Lieutenant Commander David Crothers, is a sitting at the wardroom table with his usual air of optimism and infectious grin. He is a real doer and there are no problems for him – just solutions.

I sit at the table with John and David and we are joined by Ian Richards. These are the Heads of Department, the three HODs, and the one Commander and two Lieutenant Commanders on board. They are a strong team and, as Ian sits down, the other more junior officers get up and leave. They know when they are not wanted. Their time will come.

I go over the plans for the next 24 hours and listen to any concerns they may have. We have lots of checks to do when we dive and noisy routines (blowing slop drain and sewage, discharging hydrogen over the side and ejecting gash through the gash ejector, a sort of vertical torpedo tube that is operated as such but only fires compacted gash – the naval slang for waste). This needs to be planned in so that we give as little away as possible when we are trying to get past the AGI without being detected.

We agree on the timetable that Ian has already produced with the HODs before the meeting. A submarine ship's company is a team and these are my key people in making the complexities of the boat and its operation work efficiently and effectively.

The Intercom goes. 'Captain, Sir. Officer of the Watch.' I pick up the microphone in the wardroom and reply, 'Captain.'

'We will be in the diving position in 10 minutes sir. Permission to go to Diving Stations?'

I reply, 'Yes please,' and 30 seconds later the general alarm sounds throughout the boat, followed by the Petty Officer of the Watch saying, 'Diving Stations. Diving Stations.'

Diving Stations is the call to all hands on board to go to their stations for diving the boat. Every expert is placed in his main area of expertise so that I have the very best I have in the right place in case something goes wrong. The transition from a surface vessel to a submerged submarine, and vice versa, is always a potentially dangerous time as the boat moves from one dimension to another. The boat may not be in trim (either too heavy or too light) and there will have been numerous breaks to the integrity of the pressure hull since we last dived.

During maintenance back in harbour there is a need to break into the pressure hull to conduct various checks. These break points are all part of the design of the hull, but there is still a need to check the pressure hull integrity on completion of these servicing measures in case something has not been put back correctly. Then there is the unexpected, all of which is why we go to Diving Stations to make sure that we have everyone in position to check, observe and deal with any problem.

I go into the control room and jam myself into the big padded chair with the safety straps (probably came out of a Volvo truck!) behind ship control. The Tactical Information screens are to my left, providing me with a plethora of information about the environment around me and the other sharers of that sea around me.

Ian Richards is taking reports and checking that we are ready. When he is satisfied he turns to me and reports, 'Submarine at Diving Stations. Main Vent cotters removed. Emergency Blows unlocked.'

The navigator on the bridge squints over his compass at the land, getting a final series of bearings and passing them down to the plot.

Dived, HMS SPLENDID will still be in pilotage waters, but she will be navigating by dead reckoning, SINS with confirmation visual fixes taken through the periscope.

Electronic navigation systems will come more into play in the open and deeper ocean.

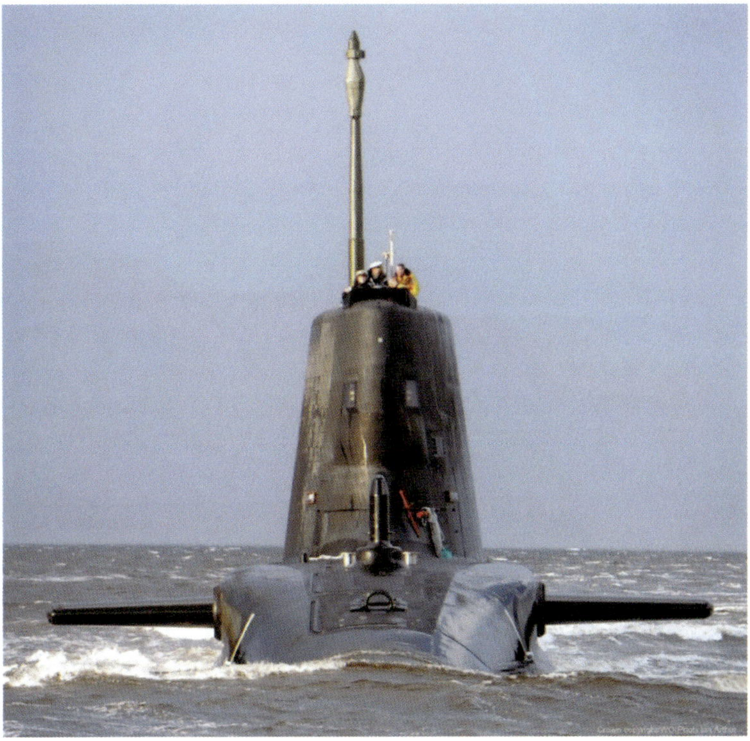

CHAPTER FOUR
TIME TO DIVE

'Come below. Shut the upper lid. I have the submarine.' I have taken back the con for diving.

The Navigator repeats the order and gives the lookout the compass repeat. He shuts the voice pipe cock, secures the dummy ends into the intercom sockets and pushes the bridge fairing covers into place before shutting the clips that keep them secured in place. He has one final look around the bridge to make sure he has left nothing behind and follows the lookout into the conning tower. He wedges himself on the ladder and pulls the large sprung upper lid shut, putting on both clips, and then pinning them, shouting down the tower as he does so, 'Upper lid shut. One clip, two clips. One pin, two pins.'

This is repeated by the signalman so that Ian Richards in the control room can hear the reports.

The Navigator tumbles into the control room looking like a drenched cat. He reports personally to me that the bridge is clear, and the upper lid is shut (submariners always 'shut' things, never close them – it was found many years ago that the word 'close' is open to interpretation when shouted or mumbled) with 'two clips and two pins.'

HMS SPLENDID is now as she is meant to be – an airtight, watertight, pressure proof weapon of war. All she needs to do now is to get into her proper element and dive!

The Petty Officer of the Watch, watched by a drying Navigator, takes a final fix on the periscope. He has been doing this every six minutes since we left the jetty. In front of me and inboard of the Coxswain on the planes, the plethora of valves and dials on the Systems Panel – more than a jumbo jet – which contains the monitors and controls for all the hydraulic, air and water systems that allow us to breathe and fight and swim. And dive.

I like to dive as soon as possible after leaving harbour. There are several reasons for this. One is to make sure all the sonar and detection systems, particularly the towed array, are all working correctly and also to reduce the chance of the towed array getting fouled by surface shipping, of which there is plenty in these relatively congested coastal waters. Another is that a dive gets the cobwebs out of the crew, reminds everyone that we are in an alien environment and helps us focus on what we are here for.

Diesel submarines are boats that spend as much time on the surface as they do dived, submerging only to do their work. A nuclear submarine is the first craft in human history that is happier under the water than on top of it.

The air on my face is not warm, not cool, 72° F. It is always shirtsleeve weather in a nuclear submarine. The towed array will be streaming out behind, neutrally buoyant when the submarine is moving, ten feet or so below the surface. Much too shallow for my liking but that is the way it is designed. It means that at periscope depth the overall length of the submarine is significantly longer than the hull itself. The boat is now at 6 knots and the measured mile beacons on the eastern shore of the Isle of Arran are abeam. There is a deep trench here – a favourite place for submarines that has been used for decades – with enough room to stretch the boat's legs. There is little tide and yet plenty of fixing marks to know where you are: a good place to dive.

Unfortunately, the fish like it too and even though the Admiralty chart states unequivocally that this is a Submarine Exercising Area, the Clyde fisherman still trawl up and down the trench and can create problems for us. There have been some tragedies over the years with submarines getting snagged in fishing boat nets and fisherman drowning and we are all conscious of being careful. There is one there now, but he is well over to the east and parallel to the course we want to follow, but we shall keep a close eye on him.

Ian Richards looks at me and I nod. We are ready.

He asks for some reports to confirm what he already knows – usual submariner's belt and braces approach. I scan all the dials on Ship Control and the Panel and satisfy myself that everything is as it should be.

Nuclear submarines do not crash dive like you see in the World War II movies. HMS WALRUS (which was built in the 1950's to a World War II design) would go down to 65 feet in 1 minute but HMS SPLENDID will take anything from 6 to 8 minutes to dive to the same depth. We tend to go down to 90 feet and then back to 65 feet so that the boat's ngle is both up and down and thus ensures that all the air escapes from the ballast tanks. The forward hydroplanes, which are below the waterline and turned in when surfaced, are turned out and slide from their sockets in the hull below the surface waterline.

Ian Richards orders, 'Diving now. Diving now,' on the intercom for the whole ships company to hear.

Then he says, 'Open 4 main vent.'

He waits about 30 seconds and then 'Open 3 main vent,' followed about 40 seconds later by 'Open 1, and 2 main vents. 10 degrees down.' I am at the search periscope, watching the air escape and the boat start to dive.

The Coxswain who is now controlling the hydroplanes as well as steering puts the hydroplanes to dive and calls out the depth every 5 feet as we go down. That way both Ian and I can judge the rate of descent. We can hear the air rushing out of the main vents even here in the control room and we then wait as the air is expelled and the water comes in through the free flood holes at the bottom of each ballast tank.

The deck tilts underfoot; only a degree or two at a time, imperceptible to someone walking along a road, but to a submarine captain as plain as the path up Ben Nevis. '6 degrees down. 90 feet and back to 65,' says Ian, repeated by the Coxswain who has the one man control rudder and diving planes yoke pushed fully forward.

The one man control, (OMC) is an ingenious device invented by a technology company called Harlands in the late 1960s, employing the same principle used in aircraft. It combines on one yoke, with the functions of the rudder (left and right or rather port and starboard to steer), and controls the fore planes and after planes in synch. The fore planes control the depth and the after planes the angle. It has an autopilot facility for both course and depth and various settings that can be ordered such as pitch angle and sensitivity of plane used. There are times when we are at speed when we disconnect the fore planes and even bring them in like an under carriage, and control both depth and angle on the after planes alone.

But now they are very much in synch and the Coxswain continues to call out the depth as we go down. We reach 90 feet and he reverses the planes and comes back up to 65 feet – periscope depth.

Ian Richards is on the main intercom again. 'The submarine is at periscope depth. All compartments carry out post diving checks and report.'

This sets in motion another long list of checks that ensures that the boat is properly configured for being underwater – after all it may be a long time before we are on the surface again. It is only the stamina of the man and the capacity of the food stored that limits a nuclear submarine's endurance.

When a submarine is submerged, the trick is to keep it neutrally buoyant and "balanced" or trimmed so that it is "level" in the water (has a "zero bubble"). There are auxiliary tanks aboard that allow water to be flooded in or pumped out. This is done by using the ballast pump to pump water out through a hull valve and flood water in through the same valve. That resolves the bodily weight, but there is still a need to trim the submarine fore and aft and this is achieved by moving water backwards and forwards through a separate trim system and trim pump.

The Officer of the Watch is in charge of "catching the trim. All these movements to "catch the trim" are controlled on the orders from the Officer of the Watch to the Panel Operator who has all the controls at his fingertips. When a boat is properly trimmed and neutrally buoyant, it can be moved most efficiently through the water. The planes, which are used to "steer" the ship vertically, will be at zero and the boat will hold its depth with a zero bubble.

There is a bit more of an art to this, but the basics are straightforward and involve ordering small movements of water in and out of the submarine through the ballast system and moving water forward or aft through the trim system. And so the "trim is caught." This is a continuous process as the ordered depth of the submarine is changed as the internal tanks of fresh water are used, the slop drain and sewage tank is filled and emptied and a plethora of other small changes happen.

I listen to the reports coming in. We are now also receiving reports from the sound room of sonar contacts. Reports from sonar and the sensors are coming in and are being matched to the picture of shipping contacts we had on the DCB tactical system screens surface picture before we dived. From now on we are dependent on the sonar, with the occasional information from visual observation on the periscope or a sensor on a mast.

Ten minutes pass and the trim is caught. Ian Richards reports that all the checks have been made and everything is settled. There have been a few valves and glands tightened and adjustments made to machinery. "Ready to go to the watch, sir" says Ian to me.

'Watch Diving, Patrol Quiet State. When we are settled on the watch we will go to 300 feet.' I reply, and this starts the changeover of personnel to the two watch system forward (6 hours on 6 hours off) and the three watch system aft (Four hours on, eight hours off with 2 hour dog watches between 1600 and 2000 each day). The different watch systems are because the engineering department 'back aft' has a different type of watch keeping routine to those forward. We have found that the two watch system for the sensor and tactical systems operators provides better continuity and better rest between watches although it is tiring after a few weeks.

We are on now on the watch. The Doctor, as Second Officer of the Watch, has taken over from the Petty Officer of the Watch on the navigation and checks the Ships Inertial Navigation System (SINS) and the automatic plot, which generates a dead reckoning (DR) position to the scale of the chart shining a pencil beam up onto the chart. The DR Plot is fed course and speed direct from the compass and log repeaters. When the fix is plotted on the chart, the Officer of the Watch goes to look to ensure he is happy where we are and orders, '6 down. Keep 300 feet.' The waters of the Clyde slap together over the summit of the fin. We slide into the deep, where the weather is always the same.

I put it in the holder on the chair and light my pipe. Smoking is still allowed in submarines and many of the Ship's Company smoke. I have been a pipe smoker for many years and I rely – selfishly – on the air conditioning system to get rid of my fumes. There is an upside as the aroma of my St Bruno flake tobacco indicates to anyone interested/or trying to pull the wool over my eyes that the Captain is safely in the control room and not patrolling the boat!

There was another reason for the early dive. The waters off the North Atlantic are divided up into sectors, under a system known as water space management. It is not unlike air traffic control, and it has the same object – to prevent mutual interference and collisions. Driving a nuclear submarine is like driving a car down the fast lane of the motorway, blindfold. And with the windows shut and with only the sound of other cars to guide you.

In water space management each submarine is allotted a block of water thirty miles long and twenty miles wide – known as its moving haven or MXA. The block travels with the submarine.

The allocation of blocks is agreed at NATO. This NATO agreement is very fragile. Many nations do not have much confidence in the NATO systems believing that some countries leak the information either deliberately or mistakenly. We have always assumed that any NATO sub-note information, in essence the planned route or area the submarine is going to operate has a good chance of getting to the Soviets. If that happens then the Soviets effectively could have a clear picture of where you are and where you are going so it is not surprising that submarines often have an 'official' (NATO sub note) position and a real one. This system has a real purpose in that it aims to avoid mutual interference and thus any chance of an underwater collision but, unfortunately, the Soviets do not pass their sub notes or whatever they use to NATO or the UK! So, although there is ample evidence that several nations do their own thing, the system does provide a level of security against a possible collision.

Today, HMS SPLENDID has NATO water space management allocation for a patrol area off the southwest of Iceland. In the shielded conference room off the Northwood tunnel last week, I had received entirely different orders. From henceforward, HMS SPLENDID will be proceeding in its own water heading for a patrol area that has nothing to do with Iceland.

Other countries of various sorts and types also decide where they go and, despite the best will in the world that underwater movements will be coordinated, the reality is that nation states operating submarines – by the nature of what they do – will decide for themselves where their submarines will go and when. That means that they will depend on their own sensors to keep them from accidently running into another submarine.

Despite what the media portrays British submarine security is as watertight as their boats and we expend a great deal of energy making sure that they are – both the boats and security. A British submarine coming out of Faslane, or an American coming out of Holy Loch, has to turn left down the Irish Sea or right through the North Channel. The Americans like the Irish Sea route, which is wide, if shallow. The British are less keen. By the Irish Sea route, the hundred-fathom line, which effectively defines deep water, lies somewhere near the Fastnet Rock at the southwestern corner of Ireland.

Most Royal Navy submarine Commanding Officers have to make a choice depending on where they are going and what they are planning to do and most prefer the North Channel, between the Mull of Kintyre and the coast of Northern Ireland, because the hundred-fathom line is only about 40 miles to its northwest and that allows access to deep water much quicker than the Irish Sea route. But the

North Channel has its disadvantages. It is only twenty-two miles wide. Its tides are notoriously powerful, its waters extremely hazardous and shallow. A cursory look at the chart, whether you are a Brit or Soviet, will show you that there are very limited routes that a dived submarine can take. Off its northern exit by Rathlin Island, the Soviet AGIs hover, combing the ether with their aerials and sitting in the middle of, what they consider, will be the preferred channels.

The shallows mean that a submarine cannot get much below periscope depth, and the tortuous channels mean that navigation is by limited use of the periscope, exacerbated by the extra length of the towed array. But, what the Office of the Watch is likely to see through the periscope, is not a hotel painted white by the Navy as an aid to clandestine navigation, but an AGI bearing down, half full of curiosity and the other half full of hostile intent, and a threat to be taken seriously.

You have no idea what the AGI is going to do. Try to pass very close and provoke a change in course or try to go close astern and cut your towed array. They certainly want to report your progress and identify you by name if they can. They also want to harass you by manoeuvring in such a way as to try to force you to change course to avoid a close quarter's situation or at worse a collision. These situations go with the territory of being a submarine Captain and we do prepare and plan possible actions very carefully. Courts Martial for a collision or losing an array has happened, but is still rare. For us it is more embarrassing that you even got into that situation. Once past the AGIs in the choke point, the passage to the patrol area should be smooth and easy.

At least it should be.

The control room was the same as two days ago, but different. Same temperature, same faces, same sounds. But everyone had settled into dived routine. The black circles had gone from under people's eyes and the Navigating Officer looked almost cheerful, because the inertial navigation system had fallen in line and was now agreeing with his fixes and dead reckoning plot.

I was feeling better myself. The indigestion I always get in the North Channel from AGIs, rocky outcrops, shallow water and strong tides, not to mention the Scottish weather, had gone. The Outside Wrecker had been pumping teacupfuls of water from tank to tank. Now we had the boat precisely trimmed to neutral buoyancy, and Barny Barnard, the Petty Officer Cook and starboard watch planes man, was flying her through the sea with featherweight touches on the planes and rudder. It is a submarine fact that for some bizarre reason Petty Officer Cooks are always good plainsmen. It must be something in the Bisto.

It was Sunday. I knew it was Sunday. Not because we had the usual ecumenical church service, demanded by the Queen's Regulations and Admiralty Instruction (QRAI) – otherwise known as the Navy's Bible – attended by about 15 souls, but because we had had grapefruit segments for breakfast.

I had read the prayers. We had sung a couple of good hymns, "Eternal father strong to save" and "Cym Rhondda" always go down well as you don't have to sing in tune.

Now HMS SPLENDID was steaming resolutely towards the patrol area at a steady 14 knots. This was a good speed as it was a compromise between getting where you wanted to go in reasonable time, but also ensuring you were sufficiently quiet that you could well hear what was going on outside. In other words, in a state where we were almost certain to hear anybody else before they heard us. We call it the sonar advantage. Back in the early 1970's we had discovered that the movement over the hydrophones created "flow induced resonance" which, at a certain speed, interfered with or blanked out the incoming noise. To correct that the boffins in the MOD came up with a large GRP (Glass Reinforced Plastic) or fibre glass dome that encompassed the whole sonar array at the front of the submarine. This created an area of still water next to the hydrophones that allowed them to still hear extremely well at a much higher speed. It was an ingenious solution and made a great difference.

At the back end, the reactor was in containment state three – a relaxed state when away from land, – glowing like a kettle deep inside its lead shielding, though nobody could, or would, want to see that. All ill-informed commentators want people to think that the reactor is always pulsing and glowing red hot. The reality is very different.

In reality it is a very benign machine about the size of a dustbin, but extremely well shielded and controlled with consummate care and attention.

Back aft there are around 14 watch keepers working 1 watch in 3, each watch of 4 hours duration. There would be an Engineering Officer of the Watch (EOOW) who would be in charge of everything involved with the reactor systems, steam turbines and steam generators and the plethora of systems that kept propulsion available to the Captain. His training to get to that position would have lasted around 7 years – more than a doctor – and he would have spent hours and hours crawling around the submarine locating valves and pipes so that he knew as much as there was to know. He would have also spent hours in a simulator ashore where every type of potential failure would have been thrown at him, some even if they were highly unlikely. But his knowledge had to be so good that he was able to deal with the most difficult situation if it arose.

In the manoeuvring room which was the control room for all the back aft machinery he had a Chief of the Watch to support him – who was also qualified to the same level, and individual highly qualified senior ratings manning the Reactor, Electrical and Propulsion Panels. One of them was Paddy Porter who was an Electrical Panel Operator. He was a delightful Irishman who always viewed things in a calm matter of fact manner. These were the key controllers and then there were junior ratings who were actually in the various propulsion compartments and who responded to instructions but also spent a great deal of their time checking and checking again, taking readings from various gauges and recording them and constantly looking for the unusual. They were a tight group and relied very much on each other.

In the submarine's mid-section, people were living and eating and sleeping. Some were on watch like those in the control room and the sound room. The sonar operators were the boat's ears slicing up sea sounds with a mass of specialist analysis equipment designed to break down every last sound the hydrophones on the sonar sets could detect. The Communications team in the Wireless Shack down on three deck led by Chief Radio Supervisor Pincher Martin under the control room were watching the constant flow of messages from Northwood coming through on tele printers rattling along at 75 bauds per minute.

In the galley – Leading Cook Preston and Cooks Jones and Sturman led by PO Cook Barny Barnard continued to produce miracles cooking three meals a day. After few days all the salad gear is gone and the fresh vegetables and potatoes start to diminish and for most the three meals a day had shrunk to two and sometimes one, depending on which watch they were on and when they preferred to eat. People were moving precisely, but quietly and with no excess of energy. The port watch were in their bunks, reading or dozing, preparing themselves mentally for the showing of the movie on the boat's

16mm reel to reel films we carried. Weapons Engineering Mechanician Steve Hogg and Chief Petty Officer Jeff Matthews – the TI – or Torpedo Instructor were reluctant to leave their babies (torpedoes) alone and were always looking for problems although there were seldom many. HMS SPLENDID was a small town moving through the pitch-black sea, as close to peaceful as she could be. Which, in reality, was not very peaceful at all.

For a nuclear attack submarine, the Cold War could turn hot at five minute's notice. SPLENDID's purpose in life was to be aggressive, to track down Soviet SSBNs and SSNs, stalk them, track or trail them, listen to their activity and the noises they made, noting their communications and habits, and recording them for addition to the great library of intelligence that the MOD tries to keep up to date. This all adds up to a better understanding of your potential enemy. "Know your Enemy" is a key element of peace time activity.

The famous Chinese General and strategist Sun Tzu in his book "The Art of War" – read and studied by most military officers of many nations – said "It is said that if you know your enemies and know yourself, you will not be imperiled in a hundred battles; if you do not know your enemies but do know yourself, you will win one and lose one; if you do not know your enemies nor yourself, you will be imperiled in every single battle."

So, if you know your enemy's capabilities and likely courses of action you have a better chance of succeeding. And it helps you decide on your own options too – what might be possible and what will not be. Again, as Sun Tzu said, "The commander who advances without coveting fame and retreats without fearing disgrace, whose only thought is to protect his country and do good service for his sovereign, is the jewel of the kingdom."

In the event of the Soviet boat preparing to fire missiles, HMS SPLENDID's role, as an SSN, was to fire and direct a Tigerfish torpedo to sink the Soviet SSBN before it could launch its missiles and potentially destroy most of the UK, North America, or whatever else they had targeted. Our torpedo tubes were already loaded – just in case. Provided the missile firing was not just an exercise. And provided HMS SPLENDID was not herself sunk by the Soviet SSN that would almost certainly be riding 'shotgun' on the Soviet SSBN. Usually a Soviet SSN [attack submarine] would be in close proximity to the SSBN [missile submarine], its mission to protect the Soviet SSBN from our torpedo attack for long enough for the SSBN to fire its nuclear missiles.

And provided our Tigerfish torpedoes worked, which was by no means certain! We normally had the tubes loaded but not flooded. However as the environment in which we were operating became more potentially hostile, defined by your position and potential of finding enemy targets, we flooded at least two tubes and made them ready. Flooding torpedo tubes made a noise and we made sure that this was done well away from prying ears.

The world of submarine warfare in the age of deterrence contained far too many provisos ever to be peaceful. So any advantage we had over the enemy – knowing from their signatures through the water which was the missile boat and which the shotgun, and what class of that boat each was – could, in the event of war, be the margin of life and death. The difference between 16 nuclear missiles raining down from the sky onto Britain or America and destroying that country entirely, and us destroying that Soviet missile sub before it had a chance to open fire. That is no small task. And one of which we were highly aware.

The officers did, of course, discuss this amongst ourselves and with members of the Ship's Company, but not formally. What we might do and when was always a topic of conversation, although I rarely came across a submariner who did not passionately believe in what he was doing.

The watch ended. The Officer of the Watch gave me his end of watch report. Men explained things that needed explaining. This was useful. But what we were really looking for was noise. We are very, very fussy about noise. Active sonar, the kind that goes 'ping,' is something you hear in war films, or when things have gone so far someone is about to shoot at you or you are about to shoot at them but using active sonar means that you are revealing yourself – and that is usually a mistake. Passive sonar on a quiet boat means that we can hear a Soviet boat before he hears us and follow him at a distance. To do this, it is crucial that we can hear him, but he cannot hear us. We call this the sonar advantage.

In HMS SPLENDID's Sonar Type 2001 we did have a significant active capability, as you will see in the next chapter, but its use declined in the early 1980s. If you really want to use your stealth and guile you need to remain passive and maximize the technological advantage you have to detect the enemy before they detect you. This is a fundamental part of operating a nuclear submarine and remains so.

HMS SPLENDID's propulsor has vanes at its forward end, to spin the water column – or pre-swirl, as we call it – so the blades do not cavitate, producing fizzy little hydrogen bubbles that can be heard by the enemy. Her engines float on hydraulic rafts. Everything attached to the pressure hull from the inside has a flexible rubber mount to prevent any knocking or chafing or squeaking of metal on metal.

On the Officer of the Watch's rounds of the boat, at the end of his watch, he discreetly checked that nobody had left a hammer wedged between a fitting and the hull. When the Petty Officer Cook Barny Barnard came back off the planes to go back to the galley he would be watching his chefs and chastising them to be careful and not to clatter a saucepan. If someone makes an unnecessary noise by mistake then he is chastised. Although he is probably more annoyed with himself. We do go on about noise and everyone is only too well aware of the dangers of being careless.

Silence is our watchword. After all we are known as the Silent Service and to make any noise on a submarine under water is still a cardinal sin. Everyone monitors everyone else and that is accepted as a sensible approach.

Things are fine. We are where we expected to be, the boat is running well and there are only a very few minor defects. There are always defects in a vessel as complicated as an SSN. But we have a zero tolerance policy to defects and as soon as they occur the repair is pursued in a serious and pacey manner. We want the machine to be working. At full potential. All the time.

HMS SPLENDID leaving Faslane

CHAPTER FIVE

A CLOSE SHAVE – HMS CONQUEROR IN 1972

HMS CONQUEROR

In 1972 I was serving as the Navigating Officer of HMS CONQUEROR, which was the fourth VALIANT class submarine built. This was my first SSN, and I had come straight from specialist training on the first Long Submarine Navigation Course at HMS DRYAD, aimed at improving dramatically the quality of navigation in our SSNs. Improvement in nuclear submarine Navigating officers training was seen as vital There had been several arrow escapes and a few groundings and it was obviously considered that with nuclear submarines now being the Navy's capital ships they should have well qualified officers navigating them. They were right!

This was a key time in the Cold War. By the early 1970s, the Soviet Union was at the peak of its power. In addition to economic advantages at home, the Soviet Union attempted to assert itself as the world's dominant superpower overseas. For nearly every Soviet success in the early 1970s, the United States suffered a setback. While the oil-rich Soviet economy continued to grow, the economy of the United States strained under the pressure of the OPEC imposed oil embargo of 1972 and 1973.

The Soviet Union had also prevailed on the international stage. Soviet-backed North Vietnamese forces expelled American troops after a prolonged conflict. The communist victory in Vietnam, coupled with US public opposition to the conflict, signalled an end to the American policy of communist containment in Southeast Asia.

The pace of Soviet nuclear weapon production greatly alarmed Washington. Fearing a Soviet advantage in the arms race, Nixon signed the Strategic Arms Limitations Talks (SALT I). The West looked to be slipping behind in the Cold War.

Commander Chris Ward was the Captain and we were the second tranche of CONQUEROR's Ships' Company. The boat had been built in Cammell Laird's in Birkenhead and had had a difficult time getting out of the shipyard due to industrial unrest and even sabotage and this led to long delays in finishing the boat.

We were all very aware that the Soviet submarine force was getting stronger and more sophisticated. There was definitely a view at the time, because we did not know as much as we would have liked, that they were bigger in size and in numbers than they actually were.

The Soviets had big surface ships with missiles everywhere on them, although nobody really knew whether they worked or not. I expect many of their systems did not, though we did not really know.

There was apprehension that we were perhaps making out that the Soviet submarine force was actually stronger than they were but, and again, I don't think any of us knew that for certain.

What I do know is that the uncertainty fuelled our concern and they were flexing their muscles and were coming out to patrol and snoop into areas that we had not seen before, including the north western and south western approaches to the UK and the Mediterranean. Our detection systems were still continuing to be developed and this was a continuous process.

Whatever the reality, the Soviet submarine force certainly felt like a threat and I became obsessed with the Soviet Union and making sure that the Soviet Union did not get its way. I was determined, like all my colleagues that we would do everything we could to play our part. I read as much as I could on Russia and how it had merged into the Soviet Union. I read numerous intelligence reports that tried to assess the Soviet submarine force capability in terms of sensors, weapons, training and their detection capability on us, as well as somewhat sketchy assessments of the tactics they might use to harass or even attack us or what they might do if we found their submarines and they detected us.

Of course, some was based on collected fact and some was speculation. Sometimes it was difficult to understand which was which. I did not have any first- hand knowledge as I had never been at close quarters with a Soviet submarine. , but it was some comfort that the Royal Navy Submarine Flotilla was made up of volunteers, not the conscripts on which the Soviets based their submarine manning. We approached everything, including our excellent training systems, in a thoroughly professional manner.

The Soviet conscripts clearly had a very different lifestyle to our own and, although I did not know any details at the time, I was fortunate later on in my career to visit Severomorsk in 1993, the HQ of the Soviet Northern Fleet and see for myself just how poor the condition of their ships and submarines really were and had been.

I think I had a view that the Soviet submariner had almost a blind faith in their state system and the motherland and their ability to come out on top. I have no idea if this was true, but conversations I had much later with Admiral Yerofeyev, the Northern Fleet Commander and his Deputy, Vice Admiral Suchkov, and a Soviet submarine squadron commander, Rear Admiral Titerenko, indicated to me that they were equally committed to their communist system as I was to mine.

We had to counter that, and all three of them told me that they were fearful of the professionalism and grit of the Royal Navy. They saw the United States as their main foe and saw the UK as more of an irritant – a pest that was always nibbling at the side. But we were still quite a large navy in 1972 and we weren't to be pushed aside.

The politics that were going on is well documented in a number of books. Some of us, including myself, were involved in a book called "We Come Unseen" by Jim Ring. It explained the relationship between the politics and where five of us were at various stages of our careers. I have no idea how we were chosen, but the five were Jim Taylor, Jeff Tall, Martin MacPherson, Toby Elliott and me. We were all of the same generation and had all been in command of nuclear submarines.

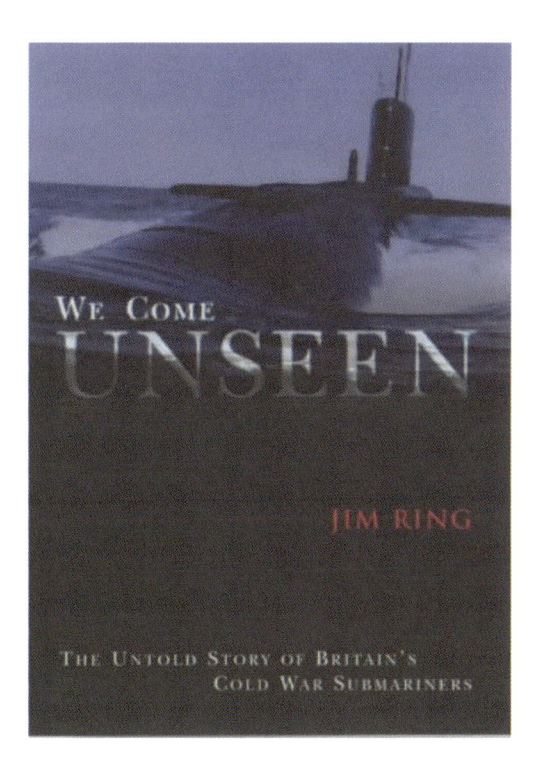

Looking back at that posed the question as to whether I realised what was going on at the time politically. Some I did. Some I did not. For example, I was not really aware of what was going on with Strategic Arms Limitation and I was not really that interested in it. It was way above my pay grade at the time anyway.

On New Year's Eve 1972 my parents had just arrived for the New Year celebrations in our maisonette in Smugglers Way, in Faslane. And then, that very day, I had a telephone call to return to the boat. I subsequently discovered that I had enough time to go back home and grab a few clothes before going back onboard. I spent all New Year Eve's night planning, with curtains around my chart table – I was the navigator after all!

This was the time when we had what was called a "Ready Duty SSN" (attack boat) and there was a nuclear submarine that was "on call." It sounds simplistic, but in reality it was a complex situation for the Flag Officer Submarine's Programming Officer. We had a rota and each boat was allocated on standby for various periods from 3 weeks to 3 months. That meant that your readiness, both materially and for the Ships' Company, needed careful thought in case you had to move quickly. It was not specified what you were on standby for, but you needed to be always topped up with stores, food and all the other things that sustained you at sea for an indefinite period.

We were told that the Prime Minister at the time, Edward Heath, was of the view that the government paid all this money for these very expensive submarines and, "when I want one, I want one!" And he wanted one that New Year's Eve. We recalled the Ship's Company and, amazingly, every one of them returned on New Year's Eve and New Year's Day in Scotland, including one from the Isle of Wight. We sailed at 1000 the next morning. Mind you I would not have expected anything less. They may have cursed and sworn, but they still got back.

The mission was to intercept a trawler, or coaster, that was transiting from the Eastern Mediterranean and was suspected to be full of IRA guns and weapons. Our job was to find it trail it and follow it back so that it could be arrested when it was close enough to do so. The mission lasted around 15 days by the time we got down to the Mediterranean and followed it back. The coaster had started somewhere in the Middle East, but was thought to be Cypriot owned and was called the Claudia. It was strongly suspected of running guns and explosives to the IRA in Ireland. The intelligence on this probably came from a combination of UK and Irish sources, but we were not told from where the information had come. The information was very limited, but we knew when it left Cyprus and what it looked like.

Anyway, I was able to project its probable track on the chart towards Southern Irish coast, where it was believed to be going, and work out an intercept position, or area of probability. The problem was that nobody knew whether the trawler would make another port call. We had been told that various embassies had been alerted to look out for it, but I suspect they were not told why. I also looked at what would the intercept position be if it stopped in Libya as it was well known by then that the Libyan Leader, Colonel Muammar Gaddafi sympathised with the IRA campaign.

We made a fast passage to the Mediterranean and passed through the Straits of Gibraltar. We then made our way to my predicted probability area, south of Sardinia. We had no more intelligence or positional information, but there was a strong chance that we would pick up a noisy coaster if it was not near the coast. And so it proved.

After 24 hours of searching we picked up the Claudia and managed to identify it visually through the periscope. We were then able to follow it from about 3 miles astern as it continued on its 8-10 knot passage. This was very simple and I am certain that they had no idea we were there. We were surprisingly pulled off in the Bay of Biscay and ordered to return to Coulport.

Later we thought that this may have been a rehearsal and, in late March 1973, the Claudia, carrying a shipment of weapons, was intercepted by three Irish Navy patrol vessels in Irish territorial waters near Pelvic Head, County Waterford. They seized five tonnes of Libyan arms and ammunition found on board. The weapons included 250 Soviet-made small arms, 240 rifles, anti-tank mines and other explosives. Later I found out that it was estimated that three shipments of weapons of similar size and makeup did get through to the IRA during the same time period and that the early Libyan arms shipments furnished the IRA with its first RPG-7 rocket-propelled grenade launchers, and that Gaddafi also donated three to five million US dollars at this time. This was one of the very first 'Ready Duty SSN' tasks and there is no doubt that it was kept very quiet. The Ships' Company were given an explanation and told that anything about this mission was to remain within the boat. Submariners are used to that!

After we finished that operation, we returned to Coulport in Loch Long rather than Faslane as we had some torpedoes to change. Within an hour of arrival Captain, Commander Chris Ward, called me in and said that there was another mission for us. He wanted me to go to Faslane and get on the secure telephone [no cell phones in those days] to the Flag Officer Submarine's duty staff officer and find out what was going on and what we were required to do.

I managed to get a lift to Faslane and I got on the phone to the FOSM duty staff officer – who was an engineer (nothing wrong with that – many of my best friends are engineers!) – and apparently there was intelligence, and a strong belief, that there was a Soviet submarine that had entered the Clyde local areas. That is inside the North Channel between Northern Ireland and the Mull of Kintyre and thus inside the UK's territorial waters by anyone's view of things. The intelligence had come from maritime patrol aircraft that had been tracking this particular submarine. These were United States P3 aircraft from Keflavik in Iceland and Royal Air Force Nimrods from Kinloss in Scotland. It was also likely to have been picked up initially on SOSUS. SOSUS stands for Sound Surveillance System and was a series of underwater arrays of hydrophones located on the sea bed and connected by cable to shore stations around the world. The system worked by the use of fixed pre-positioned underwater sonar arrays aimed at detecting Soviet submarines in the lower acoustic range (0 to 10 KHz). But the key ones were in the Greenland - Iceland - Faeroes - UK gap and off the East coast of the United States and at various locations in the Pacific Ocean.

The system was intended to find and track Soviet submarines as they came into the Atlantic and it was a very secret system that the United States shared only with the United Kingdom. It was a key long range early warning system and was an extraordinary scientific and engineering achievement. More to the point, we were extremely fortunate that the United States trusted us to share SOSUS and, indeed, there were shore terminals based in the UK.

SOSUS did not provide real time information as we know it today. It took about 20 minutes for the detection to be transmitted from the array through the shore terminal and then to Northwood and be analysed and turned round and put on the submarine broadcast. We considered 20 minutes to be incredibly fast then, and so it was.

Of course, at that time not only was Faslane the home of the UK Polaris submarines, but the United States also based a large number of their Polaris submarines from a Depot Ship moored in the middle of Holy Loch, off Dunoon, in Scotland.

I asked the FOSM Duty Staff what our orders were. 'Well,' he said. 'I'm not sure. I suppose, chase it out!'

I was horrified that a Soviet submarine should consider, let alone be able, to enter the Clyde Inner areas which were absolutely our back yard. How dare he come in here? We had to get rid of him.

And yet I took it as perfectly normal that we could and would operate in International Waters in the North Norwegian and Barents Seas – the Soviet's backyard. It was just we were not used to this type of aggression in our home waters. Nor was it expected, even though we knew the Soviets wanted to keep track of our SSBNs.

I went back to Coulport and, within 8 hours, we were at sea again, going down the Clyde. After we sailed more information started to arrive by signal and we sat down and tried to decide how we were going to approach this situation.

Obviously, the first thing to do was to find it. Then, assuming we had done that, just how were we going to "chase it out"? The intelligence began to indicate that this was a Victor class SSN and she was approaching UK territorial waters although at this stage she was still outside the UK 12 mile limit but, by my reckoning, inside our 200 mile limit. We started to receive vectored reports from the maritime patrol aircraft.

There was no precedent for this and nobody knew how to do this. We were on our own.

What we did know at that stage, from previous interactions, was that Soviet submarine tactics were likely to be very aggressive. But that also indicated that these tactics could be a response to both the US and UK interference to what they perceived as their own operations and that their ability to detect us was not likely to very good. Moreover, they possibly could not hold and then track us on sonar as well as we could hold and then track them. But, and then again, this was thought to be a new Victor class submarine and we did not really know her capabilities.

Soviet Victor III Class nuclear submarine

How should we prepare for this? We didn't have any specific Rules of Engagement [RoE] in case things turned nasty. We operated under a set of standard National Rules of Engagement, but these were rarely changed. We pulled out those and it did not really cover what we were probably going up against. These days a submarine captain would demand to have RoEs – prepared by the MOD and politicians – so he knows what he is permitted to do and not do. Politicians have a long and trusted tradition of grabbing the glory when something turns out well, and blaming the junior guy on the spot when it goes pear-shaped. Rules of Engagement are therefore also designed to protect the Commanding Officer as well as the politicians in the event something goes wrong.

We would be under the Operational Control [OPCON] of

Commodore Clyde [COMCLYDE]. We knew we were not authorized to fire a torpedo. But what should we do if one was fired at us? We did not know whether the Soviets were actually authorised to fire torpedoes at western submarines, either in self defence or as a tactic to shake someone off.

There were lots of suggestions, on both sides of the Atlantic, that there could be situations when the Soviets might employ such tactics, but the general view was that this was unlikely. However, we needed to be ready for all eventualities and would ensure that our torpedo evasion procedures were practiced both in the shore Submarine Command Team Trainer (SCTT) and at sea. We did not know what might provoke the Soviets into firing a torpedo, but thought that they were unlikely to do this in international waters.

However, we did not really have a close quarter's procedure and it was very much left to the Commanding Officer to decide how to act depending on the Soviet and our own course, speed, depth and aspect. It was in The Hunt for Red October that Tom Clancy concluded, probably correctly, that, "the submariner's trade required more than skill. It required instinct, and an artist's touch: monomaniacal confidence, and the aggressiveness of a professional boxer."

We spent half an hour considering the likely options and reactions of the Soviet submarine, including what he might do when he was actually in the Clyde Inner areas [i.e. inside the North Channel] and how he would react if he thought we had detected him. The Torpedo and Sonar Officer [TASO] was directed to urgently review the "what ifs" and report back to the Captain in 4 hours' time.

After a series of discussions with the First Lieutenant, to which I was included, the Captain decided that he should have at least two tubes loaded and have the bow caps [the torpedo tube outer doors] of two tubes open. That seemed a sensible decision to me. It was one I was to remember several years later when it might have been me on the receiving end of a Soviet torpedo, when I was the one being 'difficult'.

One of the main aims throughout our operation of nuclear submarines was to maintain what we called the "sonar advantage". In other words, we would detect and track a Soviet submarine at a greater range before they could detect us. This would allow us to establish course and speed and range, which are the basic parameters of any fire control solution [the details you need to know to have any chance when firing a weapon of it hitting the target] earlier than the Soviet could do the same on us.

Assessing depth on sonar was not really possible at that time and we did not have the sensors that could do this.

We were able to talk direct to the Nimrods by secure short range UHF and VHF radio and obtain the latest information as well as getting constant reports from Northwood on the submarine VLF broadcast on SOSUS information. Remember SOSUS is a passive sonar system that indicates a "presence" of a submarine, or at least some source of recognisable submarine noise, but it is not a precise location. Instead it indicates an area within which a target can be found and gives a very good start to any search and follow up.

We did not use HF radio as that was too easily intercepted from long range. There was the potential that a Soviet submarine, if it was at periscope depth, could pick up those transmissions as of course might an AGI or Soviet listening station. The fact that they could not understand them as they were encrypted was immaterial. If they could intercept them this could give away our position, at least to within a few miles.

The reports indicated that the Victor was pretty close and approaching the North Channel. The North Channel is the stretch of sea between the Mull of Kintyre at the southwestern tip of Scotland and the northeastern shore of Northern Ireland, off Rathlin Island. It is a very dangerous piece of water with many navigational dangers and very strong tidal streams, not to mention awful weather for more days than not. It is a tricky piece of water for a dived submarine. We had dived off the island of Ailsa Craig and were approaching the area at periscope depth in a cautious manner. At that time our charts were not very good and had really been designed for surface ships. The overlap between charts was poor and invariably at different scales and you needed around three charts to get through the North Channel. You went from a large scale to a small scale to a large scale chart, which did not make it very easy when you were trying to navigate precisely through a navigational difficult area.

Tidal streams do affect submarines. When they run at 3 or 4 knots and change direction, depending where you are, it provides a further uncertainty – particularly if you are deep. Of course the hour by hour tidal predictions provided by the Hydrographer of the Navy are very good, but you need to pay attention.

After much discussion on the best way to approach this problem the Captain, Commander Chris Ward, decided that the best way was to let the Victor know we were looking for him. This made a lot of sense, not least because the North Channel is very noisy from a sonar perspective and it would have been very difficult to find him passively on sonar using that way alone. We started out searching using our bow mounted sonar Type 2001 in its active mode, which meant that we were transmitting a very loud "pinging sequence of noises" into the water. If the sound made contact with something [like a submarine] the echo returned and was detected by the sonar and displayed on a screen similar to underwater radar. That would give us a bearing and a range. The initial designs and raison d'etre for building nuclear attack submarines was to "support the Fleet". The submarines' role was that of an outer screen in front of a surface Carrier or Battle Group. Their mission was to both deter and detect submarines trying to get into a position to attack the Group and this mode of active sonar was originally intended with that role in mind. Protected by friendly surface ships and their aircraft, it mattered very much less that an enemy submarine knew where you were from the sound of your active sonar.

But, by the time we had built these submarines, this operating philosophy was losing credence as it became clear that the best way for a nuclear submarine to operate was alone and passively. We are not known as the "Silent Service" for nothing and the principle of remaining silent dominated submarine tactics for the next 30 years, and still does today.

But this was a very different situation and one that nobody had encountered before. There was, quite simply, no known tactic or procedure for dealing with such a situation. As the only instructions we had were to "chase the Victor out", then it made sense to go active and do just that. We were also in an area of high underwater background noise and that would have made passive only detection of another, inherently silent, nuclear submarine all the more difficult.

Underwater background noise is made up of shipping traffic noise from propellers and machinery, which carries a surprisingly long way. Like 'biological noise' from snapping shrimps, fish and other biologics and noise from waves and seas against the shore – even though that shore could be a number of miles distant. We often call it traffic noise and there are some places where it is very loud – like the Southwest approaches of UK and some where it is very quiet like Loch Goil and the top end of Loch Fyne near Inverary, which is why we have a submarine noise range there.

The Captain ordered, 'Keep 235 feet. Course 310°. Speed 7 knots.

Action Stations.' We decided to go to an anti-metric depth as we knew that the Soviets used metric depths, while we used feet. If the Victor was at 50 metres [165 feet] we would need to keep to either 235 feet [165 + 70 feet - our size from top of the fin to the keel plus a safety margin) or 95 feet. If the Victor was at 40 metres [131 feet] we would need to keep to 201 feet or be at periscope depth. The mission here was to find the Soviet submarine, not to have an accidental collision with him, hence the anti-metric depths to minimize the chances of this happening. Remember, back then we had no means of judging an object's depth, only its range, heading and speed.

The Captain decided that we would go to 235 feet and work on the assumption that the Victor would probably operate no lower than 50 metres. The depth of water just about gave us sufficient margin to do this, but it would be uncomfortable being so close to the seabed in a navigationally constrained area.

'Captain to Sonar – Active transmissions. Ripple All Scale 40 – make the Captain's key,' ordered Commander Chris Ward. The Type 2001 active sonar transmitted and the noise reverberated throughout the submarine.

We had played our best card and in the same instant we had essentially said to the Soviet submarine – "Hey look we are over here." If he was within 30 miles it was inconceivable that our transmission had not been heard. Moreover Sonar Type 2001 in any active mode is extremely loud and there was not the slightest chance that we would not be heard and the Soviet would have a bearing on us within two transmissions. Within about five transmissions he would have the makings of a fire control solution on us.

After the first transmission the Officer of the Watch on the Active Display shouted out 'Contact bearing 300°. Range 5000 yards.'

It had not taken long before we had a returning echo and we immediately knew we had found him, fine on the port bow, at a range of 5000 yards. We were doing 7 knots.

'Passive search. 15 degrees of 310° and report' said the Captain.

The First Lieutenant reported to the Captain. 'Submarine at Actions Stations. Containment State 1.' Containment State 1 meant that every possible protection measure for the reactor plant was put in place and the tunnel doors were shut. Passive sonar started searching the bearing and, within a minute, reported, 'Passive contact bearing 300 degrees. Initial classification is a submarine – possible Victor class.'

'30 second passive bearings and active contacts to the plot,' said the

Captain. 'Navigator, get these plotted as soon as you can and give me a course and speed.' I felt under great pressure. You have to be quick to plot 30 second passive bearings using a parallel rule and then also correlate those with the bearings and range coming from the active display. I was plotting these as they were reported, together with bearing and range from the active echo returns as fast as I could. This took around 20 seconds of the 30 seconds between reports, which left 10 seconds for analysis between reports.

I suspect the Captain would have liked 15 second bearings, but he appreciated that this would be too quick to be able to plot them with a parallel ruler and dividers and then look for the possible matches for course and speed using the multipoint dividers. There was no computer assisted analysis equipment or fancy software like I subsequently had later in my career to help me out. I was frustrated that I could not give a better service to my Captain but, in an effort to help, I suggested to the Captain that we go to 15-second bearings and I would plot as fast as I could.

They started to come in and I was able to speed up the process and match particularly the course and speed. I was using the active transmission range as the best starting place as it was going to be the best information we had on range. After about 2 minutes I came up with, 'Bearing 300° - range still steady. 4000 yards at a possible speed of 18 knots. Closing speed between both submarines is 25 knots'

The next two reports made it even clearer that the bearing was still steady and the Victor 3 had speeded up. It was doing at least 18 knots and coming straight towards us. If the bearing remained steady then a collision was going to happen, although of course we did not know what depth the Victor was keeping.

At this time no one really knew how Soviet submarines would react in these situations, but we had to assume that that they would rush down the bearing. There had been several situations in the North Norwegian and Barents Seas where Soviet submarines had done this and, although it did not really make any tactical sense except to frighten off the opposition, we were aware that it was the aggressive stance in vogue in the Soviet Navy at the time. And that is just what the Victor did!

'Come right to course 330°,' said the Captain. We had to change course to try to get the steady bearing to move left or right and get away from a steady bearing and a potential collision. The Captain had altered course 20 degrees to starboard to 330° to try to get the bearing to move left. I hoped that he had turned the right way! The best analogy to this is coming up to a roundabout in your car and there is another car coming from your right and you have to decide whether to give way or keep going.

On an everyday basis you make judgments whether to stop, or cross in front of the oncoming car. But, if the two cars remain relatively on the same bearing, they will collide. It is exactly the same at sea, whether dived or on the surface.

Another 2 minutes and the report was, 'Bearing 300°. Range 2800 yards. Target course 120°. Speed still 18 knots.' The bearing had not changed. This was getting scary. The Captain was calculating in his mind whether to again change our own course, speed, or depth and came over to my plot. I was doing the same thing and my mind was in overdrive. 'Are you sure about the speed, Pilot,' he said. I replied as confidently as I could 'Yes, sir. Nothing below that fits the bearings and ranges. 'The next two reports indicated that the bearing as still steady and the range was still closing. There was no point in stopping active transmissions as we would only deny ourselves valuable information and, by now, it was abundantly clear that the Victor would have our transmissions ringing in his ears.

'Come right to course 350°. Speed 8 knots,' ordered the Captain sharply and we started to move to starboard. The next report was 'Bearing 298°. Range 2000 yards.' Followed by, 'Bearing starting to move left.'

I wiped my brow on my cuff, but we were not out of the woods just yet. 'Bearing 297°. Range 1700 yards.'

'Bearing 297°. Range 1400 yards.'

'Bearing 296°. Range 1000 yards.'

I followed this with, 'Best solution. Course 128°. Speed 18 knots. Bearing moving very slowly left.'

The Captain was concentrating on the reports and then shouted, 'Shut bulkhead doors. Stand by Collision. Speed 6 knots. Come right to course 010°.'

Reports were coming in thick and fast and the tension in the control room was very discernible. I did not have time to look up and see what else was going on, but I could feel it. The Captain's voice reflected the tension.

'Bearing 295°. Range 750 yards,' came the report from the sound room. 'Bearing 293°. Range 400 yards'

We had certainly got the bearing moving left, but we still did not know the Victor's depth. We just had to keep the bearing moving left to avoid a collision. In this game of underwater chicken we had - sensibly – blinked first! and that could have saved our bacon.

Then, in a rush, came the sound room reports: 'Bearing 285°. Range 300 yards –

'Bearing 275°. Range 200 yards –

'Bearing 260°. Range 200 yards.'

This was a great relief as we had really got the bearing moving fast left, which meant that, although this was going to be close, we were unlikely to collide unless the Soviet submarine changed course to port towards us. I was listening hard to see if that might happen.

I remember thinking, what on earth did the Soviet think it would gain by this tactic, apart from frightening us – and he had certainly done that. He could not have possibly heard us passively at that speed and was thus responding to our active transmissions.

Passive sonar blanked,' came the shout from the sound room. That meant that the noise was so great that it had overwhelmed the sonar system and the operators were unable to get a significant bearing as they had all round noise. We also knew that meant he was close – very close and we were totally dependent on holding active contact.

And then we heard the noise – a very loud increase in background noise - on the "Underwater Telephone" sonar.

He WAS close! The boat rocked slightly.

It was strange situation because we all "felt" it, but could not define what it was we had felt. He was abeam, but we had avoided a collision. But what would he do next?

Within 30 seconds we had another report from the sound room 'Target regained. Best Bearing 190°. Range 400 yards. Fading.'

My plot confirmed that the Victor had passed around 3-400 yards on our port beam and we still did not know his depth. But we could not relax. He was likely to turn around and come back, but now he was in the stern arcs of our Type 2001 sonar, both passive and active [you will recall that the Type 2001 bow sonar only covers 120 degrees either side of the ship's head. We had the Under Water Telephone and rudimentary sonar in the back of the fin, looking aft, but it was not very good. We were not completely blind, but we were not in a good position.

The Captain ordered, 'Come right. Course 080°.'

We had to alter course to ensure that we could keep the Victor in our bow sonar arcs.

'Stop transmitting. Break the Captain's key' - which stops the 2001 sonar transmitting - ordered the Captain. He had decided to stop transmitting to give us a better chance of picking up the Victor passively again. We could always go active again if required.

I have to say that at that moment, with poor passive performance, I was not sure that this was a good idea, but the Captain was right.

By this time we were on course 080° again Passive sonar soon picked up the Victor and reported, 'Bearing 180°. Contact slowing down.'

Was he turning round or was he just trying to get away? We did not know. We needed to continue to keep analysing the possibilities.

'Course 090°. Speed 6 knots,' ordered the Captain.

We received two further bearings of 180 and then sonar reported, 'target speeding up.'

The crazy bastard. He was coming back at us and we had to be ready for another close quarter's situation.

'Bearing 190° –

'Bearing 194°.'

He was tracking back up our starboard side now that we had altered course.

The Captain came and looked at the navigational chart. We had been keeping our position by estimated position. That was dead reckoning based on our course and speed, adjusted for tidal stream. We had been deep for around two hours in very dangerous waters and we had to allow a margin of error on the position we had. We call that the "pool of errors."

I showed him my estimation of the pool of errors and he seemed satisfied with where we were and the error situation and said, 'Captain to Sonar. Active transmissions.

Ripple All Scale 20 – make the Captain's key.'

He had decided that the passive picture was not good enough. If the Soviet had turned round, we needed a better picture of what was going on. So he had decided to go active again. If we were going to "chase him out", we had to make it clear to him that we knew where he was.

After the first transmission the report was, 'Bearing 200°. Range 3000 yards – moving out of the sonar beams.'

We had to come right again to keep him in our coverage.

The captain ordered, 'Come right. Course 130. Speed 7 knots.'

Over the next few minutes the reports came in from the sound room: 'Bearing 205°. Range 2600 yards –

'Bearing 214°. Range 2200 yards.–

'Bearing 220°. Range 2000 yards –

'Bearing 230°. Range 1800 yards –

'Come right. Course 180°,' said the Captain. We had to keep altering course to keep the Victor in our sonar arcs.

I had been plotting furiously and analysing to see what the best assessment I could make of the speed. It was furiously difficult and I struggled to get a match through the bearings that I was confident enough to shout out.

'Bearing 240°. Range 1700 yards.'

I decided to say something. 'Best speed 14 knots,' I cried out.

'Are you sure,' snapped the Captain and I were joined at the chart table by the First Lieutenant who cast a critical eye over my workings and plot. I had the makings of the Victor moving in a northerly direction, but it seemed that he was doing less speed this time.

'Bearing 250°. Range 1600 yards.' Came from the active display operator. 'Our best target course 330°. Speed 15 knots'

'Captain to Sonar – change active scale to Scale 10,' said the Captain. This reduced the power of the transmissions slightly and meant that we should have a better picture close in to us.

By this time my plot looked like a spider's web, but I did not want to lose any history and I did not want to change the paper and start again. So I changed the colour of the pencil I was using.

'Bearing 260°. Range 1600 yards.'

'Come right. Course 230°,' ordered the Captain.

We had to keep following him round. It was clear that he was not going to be so close this time, but we had to ensure that we held contact and were able to track him.

'Bearing 270°. Range 1600 yards,' followed by 'Bearing 275°. Range 1600 yards.'

We had steadied his range, which meant he was not closing and we were hoping that his range would now open up.

I gave another assessment of course and speed. 'Plot suggests target course 330°. Best speed 15 knots.'

Another couple of minutes passed and we had more reports: 'Bearing 280°. Range 1700 yards –

'Bearing 290°. Range 1800 yards –

'Bearing 300°. Range 2000 yards.'

He was definitely opening now, but we could not stop transmitting active in case we lost him. A few more minutes passed and we had a report of; 'Bearing 310°. Range 3000 yards.'

From the sound room came – 'Target speeding up. Loud cavitation on the bearing.'

This was good. It told us, first, that he had not reduced speed and also that he was noisy at medium speed, which meant that his propellers were not "tuned" to ensure that they did not cavitate.

We continued to track the Victor for the next 30 minutes, by which time the Captain had opened up bulkhead doors and gone back to Containment State 3. But we remained at Action Stations.

I asked the captain to come and look at the navigational situation and suggested that we came up to 180 feet and that we should go to periscope depth for a fix as soon as we could. My 'pool of errors' was getting exponentially bigger and I was feeling ever more uncomfortable about my navigational position. But now was not the right time to go back to periscope depth as we might lose the Soviet and we needed to be sure that we were indeed chasing him away.

It was also clear that if the Victor was going to continue on his northwesterly course he was moving out of the area and we would have done our job. I wondered whether there was a Nimrod on top of us and whether he had logged some of the last period of activity. We had not detected any active sonobuoys that might have been dropped from a Nimrod, but they could be just using passive ones, which was more likely. It would also be good to give any Nimrod an up to date position of the Victor so that they could track him out of the area.

'Bearing 310° Range. 5000 yards –

'Bearing 310°. Range 6000 yards –

Half an hour later, when we had changed Active transmissions to Scale 20, and the reports were: 'Bearing 311° Range 12000 yards', it was clear that the Victor was retreating. Shortly afterwards Active Sonar lost contact and the Captain decided that we should stop transmitting and have a good passive search before returning to periscope depth.

'Stop transmitting. Break the Captain's key,' said the Captain followed by: 'Fall out Actions Stations. Well done everybody.'

The First Lieutenant went on main broadcast and gave a short summary of the encounter with the Victor and explained that we would be keeping a watchful eye in case he returned.

We did a careful passive search and had intermittent faint contact with the Victor, but then we lost him at about 15000 yards. We established a datum, or last point of contact, that we could pass to the

Nimrod.

Within 15 minutes we were back at periscope depth. My fix showed that we were about a mile from where I thought we were. That was a bit disappointing for me as I thought I had been a bit more accurate than that, but it is a notoriously difficult area and the tidal streams do not always go as predicted.

There was a Nimrod above us and we passed our datum and other relevant information to him on UHF secure. There was also some SOSUS data on the submarine broadcast, although it was a bit out of date. The acoustic data confirmed that the target was a Victor 3 Soviet submarine, which had been classified by its tonal signature and that we had detected similar tonal information to our passive sonar which had detected and tracked him. The Captain waited about an hour and we started transmitting again on active sonar and did so right up to the 100 fathom line, well beyond our territorial waters and well clear of the North Channel and our 12 mile territorial limit.

The sound room team had done very well indeed, but I suppose that you get so confident in the capability of your equipment and the training and ability of your operators at every level and in every department in the submarine that you expect that level of expertise and come to have total confidence in what they are saying.

Yes, you are driving around blind, but it does not feel like that. On reflection, I don't think I ever sailed on a submarine after a maintenance period without there being some new piece of development equipment to try out. Not being able to see is not an issue to most submariners and we learn to trust our equipment and we use our sensors to the maximum capability. The nearest analogy I can give you to driving a submarine is to drive your car down the M1 on a Sunday morning in the middle lane with your eyes shut, but with some traffic coming in the opposite direction and some crossing the motorway!

But that was our job and we were happy doing it.

The atmosphere in the control room was always very tense. Chris Ward was an extraordinary Captain whose attention to detail was leaning on the pedantic, but I did learn a great deal from him and he was very supportive of what I did.

I was fortunate with Chris Ward as there was one thing I could do which he never mastered, I had an electronic radio fixing aid called Loran C and I could always pull a navigation fix out of Loran C, which was not that easy. So, I always worked on the basis that, if I could keep him from understanding the foibles of Loran C, I would have his confidence. I believe that I did, both as a navigating officer and officer of the watch.

Once the Victor 3 incident had gone by Chris Ward was clearly satisfied that we had done what we had been asked to do. Over the next 12 hours we received reports from both SOSUS and the RAF Nimrods that indeed the Victor had continued to move away towards the Iceland Faeroes Gap.

Suffice to say there were many huge lessons that came out of this incident. It was not until this encounter that we realized that we were not doing this very well.

Nuclear submarine operations were entering a much more central effort to the UK's response to the Cold War and we had to raise our game. So the CONQUEROR's Victor 3 encounter was a huge wake up call to everybody.

Against that, we had not really learnt much more from the incident about Soviet submarine tactics, except that they were prepared to be aggressive – perhaps because they did not have the sonar advantage. But we now knew they stopped short of firing torpedoes. They were of course in our neck of the woods and their response could be completely different in their own back yard.

I often wonder, if we had not gone active, whether we would have detected them passively. I suspect that we would. But then we would have found it very difficult to "chase them out" if we had not demonstrated to them that we knew where they were through active sonar.

The Victor 3 was a big step forward for the Soviet submarine force and they were becoming quieter and faster, but we still had the sonar advantage. The fact that they were now prepared to enter UK water, within the 12 miles limit, showed a new confidence that they could – perhaps – counter what the United States Navy and we were doing elsewhere and close to their own back yard. This was also important as this incursion was a direct threat to both US and UK Polaris submarines departing from the UK and, in the original criteria for SSNs, the importance of defending SSBNs was a key item. And that was one that was clearly not lost on the Soviets.

The confrontation was analysed by the Strategic Submarine Performance Analysis Group [SSPAG] who were charged with analyzing all Polaris and subsequent Trident patrols to make sure nothing had been missed and that our patrols had not been compromised in any way. They looked at everything, including FOSM directives,

Command and Control by COMCLYDE, water space management, communications, intelligence both in quality and timeliness, and the whole business of navigation and charts.

The most important result of this comprehensive analysis was the urgent need for centralized Command and Control, communications, and Intelligence [C3I]. I am pleased to say that, although their report was pretty damning, their recommendations were accepted in full and action to change these things was put in train without delay.

There was significant opposition from the local area commanders as they had run their own local sea areas for years and had experienced staff at each one – in the Clyde who ran both the inner areas inside the Mull of Kintyre and the Outer areas off Londonderry into the Atlantic, as well as those off Rosyth, Plymouth, and Gosport.

But meeting the requirements of a nuclear submarine in the Cold War meant that we had to change and get much smarter.

This led to the formation of Commander Task Force 311 [CTF 311] at Northwood, where all operational control of submarines outside local areas was assumed by the Commander in Chief, who had his operational headquarters there. The Commander in Chief also had operational control of the Polaris submarines executed by CTF 345 and there was already in place a centralized C3I for these boats at Northwood. The submarine broadcast was keyed for transmission from the Rugby and other transmitters from the Polaris communications centre there.

Additionally the NATO water space management mutual interference plot was run from Northwood, the Fleet Weather Centre was at Northwood, all the surface ships were run from Northwood and, crucially, we also had a representative of COMSUBLANT, ensuring we were able to have a close relationship with the United States submarine commander for the Atlantic [COMSUBLANT] based in Norfolk, Virginia. So Northwood was the obvious place for CTF 311.

I am not sure who was directly behind this decision but, as you can imagine, it did not go down well with Flag Officer Submarines who was still based in Gosport as this reduced his control of his submarines significantly. It was not until 1978 that the then Flag Officer Submarines, Admiral Sir John Fieldhouse, moved his entire staff from Gosport to Northwood with six weeks' notice.

The setting up of CTF 311 was given to Commander Tom Green, and Lieutenant Commander Chris Meyer, who had been my First Lieutenant in my first submarine HMS OPOSSUM in 1966. I relieved

Chris at Northwood in 1976, having just left command of HMS WALRUS. This was a very exciting time, trying to put into action all the procedures that would ensure a fast, efficient and professional service to our nuclear submarines which were increasingly being involved in Cold War missions of various sorts.

CTF 311 was extremely well led by Tom Green and then moved forward again by, then Commander, later Captain Richard Sharpe and then Commander, later Captain, John Speller. It was my privilege to work with both of these two outstanding officers. Both had been at the sharp end. Richard Sharpe, as Commanding Officer in HMS COURAGEOUS and John Speller in HMS SWIFTSURE. Both had seen both the value and sense of centralized command and control. They were both brilliant officers with significant personal experience at sea and I was fortunate to come under the magnetic spell of both of them at a key point in my career. I cannot speak too highly of them and, as well as continuing to improve the service to submarines at sea on difficult operations, I learnt so much from them.

However, perceptions changed markedly in 1977, when Tom Mangold produced a Panorama documentary called the "Deep Cold War." In this programmed he tried to describe what was going on in Anti-Submarine Warfare in general, and in submarine warfare against the Soviets in particular. He started to talk openly about the existence and the broad capability SOSUS, but without saying exactly where it was.

As far as I was concerned, working in CTF 311 in Northwood and being heavily involved in the use of SOSUS in support of our submarines, he blew SOSUS wide open. I was absolutely horrified and could not believe what I was seeing and hearing. Why was he saying this? Why was he jeopardising what we were doing? Why was he giving away something that was so valuable to us?

I am quite sure, on reflection, that the Soviets knew that something was going on, although the pattern of their movements did not indicate that they knew the specifics.

Later, in 1993, when I was a Commodore and Chief of Staff to Vice Admiral Sir Toby Frere as Flag Officer Submarines, I asked both Admiral Yerofeyev and Vice Admiral Suchkov during my visit to Severomorsk how much they knew. They said they knew that there were underwater detection arrays, but they did not really know where they were. They assumed that they would be at what were called the "choke points" in the Greenland – Iceland – Faeroes - UK gaps and they were not far wrong.

I thought at the time that SOSUS, both its existence and capability, was a closely guarded secret and we treated it as such in CTF 311. After the Panorama programme we had to assume that the Soviets had a much better idea of where these arrays were located and we monitored patterns very carefully to see if anything had been compromised. There did not seem to be much of a change and we continued to use SOSUS to vector our own submarines onto Soviet target submarines.

I still do not know to this day where Tom Mangold got this information. Again, during my visit to Severomorsk in 1993 in conversations with Admiral Yerofeyev and Admiral Suchkov, they told me that the CONQUEROR/VICTOR 3 incident and the Panorama programme had made them more circumspect in their operations and had also led to a faster improvement programme in submarine noise reduction. They also confirmed that their submarines were only authorised to use torpedoes in self defence in International waters. They did not answer my question about their rules inside their own territorial waters...!

CHAPTER SIX
CASING RATTLE

I lie back on my bunk, dozing and think of what my family is likely to be doing now. I suspect I am not alone amongst the other members of the ship's company. I worry about her, even though there is little I can do out here in the deep water with no way of contacting her or hearing what is going on. Submariner's wives are a tough lot and have to put up with much.

The introduction of Polaris submarines meant that everyone going on a patrol was required to indicate before they left what they would like to happen in the event of bad news from home. The options were:

1. Be told immediately.
2. Be told 24 hours before return to harbour or
3. Be told on arrival in harbour.

These were tough options and, although I never had to be the bearer of bad news in my time in command, I am not sure whether I would have told a member of my crew bad news about their family a few days out when there was 60 plus days to go before our return. Most opted to be told 24 hours before return to harbour, based on the fact that there was nothing you could do about it and you were unlikely to be airlifted off for compassionate reasons. Since the end of the Cold War things have eased considerably and there is a much more pragmatic approach these days.

The submarine carried on, six hundred feet down, under two thermoclines, nineteen thousand feet above the bottom of the sea. In general a thermocline is where the sea water temperature changes with depth and can have a marked effect to both passive and active sonar's predicted and actual ranges. Sea water temperature decreases from the surface to the deepest levels, except in high latitudes where the configuration can be more complex. There exists in most ocean areas (apart from polar and sub-polar oceans) a zone where the rate of decrease of temperature is much larger compared with that above and below. Depending on the geographical location, the thermocline depth ranges from about 50m to 1000m. A simplified view is to consider the thermocline as the separation zone between the sea water temperature on the surface and in the deep. However, the thermocline depth varies from geographical region to region, and with the seasons, especially in the mid- latitude regions where a secondary and much shallower thermocline (above 50m) occurs in summer.

In high latitudes, a thermocline may appear only seasonally. We take temperature readings regularly – every time we move from deep to periscope depth and vice versa with an instrument called the bathythermograph or bathy for short. There is a recorder in the control room and these records are very valuable not only immediately but also for long term analysis by the Hydrographer, to which all records are sent. For immediate use they allow the prediction of sonar ranges in any area and are a vital part of the sound room armoury.

I remember only too well as a Sonar Officer wrestling with the complex calculations that were required to come up with realistic range prediction information. Nowadays, of course, this is all done by computer, but I am convinced that all the records we sent to the Hydrographer, each card annotated with a position, went a long way towards our understanding of the ocean and how we can exploit it in sonar terms.

A tap on the door.

'Come.' I sit up. Blink. The CO is not disturbed if there is not a good reason.

It was the First Lieutenant, Ian Richards. He looks pale and unhappy which was a bad sign. 'Nick Slide's got something, sir,' he said. Leading Seaman (Sonar) Nick Slide is an experienced sonar operator. He has a dark hair and a fresh face and he looks as if he belongs in a recording studio, an impression reinforced by the fat earphones clamped on his head. He is known as Batman, because he can see in the dark, using his ears. I got up and went with Ian to the sound room.

'Well?' I said. 'What do think?'

By which Batman (for whom no question is a simple one) probably understood me to ask, where is the noise on the frequency band? 'Everywhere, Sir,' he said. Nick Slide handed me his earphones.

I heard the roar of the sea. And another sound. Someone was

ringing a bell out there.

'It sounds like tapping on or under the casing, sir,' said Ian Richards.

'Thank you,' I said, because he was in danger of doing the thing they teach you not to do at Dartmouth, which is supply too much information. He was doing it out of nervousness. Understandable nervousness. Somewhere out there, under the casing on the outside of the boat, an end or a bight of rope had worked its way out of its frapping, or a pipe clip had come loose. Now it was waving in the eddies, clattering against the steel. It was the kind of sound that on a moored yacht would have woken you up and annoyed you for thirty seconds before you went back to sleep. On a submarine it was the kind of sound that says to any other submarine within fifty miles, "look, I'm over here."

Thanks to the Waterspace Management system, any submarine within fifty miles was going to be an enemy. This was not a good thing.

The control room was suddenly full of life and movement. The OOW, Jeff Thomas, had already reduced speed to 4 knots and gone to the Search Quiet State, which was the signal for pre-arranged noise monitoring teams to go round shutting down unnecessary equipment – fans, pumps, whatever, as we tried to identify the source. Back in the control room Ian and I waited.

Then the reports started to come in. As if he knew this was a rattle, Petty Officer Danny Fisher, the Second Coxswain, appeared in the control room. The Second Coxswain – usually a sonar man – is a quaint old submarine term for the Petty Officer who was in charge of casing maintenance and the Casing party. He is responsible for its maintenance, painting and, when securing for sea, ensuring that everything underneath the casing is properly secured. Someone from the sonar department has a very much more personal interest in having the submarine's own noise is minimal which is why a sonar man is in charge. Now, with a noise under the casing, it was his name and reputation on the line. And it would be him who would have to fix it.

Next, the forward, bow, party after checking the boat assured the First Lieutenant that the tap was starboard side in the torpedo compartment.

Leading Cook "North End" Preston was just as sure it was above the galley.

The engineering party considered that it was in the back end of the tunnel, port side. It was possible that they were all right, but by no means probable. The day before we had sailed, the Casing Officer, Sub Lieutenant Toby Spreckley and Petty Officer Danny Fisher, the Second Coxswain had been over the space between the casing and the pressure hull, inch by inch on what we call a "casing crawl" making sure that nothing had been dropped or had been badly secured, or was flapping in the breeze. Given that it was a given that they had done that check comprehensively, the noise must be a loose mooring rope – the very last things to be tied off as we left the Wall. And there were no mooring ropes close to the galley. Furthermore, Leading Cook Preston was known to be a man who sometimes exaggerated things. The only person showing any degree of certainty in the engineering party was Leading Mechanical Engineer Mechanic (LMEM) Carter who, as a young man seeking to make his mark, was perhaps trying too hard. The bow party had it, then.

There was a silence, except for the hum and the sound of essential machinery, and much of this was electrical noise. Everyone in the control room was waiting for me to give an order. We were in the cold and nasty North Atlantic. Apart from the bell on the hull, there were no man-made sounds.

We needed to do a 'rattle check'.

In theory we could run east into a fjord in Norway and do it in flat water. But we would lose time, and we would certainly be reported by a public-spirited Norwegian (they all are), and forced to identify ourselves. Norway was not an option.

The weather forecast was not too good and the wind was strong from the NE, force 6 when I had last looked through the periscope some three hours ago when we had been at periscope depth to read a broadcast routine and take a Satnav fix.

'We'll go up and have a look – we have to find the rattle,' I said to Ian. 'Get the team together and let me know when everybody is ready.' This involved the Casing Officer, Second Coxswain and the Assistant MEO – Lieutenant Tony Rowe - getting themselves sorted with bags containing torches, wire and rope ends - to tie things down - an adjustable spanner, a hammer and rubber and wooden wedges. The bags were always ready but they had to get dressed and get the lifelines on and ensure they had a plan of attack. Ian would supervise from the bridge and Ian Mackenzie would ensure that all our sensors were watching and assessing any potential addition to our party. I did not want to hear or see any sonar contact or, more to the point, any surface ship or aircraft while this was going on. Submarines are vulnerable on the surface, outside their natural environment, and also much more liable to detection. I was in the North Atlantic Ocean and well within range of a potential Soviet patrolling aircraft. In actual fact, I did not want to be seen by anyone – friend or foe.

The trouble is that when there is a rattle it is so difficult to track it down to a specific area. A pressure hull is a magnificent conductor of sound and that is why the design of the submarine included every piece of machinery being resiliently mounted to separate the machine's noise from the pressure hull. The main engines are resiliently mounted on a hydraulic raft which is very ingenious. To check the whole casing could take an hour or more. I was not prepared to give them that long.

We came round, beam to sea – north east. The planes man heaved gently back on the OMC yoke. The deck angled up underfoot. The control room was quiet, shirt sleeve weather as usual. Visibility in the snow flurries would be poor. Ideal for remaining undetected on the surface, except for the winds: NE, force seven to eight. The depth gauge wound up steadily. At five, four, three hundred, two hundred feet there was no sense of outside movement, only the angle of the deck against the feet. The bathythermograph trace showed us going through two temperature layers. We could not feel them either, but they affect the way sound travels in the water, so I had a corner of my mind in the sonar room. Nothing. An empty piece of sea. The only worries would come from the sea itself.

As we went through a hundred feet, there was still no movement in the deck. At sixty feet, periscope depth, the boat was corkscrewing gently.

The control room was filling up with men in survival suits and deck boots and lifejackets and harnesses and bags of "solutions." The First Lieutenant put up the periscope, made a 360° scan. The deck bucked at him. The ECM people reported- nothing. HMS SPLENDID was not on anyone's radar. All clear.

'Sea state,' I said.

'Eight to ten feet over a ten-foot swell, but it is difficult to see the direction as there's no real horizon,' said Ian. This was very marginal for a casing run. No Commanding Officer likes putting men on the outside in the open ocean and the difficult sea conditions meant that the boys would have to be careful. But at least a black night was good cover. The boys should be able to find their ways around keeping the torches to look under the casing and make repairs. I had decided.

'We'll go up and have a look. Surface when you are ready, No. 1.' A few more checks and some questions and hopefully answers.

'Surface,' said the First Lieutenant. Compressed air at 4,000 psi roared into ballast tanks as we moved quickly from one medium to another – dived to surfaced.

The Outside Wrecker had checked the main vents were shut and blew the tanks. The planes man kept the submarine on course and, so we thought, beam to sea. The boat went up like a lift, but pitching and rolling horribly. A glass crashed in the wardroom pantry – would they ever learn to stow properly for sea I thought? We were on the roof.

Anyone watching (there was nobody) would have seen a grey-black sea toothed with white water. From that sea rose a slim periscope, then a black fin, then the fat black cigar of the hull in a white fury of bubbles. The fin was lurching wildly from side to side as the boat rolled. Down in the control room we all heard the bang as a big sea hit the fin beam-on. I went to the periscope and looked hard. The wind had gone round in the last few hours and we were now more head to sea than beam to sea. I should have had a better look before surfacing. It was too late now. The boat heeled far, far over to port, ten, and another ten more degrees. More glass broke. In a surface ship, it would have felt threatening. In the submarine it felt lethal. Another roll tried to throw me onto the chart table.

'Port thirty five. Revolutions 50,' I said sharply and more annoyed at myself for not assessing the swell right. 'Steer 315°.'

'Port thirty five. Revolutions 50. Steer 315°,' repeated the planes man with some urgency.

He gave the boat full port rudder.

The compass needle crawled round the dial. The motion changed from a corkscrew to a roll. The needle came round to 315o, steadied. The corkscrew was now a slow seesaw roll which was much easier for control.

I called out, 'Speed now?' 'Six knots.' came the reply.

'OOW. Reduce to 4 knots,' I said. 'Open up when you are ready.'

The OOW waited a minute, maybe two, while everything settled down.

'Open Up.' He shouted. Followed by, 'Upper lid open.' The conning tower hatch opened. Cold air rushed in.

The control room emptied. First Lieutenant first. Then the men in survival suits carrying their bags of tools and T-bars to open the casing panels to get access to underneath the casing.

Leading Seaman John Boddy checked them as they went into the tower and put their names on a board with a chinagraph pencil. We used every possible method to make sure we knew where every man was. There have been a few occasions over the years when people have been left outside the submarine when it has dived and I did not want that to happen!

A dustbinful of water came down the hatch – it always does when you open up - and is something you can't really avoid as there will always be some water in the fin after surfacing. Ian Richards on the bridge reported that he had the watch and ordered 'Casing party on the casing. First and last man out, shout to the bridge.' The order was repeated up the tower and the casing crew worked their way through the pipework in the fin in pitch black and the Second Coxswain finally got to the fin door. He went out, first clipping his harness onto the ice rail that runs along the casing. If he was washed overboard now he might have a chance. He was followed by the rest of the team who scuttled down the deck, the breeze tearing at their survival suits, billowing their harness straps.

Clip the harness onto the ice rail, crawl forward.

The First Lieutenant on the bridge yelled, 'Look out,' as the nose went down into a wave. Icy water sluiced aft.

'Hold on!'

The wave went away. The boat ploughed forward slowly, keeping pace with the snowflakes dancing in the lee of the fin.

Petty Officer Danny Fisher shoved his T-bar in the lock of one of the casing plates, turned it and pulled back the cover to open up access under the casing. Able Seaman 'Oily' Rigg shoved his hands in the opening. The water bit at his ungloved fingers as he ran them over the mooring warp coiled away over the bollards, the frapping that held the turns of big line hard as stone, the ends neatly tucked.

Rigg's head was seen to be shaking in its hood. All secure here. He hauled himself back by the lifeline. Petty Officer Fisher closed the panel, and secured the latch, ignoring the wave that washed up over the submarine's bow and covered him to the knees.

He moved on to the next panel, turned the T-bar. Rigg put his hands in again, started his braille examination of the lines. HMS SPLENDID's bow went into the back of a swell. The swell came down the deck tall and slow. Able Seaman Rigg disappeared in the black crescendo of water. When the water went, he was dangling over the side by his lifeline. Petty Officer Danny Fisher and Lieutenant Tony Rowe and Sub Lieutenant Toby Spreckley pulled him back.

He seemed to be swearing. Still swearing, he stuffed his hand into the open panel, following the turns of the frapping with his numbing fingers.

And there it was: a three-inch end of the frapping, with a steel piece in the eye of the rope that had come un-tucked, tapping against the smooth steel of the pressure hull. The word passed from Able Seaman Rigg to PO Fisher; from PO Fisher to Sub Lieutenant Spreckley, the Casing Officer. I say the word but it was a loud shout above the noise of the sea.

HMS SPLENDID ran on, head to sea. Vulnerable – not where she should be.

The casing crew had the panels off. They were re-frapping the line. A little group perched precariously on the boat's smooth casing, washed by the big cold seas sliding down the hull. Ian Richards yelled down that they had found the problem. 'How much longer' I said back, knowing that Ian could not answer that. It would take as long as it took. I really hated this sort of thing. All sorts of scenarios go through a Captain's mind when you have put your people in a vulnerable position and you question whether you should have risked them to such a task.

Petty Officer Danny Fisher did his stuff with the T-bar and waved a thumbs up to Ian Richards on the bridge. Ian waved them back and the Casing party all moved slowly along the ice rail back towards the fin door. Just then Able Seaman Rigg pauses to empty the water out of his hood, immediately followed by a huge wave that engulfs him again. He emerged, still working his way aft and shaked his head. Danny Fisher was waiting by the fin door and ushered him in before yelling to Ian on the bridge, 'Casing party inside the fin. Shutting the fin door' and disappeared himself, following the others back through the fin door and down the conning-tower hatch. Petty Officer Danny Fisher clipped the fin door firmly shut and shouted up to the First Lieutenant on the bridge.

Ian passed the information back to the control room. I sighed in relief.

Snowflakes stung the skin on the Ian Richards face as he received the report from Leading Seaman John Boddy in the control room that all hands were below. I ordered Ian on the intercom to, 'Clear the bridge and come below.' Ian acknowledged the order and took a final 360° look from the bridge.

He came down the conning tower fast. 'Upper lid shut. Two clips. Two pins,' he said. His face was bloated from the suit's neck seal, his eyes red from the battering of the spray.

'Steer 045°.' You surface a submarine head to sea. You dive a submarine beam to sea.

'On course 045°,' said the planes man.

We went through the diving motions again, following the same routine as earlier, but much quicker this time. The nose went up, crashed down, the fin shuddered to the bang of a big wave. It seemed to take an age to get down to Periscope Depth where the Second OOW – the Supply Officer, Jimmy Fergusson, from Plockton in the Western Isles - grabbed a quick satnav fix and then, to the relief of everyone, the officer of the watch, at my direction, took the boat back down to 300 feet. We had to check now that the rattle had gone or we would have to go through the whole of the last thirty minutes again – and no-one wanted that, least of all me.

There was a smell of vomit. Some submariners have difficulty keeping their surface sea legs.

HMS SPLENDID sank out of the bucking, rolling upper layers into the deep. It was calm down here, and the weather was always the same. I went to the sound room and looked in the door expectantly. 'Anything?' I asked. Chief Petty Officer Jeff Thomas was in the sound room with Petty Officer Sonar, Roger Crafts. They were both listening intently and scanning the various screens closely.

'Nothing so far, Sir' said Roger Crafts.

I went back into the control room and said to the OOW, 'Increase speed to 8 knots.'

I waited anxiously. 'Sonar report?' I said 'Nothing,' came the reply.

I said to the OOW, 'Increase speed to 12 knots.'

I watched the speed increase and waited until we had settled at 12 knots before asking Sonar again, 'Can you still hear the rattle?'

There was a pause and then CPO Jeff Thomas reported, 'the rattle has gone.' We had found the rattle and it was not there anymore. We slowed to 4 knots again for a final, good, listen and there was still no sound.

We were back on course making towards our patrol area. I pressed the intercom button. 'Do you hear there. This is the Captain speaking. Thank you, everybody,' I said. 'Normal service has been resumed. Well done to the Casing party. The Chief Stoker is pleased to announce the showing of Star Wars. There will be choc-ices between reels. Well done. You have earned them.'

I pulled Toby Spreckley aside and told him we were lucky to be able to sort out that casing rattle, but to remember the next time he does a casing crawl and secures the submarine for sea after leaving harbour, that very detail must be checked.

He looked sheepish and apologized.

I said, 'Just learn and remember the lesson, Toby.'

HMS SPLENDID underwater

CHAPTER SEVEN
GETTING IN CLOSE

Passage to the patrol area is about settling in, but it is about continuing to train too. As we head up the Norwegian Sea and around the North Cape HMS SPLENDID's departments are fully operational, without compromise. The reactor's primary systems and the secondary systems are working well and the submarine is at a more relaxed Containment State with one tunnel door above the reactor compartment wide open to ease access when in a more relaxed state.

The Containment States offer a level of protection that changes in severity as you move from 3 to 1. Containment State 3 is the normal state at sea, out of sight of land, where collision is less likely than in inshore waters. We had sailed in Containment State 1 and would only use it again if we were in a close quarter's situation or anticipate a possible collision.

The catering department is displaying their usual imagination, with cans of cold Fanta after a hot and furious fire drill. Training is continuous. There is attack team training twice a day and the torpedo crews are doing loading drills.

The signal traffic was all encrypted in Code groups for security – all our traffic was classified in some way, some more than others, but everything was encrypted. This meant regular changes of code in the submarine wireless office every 4 hours, - but this could be changed if circumstances were deemed to require change more often - is pouring in from Northwood.

We have streamed the Floating Wire Aerial now – a ¾ inch diameter long piece of cable that goes from inside the boat through a series of glands out through the back of the fin. This allows us to read the VLF broadcast when deep without coming up to periscope depth. The wire is positively buoyant and so runs up close to the surface where it can pick up the VLF.

In one of the many intelligence signals it was reported that the cloud had cleared for an hour and the satellite had had a good look at the Kola Peninsula, including the great Soviet naval bases at Murmansk, Severomorsk and Polyarny. Apparently there were four Delta class SSBNs out at sea, and six SSNs. And there was a whisper from, who knows where, that something new would be doing trials in the Soviet training areas.

HMS SPLENDID was to gather intelligence, using our own discretion with regard to standard National Rules of Engagement. This was Northwood's way of saying that we were to get as close as possible to anything interesting and watch it like a hawk, but obey the national rules of engagement. If this involved going close to, or into, territorial waters, Northwood would naturally deny all knowledge and I would be on my own. But Britain definitely expected.

The Wireless Office team in their tiny office under the control room knew that something was happening. For one thing, they did the decoding. For another, something was always happening when the VLF messages came in so frequently, and from the west. The transmitter was in Rugby. If you were east of Rugby as we were, heading towards the Soviet Union, you were more than likely in the North Atlantic, Norwegian or Barents Sea which, in submarine terms, was bandit country.

The Ship's Company did not know our exact destination, but it is impossible to keep location from the crew. To start with it is important for confidence in a submarine that they know where they are. Also, it is impossible to shield this information when the chart is on the chart table on the side of the control room, where traffic of people is always passing by, going about their business.

Sea water temperature will tell you a lot and this is available in the engine room, in the sound room and on the bathythermograph. In an SSBN it is totally different as the exact location is known only to a few who work in a separate compartment called the Navigation Centre.

It is fair to say that, as CO, I myself was not at that moment feeling particularly relaxed either. I looked at the chart with the First Lieutenant. The Soviet training areas are a mixture of shallow and deep water channels, very much like the Clyde areas off the West coast of Scotland. "We'll go to Piccadilly Circus," I said.

Piccadilly Circus is the slang name given to an area outside territorial waters where several possible routes and channels join into one large area. There is a naval base at the inshore end of each of the channels and this makes it a natural choke point for me. But the Soviets recognise that too.

The chances of picking something up are good, but you also have to be on your guard in case you are the one who is picked up instead.

Ian says, 'And if someone comes out of one and heads in for the other?' 'We'll follow him,' I reply.

'Are you happy with the rules of engagement?' asks Ian inquisitively.

This is not Captain Bligh's Navy. A good Executive Officer will always be available to test a CO's theories, play devil's advocate for his "what-ifs."

If you decide after a particular frustrating day or event that you will flash off a signal to the Commander In Chief Fleet, or use particularly strong and flowery language in your signal draft, Ian would say, 'why don't I put this away and we can look at it again in the morning?' Inevitably you agree and the next morning a great many amendments are made, or you decide not to send it at all.

I am comfortable with what the rules of engagement say I can and cannot do, but there are always margins and blurred edges. Calculated risks may have to be taken. 'Naturally,' I said. 'We will take advantage of any opportunity that presents itself.'

'Naturally.' says Ian with a wry smile on his face.

'We'll get close at sunrise and take it from there. When is sunrise?'

Ian looks at the board above the navigation plot and reads out, 'Sunrise 0813. Sunset 1306.'

Another very short day in these high northern latitudes, well inside the Arctic Circle [i.e. above latitude 66°].

'So we will plan to go to Action Stations at 0730. Tell them then, not now. Might as well have everyone fresh and bright.' I reply.

Ian nodded. No sense in getting everyone keyed up before there was any need.

Intelligence more often than not tends to give you an indication rather than precise information. The chances were that something would happen. But the chances were that we would have to wait a long time for it. Submariners are used to waiting. This waiting game was brilliantly described in the amazing film Das Boot, where the U-boat crew spent hours and days waiting for something to happen and then they were pitched into 20 minutes of frantic activity and terror as the depth charges dropped all around them. That book and the film in particular explain in graphic detail the highs and lows of being a submariner – in any era.

I looked at the navigation plot, satisfied myself on where we were and where we were going, spoke to Petty Officer Sean Runham, looking after the navigational plot, put my head into the sound room and had a few words with the on watch team in the sound room, to take stock of the sonar conditions and lack of activity, and decided that there was time for a shower.

That was a luxury that one never had in diesel submarines and it is a huge plus in nuclear submarines. It is not a 5* shower, but it is pretty good and although one can bask under the jets of water, the submariner does not waste water – old habits die hard. I then went to my cabin and lay down on my bunk and dozed again. Submarine CO's seldom sleep – they doze. I got up several times in the next few hours and walked into the control room and looked at the plot. All was well and the boat was humming gently to itself as it nosed through the water.

By 0645, when I went into the control room, it was full of people: CPO George Elwood, the Outside Wrecker perusing the dials at Ship Control – air, water, hydraulics and numerous other indicators showing red or green; at the plot Ian Mackenzie, the Navigating officer, checking things at his navigational table; Roger Colborne, the Coxswain, on the One Man Control that steers the submarine and controls depth and angle.

Ian was there too. I caught his eye.

His heavy black eyebrows lifted a quarter of an inch.

After our talk last night, he would not have called action stations until the hour specified. But you cannot hide anything in a submarine. Three quarters of an hour before anyone had said anything, the crew had gone to Action Stations of their own accord.

I went and sat in the Captain's chair in the control room. Steward Savage appeared with a cup of black coffee and people began to tell me things. There was plenty to tell.

HMS SPLENDID's blunt black nose was pointing straight towards Piccadilly Circus, although we were still some way away. The hydrophones on the fixed sonar array behind the GRP dome on her bow were picking up a barrage of information. The sonar team made it all nice and plain and there was a constant stream of sonar data being sent to the Tactical Systems screens in the control room. The boys on watch there were analyzing the data and trying varying solutions of contact bearings with the aim of assessing their target course, speed and range and trying to pick one of more than passing interest.

In the area for which we were headed was the unmistakable high quality twin screw whirr of a frigate: a frigate steaming hard. Not, one hoped, for our benefit. There was a heavier rumble from the direction of the shore. Tugs – perhaps? Tugs sounded promising as they often assist submarines in the initial stages of manoeuvring out of port. And, behind it all, the whispered signatures of submarines.

These waters were always thick with submarines, working up, on exercise, or starting out for patrol.

At the moment though there was nobody close, except the frigate though. That was good.

Having spent several minutes listening and talking to the TS operators and preparing to go to periscope depth, I was now happy that it was safe to move from deep to PD. 'Revolutions for 7 knots,' I said. 'Periscope depth.'

We started to rise and that transition is always a stressful time. You believe that you have checked everything and yet.

You never know exactly.

We slowed down as we approached 65 feet and the Coxswain leveled out as Jeff Thomas, as the Ship Control Officer of the Watch, concentrated on the trim of the boat.

I raised the attack periscope and was watching right ahead as it broke the surface. A quick all round look. 'Nothing in sight. Down attack. Keep 63 feet. Up search.' The search periscope was shorter, but had all sorts of electronic gismos on it, as well as providing better binocular vision.

The sea up here is always grey and dark. Ten degrees off the bow was a darker patch of darkness. The bearing corresponded with the frigate and I looked harder down the bearing. Electronic Counter Measures alarmed and the bearing tied in. The frigate was using her radar.

'Down search,' I said quickly. Down came the periscope with a hiss of hydraulics. I looked at Ian and knew he was thinking the same thing as me. Was that a detection opportunity? It might have been but the intensity was low and it was unlikely. But it reinforced the need for caution. I doubted they had spotted me. 'Keep 180 feet,' I said.

Down went HMS SPLENDID into the dirty water, full of Arctic river debris. But I had at least managed to see that there was no indication of surface ice. It is too easy to ram an iceberg at these depths and ice doesn't always show on sonar. On we hummed, quiet as we could. We were doing six knots heading for that broadside of noise, tracking the frigate as it moved away from the boat.

The sonar operators were chattering into their headsets giving more and more information to the TS operators. The cacophony of background noise was still there. The team continued to report, analyse and assess what was actually going on.

Who was there? Where were they going? What were they doing? There seemed to be the possibility of several submarines and a mixture of noise in the direction of the coastline.

Ian and I talked over the situation and concluded that the frigate which was only about two miles away at the most, but appeared to be moving away. It had been 10 minutes since I had last looked and I decided to look again.

We did a quick clearing of the stern arcs by altering 70° off course, staying there for about 6 minutes and then returning to the previous course, and then I had a good all round sonar picture as well. I was content that it was safe to come back up.

'Take her up,' I said. 'Periscope depth.'

The Coxswain hauled back on his yoke. The lens broke surface. I was using the attack periscope again as I wanted to minimize my exposure, and the top is only the size of a Coca-Cola can.

In my "all round look" [ARL] I had seen the frigate, but continued the sweep to ensure there was nothing else close. I didn't expect there to be anything other than the frigate, but you must do an ARL as a first look to clear yourself from everything around you for 360°.

The frigate was bigger in the periscope grid, 5000 yards away, sixty degrees off the port bow and I was on his port quarter so he was going away as we had assessed from sonar before we came up. I calculated the look interval (when I needed to look at him again) in my head and I passed the accurate visual bearing and range to the operators. It was inserted into the tactical system that continued to track its movement with the continuing help of sonar information. The bearing had opened and she was moving away from us. She was on a mission, but we were not it, which was nice to know. Frigates carry choppers and a chopper will hover and dangle a sonar hydrophone on a long cable into the sea and be very dangerous. What a helicopter can do, and nothing else can do, is hunt in one place one minute and be somewhere else the next minute. And we have no real way of predicting what they will do. We do not like choppers. They are very unpredictable and they carry anti- submarine torpedoes. One more sweep of the periscope; the frigate was continuing as expected, still bustling along. No worries there for the moment, then.

Anyway, there were other things to think about, because the sonar operators were reporting a strong contact that they had classified as a submarine. The sonar traces, electronic library and years of experience had provided a classification and indicated that it was an Alfa class SSN: fast but noisy. But it was making too much noise, even for an elderly Alfa. And it was not the right kind of noise that we were expecting.

There was something else there too. Its sonar trace did not look like anything the sound room held in his library or any of their heads.

Ian looked across the control room at me. It was warm and humming and as calm as usual. I said quietly to myself, 'Bomb burst?'

'Five minutes to Piccadilly Circus,' says the navigator.

'Let's have another good look around on sonar,' I said. 'Go to port first.' Jimmy Fergusson started the maneuver and Ian took the intermittent attack periscope looks.

A submarine's hull mounted sonar is effective in a 120° arc on either side of the nose. There is a sonar set on the aft end of the fin to look backwards, but it has to look through the propulsor and the greater noise at the after end of the boat, so it is none too sensitive. You need to check by other means what is behind you, which usually means turning round and having a look. This always changes the coverage of the towed array.

The Coxswain put on port rudder, banking the boat into the turn. HMS SPLENDID came round 180°, quiet, sonars listening. Tiny Holmes, the TASO and Tactical Officer of the Watch, was murmuring in my ear, identifying the twin screws of the frigate and more surface ships to seaward. Then he said, 'I have a definite contact. Possible SSN.'

'Bearing and Range?'

The target analysis rating on my left said, '11,000 yards. 32° on the port bow.'

'Track it.'

'Tracking.'

The tactical systems team took a fix on the contact, then another, then another, plotting the angle of incidence of the sound waves on HMS SPLENDID's sensors. 'Still 032°,' he said. 'Range 9000 yards.'

The contact was heading towards us and the bearing was steady. This means, if it stays that way, you will eventually collide. But so was another channel, five miles to the east.

I went over to the plotting table. The crosses of the contact's position on the chart were approaching a bend in the deep channel. If the next fix was out of channel and still heading towards us, the contact was on our case and it was time to fade away. Some captains would have started to fade immediately. But it had taken a great expenditure of effort and teamwork to get here. I held my nerve and decided we would wait and, although sonar was classifying it as a possible Alpha class, they were not completely sure. The next fix was in the channel. It looked as though he was navigating, not chasing.

'Back on base course' said Jimmy Fergusson, in a voice completely level. Sweating slightly, we proceeded to Piccadilly Circus and went deep to 235 feet. And we waited. 235 feet is an 'anti metric' depth. The Soviets keep metric depths, so it is important avoid a depth in feet that is similar to the likely depths that a Soviet submarine might keep. For example, 50 metres is 164 feet; 75metres 246 feet and 100metres, 328 feet. You have to add on your draught (keel to top of fin) say 70 feet to ensure you have separation. It is not an exact art and there is not much room for error, but we know from intelligence that the Soviets tend to keep 50 metres and 100 metres and, although 235 feet is a little close to 75 metres, it is a calculated risk. As long as you do not stay at a metric depth your will probably be alright.

We are at 4 knots max now, moving stealthily and steadily, ready to react at any moment to a change of circumstance. We have changed to the search quiet state to maximize our detection opportunities and keep our own background noise as small as possible.

The search quiet state involves cutting out any machinery that is not completely necessary and keeping all noise within the submarine to an absolute minimum. This ensures that any signature you are giving away is a small as possible and has the shortest possible detection range for any opponent. To stay in this state for more than a couple of hours changes how we operate and thus, when you choose to initiate the search quiet state, the time you stay in that state must be carefully considered. The fact that the air conditioning fans are switched off helps to concentrate the minds of all and, if you are not on watch, everybody knows to settle down and keep quiet whether it is in a bunk or in a mess deck No music. No films. Just keeping as quiet as we could.

Sonar and target analysis continue to issue a stream of updates. The Target Motion Analysis computers are constantly recalculating as each new bearing or piece of information comes in. They are good computers, but it is still the man who has to make the decision. Experience at sniffing out the enemy does count for a lot in these circumstances. The noisy tugs were approaching, range 8,000 yards, and the plot made it quite clear they were coming our way.

Forty minutes had passed and I really needed to have another visual look and so decide to go up to periscope depth, quietly - very quietly - with just enough revolutions to hold the boat as stable as possible. Sonar continued to report the two tugs moving away, blowing black diesel fumes. It was difficult to make out but they were towing something boxy with a squarish superstructure. A target barge? Away they went, northeast, into the blackish murk that pressed down on the Barents Sea. I wanted to return to periscope depth again but we were getting a very good picture from sonar and the tactical plots. The frigate was still tracking away and was assessed as being at 10000 yards now still opening.

'Here they come,' said Tiny Holmes.

'An Alfa making that noise?' said Roger Crafts from the sound room. 'And probably another frigate. In the channel.'

'Try an Alfa and something else,' said Ian.

'Good point,' said Roger Crafts. A pause and then. 'Blimey. There is something else.'

'What is it?'

'Never heard anything like it before...'

But it had become clear that there were not one, but probably two, submarines coming towards us. And you could bet that when they got to Piccadilly Circus one would go one way, one another, and the frigate another. That was your bomb burst. Designed as a pre-planned tactical move, or was it to confuse any watchers like us? 'Never heard one like this before,' said CPO Jeff Matthews from the sound room again. 'I am going to do some more quick analysis and work this out.'

Trailing an Alpha and sussing out what he was doing and why would be good. Trailing something new would be even better. But what was it?

Ian and I did another check of the plots and discussed options and we started the process of clearing ourselves to return to periscope depth. The transition from deep to shallow can be dangerous if you cannot detect what everyone on the surface is doing. The onset of super tankers with their huge draft and massive hulls, which blanketed the sound of their propellers, was a real danger. But then I was not expecting a super tanker here. But I did need to be careful. A few more reports from sonar to completely clarify the picture as well as we could. A stern arc clearance to check there was nothing behind us. And return to the course I wanted to come up on.

Once satisfied I ordered, 'Periscope depth,' again and asked Ian to take the search periscope as we needed to use all our sensors to evaluate the situation.

Ian did a quick all round look and reported that the frigate was still on the murky fringes of vision.

'Air up,' said the ECM operator. 'It's a Badger.'

Although the Tu-16 'Badger' aircraft began life as a high-altitude, free-fall bomber, come the mid-1950s it was equipped to carry early Soviet cruise missiles The Tu-16 was also built in numerous specialized variants for reconnaissance, maritime surveillance, electronic intelligence gathering (ELINT), and electronic warfare (ECM).

Rather like our own Nimrod aircraft, slow and slightly old fashioned and somewhat ungainly. But they were very effective.

The Soviets would not be taking all this trouble unless there was something going on. Maybe, just maybe, they had something good to hide.

We continued to watch, track and analyse and nobody relaxed. The visibility was not that good and although the sun was trying to come out but there was nothing visible now. The frigate had and tugs had gone out of visual range and the sound room reported that the 'Tugs are still moving at 4 knots.' Sounds as though they are still towing the target barges' – to wherever they are going but we don't know where. But we did have a good position for them both and Ian Mackenzie put the spot on the chart and a datum [A datum is a point or location where detection has been made] was inserted on all the tactical systems screens.

'Target ETA Piccadilly Circus, 1040,' came the report. Meaning that the target would arrive at there at 1040. We had plenty of time. We continued to listen, watch, analyse and wait for developments.

There were many dry mouths in the control room.

I turned on the internal intercom, conscious that it was unlikely to be heard outside the submarine. But the cause justified the means. As a Captain you need to keep your Ship's Company informed of what is going on and your intentions. They are dependent on you to do so and I would not have it any other way. Moreover, you never know, they may have a snippet of information that they were not too confident of and it might increase their confidence to say something that could make a difference.

'This is the Captain speaking. We have an unidentified, possibly new, Soviet boat that we want to take a close look at,' I said. We don't know what he is doing – it may be a missile test it may be something else. Weather conditions are reasonable. We have him on sonar but not visible yet but we will follow him and gather intelligence and pictures as circumstances permit. If he looks as though he is going to do a missile firing then we will try to see that. We will remain in containment state one, but stand down from action stations to diving stations for the moment. We'll return to action stations as and when necessary. Please keep noise to an absolute minimum. That's all for the present.'

This was sufficient information for the Ships' Company to understand what was going on, but also give them a break for a coffee in the certainty that they would be closed up again soon. There was the sound of men falling out, changing round, the surge of noise that came with the release of tension, the murmur of Chief and Petty Officers quieting things down. There was nothing to do but wait, listen and watch.

And be quiet.

I decided to stay at periscope depth. 'We need to have something visual really before we decide what to do,' I said to Tiny. 'Stay at periscope depth and keep a good watch out but go deep again if you feel uncomfortable.' Tiny Holmes nodded that he understood and took the periscope. I could see the concentration on his face.

At 1040, Tiny reported that the frigate was passing about 6000 yards away from us in the murk, but there was no sign of helicopters, no active sonar and no visual correlation of our sonar picture. This did look as though they did not know we are here which is obviously good news – but I was equally aware that that could change in a moment's notice and we must be alert. Petty Officer Roger Crafts came on the intercom from the sound room and said 'They're using the underwater telephone'. The onboard specialist Russian speaking communications team was trying to decipher what they were saying.

Underwater telephone is a simple system that allows you to pass either speech or groups of letters using a specialist sonar set – indeed we have one fitted ourselves - but you only use it to transmit if you are sure who you are talking to. You have to transmit of course and you are inevitably giving things away to anyone else who might be listening. For us it was a very good source of intelligence, especially as to the future movements of units.

I walked to the sound room door – a good place to hang out – and asked, 'What are they saying?'

Alexander Peters, specialist communications technician, was in the sound room with a pair of headphones on. He was listening, rewinding and re-listening to the tape. All the sonar sets are recorded continuously.

Alex, a fluent Russian speaker, took off his headphones and matter of factly said, 'they will surface at 1130. They are on a trial and will return to harbour around midnight.'

'Thanks Alex. Good stuff,' I replied.

'Alfa, course 004 Speed 8 knots. Range 8000 yards,' said Petty Officer Sean Runham from the tactical desk, continuing to use his light pen on the screen so fast that I could not keep up with his movements as much as I tried. This guy was a real expert and I had learned to trust what he reported. He would have analysed the data to death to make sure he was right.

Then Roger Crafts came up with 'Unidentified sonar contact – probable submarine and also a frigate, tracking southeast. Targets splitting' Jim Fergusson on the periscope added 'nothing in sight – visibility 6000 yards.'

So there was the expected bomb-burst, or something close to it.

This Soviet tactic had been seen many times before and had confused watchers in the past. History had indicated to the Soviets that they could be being watched, even in their own waters.

This also means that, as a Commanding Officer, you have to be even more careful and mindful of not getting into a dangerous situation. The Soviets are always looking for enemy submarines and do not just go through the motions.

An enemy submarine watching from the logical place, out at sea, would have assumed that the Alfa and the unidentified contact were the same boat. Then, suddenly, the boat would have split into two boats, leaving the enemy submarine wondering which one to chase.

But bomb-bursts did not work if the enemy submarine was parked in a close quarter's position, close to Soviet waters.

'Steer 130°,' I said. 'Revolutions for 4 knots.'

HMS SPLENDID turned slowly and slid through the mucky water, down the eastern limb of the channel and into a deeper stretch of water.

Steering 130°, at four knots. Just over one hour's steaming would bring us on the edge of Soviet territorial waters, so this had to be thought through again. Plenty of time till then, I thought, biting into a ham sandwich with extra mustard, though the ham sandwich did seem harder than usual to swallow.

But we had the unidentified submarine being held reasonably well by now. It was time to go deep again as I did not want to close at periscope depth and we could get a more settled picture as we closed as on sonar alone.

I took the periscope from the Officer of the Watch for a quick all round look myself and then handed it back before going to the sound room door to speak to Roger Crafts. 'Are you holding this contact well?' I asked and he replied 'Yes I am Sir. It is getting louder all the time.'

When I got back to the control room the tactical systems plot had a good course and speed on the target and I started to move to very slowly get up onto the Soviet boat's starboard side, in a controlled and precise manner, keeping out of the noise of his screw so that it would not muffle any other sound.

Reports were coming thick and fast from the sonar operators, refining every detail. The guys on the target motion analysis computers were constantly refining the sonar bearing into a "solution" of the Soviet boat. That is its course and speed.

Depth was always a more of a dilemma. Being at close quarters with another submarine, when you do not know their depth, is a dangerous situation to be in. And it is very difficult to ascertain another submarine's depth. An underwater collision can (and in the past has) sink a submarine as quickly and effectively as any depth charge, torpedo or anti-submarine missile. The fact it would be unintentional would not change the end result: dead submariners.

The frigate was being held on sonar ahead of the unidentified submarine, on his port bow but there was still nothing visual. I wish we could see something! The sonar men sucked in the submarine acoustic signature from top to bottom of the frequency band. 'We are running a bearing on one of his lubricating oil pumps,' said Roger Crafts.

This meant that he could identify the sound characteristics of the lubricating oil pump and track the sound from this specific source. This is not done aurally alone, but by sophisticated computers supporting analysis of every frequency detected.

Twenty-three minutes later, three miles outside territorial waters, Alex said, 'He says on the underwater telephone he will surface now, to check missile installation.'

So he was coming up and this could be our chance when we knew exactly what depth he was at.

Suddenly Roger Crafts reported on the intercom from the sound room 'He's blowing his tanks.' Pause. 'Target surfacing. Now.'

I said, 'Officer of the Watch. Go to Action stations.'

Again there was the discreet stirring of men taking up positions for battle, the muffled clang of watertight doors closing in a controlled manner, the murmur of men reporting and confirming they were at their stations and their state of readiness.

In less than 2 minutes all compartments were reporting in that they were closed up and ready.

The manoeuvring room reported that we were in Containment State 1. The speed of all this was no less than I expected but at the same time indicated that this team was so professional and understood how we should all respond and act.

Soviet Alfa submarine in dry dock

CHAPTER EIGHT
UNDERWATER LOOK

The surfaced submarine and the frigate were steaming ahead at four knots and sonar and the tactical plots had a very good handle on them both and I was very content that I knew exactly what was going on both actually and relatively to HMS SPLENDID. But I wanted to see it before I went deep again. If they were preparing for a test firing the submarine's crew would be busy. They would also be noisy and disorganized, because while Soviet officers were generally good, their crews were mainly conscripts.

Soviet Typhoon Ballistic Missile Submarine

I took the periscope and, after a really hard look along the target's bearing I could just about make out the shape of the Soviet submarine on the surface, it was impossible to establish what class or type she was. But it was big and it was on the surface and we were in a good position on his quarter. I could just about make out what I took to be the frigate but could not be sure. I handed the periscope back to Tiny

Holmes and told him to watch them like a hawk and moved towards Ian and said quietly, 'We have an opportunity for an underwater look here. What do you think?' We discussed the pros and cons for a few moments and agreed that it was worth a try.

'Pilot,' I said, looking over the Navigating Officer's shoulder. 'How much water for the next four miles?'

'Thirty fathoms,' he said. 'Shelving to twelve after 7500 yards.'

'Very good. If the target remains on this course will it remain outside territorial waters?'

'Yes, sir. It will. But the depth of water is the problem.'

'Yes. I know,' I replied rather more sharply than I should have. 'But we will remain outside territorial waters – they are now 6 miles away?'

'Yes, sir,' the Navigator replied.

The boat was moving at four knots. I had an hour and 4 miles before I ran out of water.

'Officer of the Watch – hand over the look to the First Lieutenant.' I wanted my best man on the periscope now and Ian was the best and most experienced and that freed up Tiny Holmes to go to his action station where he would be more familiar with what was required. And I needed him there.

'What can you see? What are conditions like?' I said impatient for information. 'Conditions are good enough for us to take photographs,' he said. 'Starboard side will be lit more than the port.'

'Very good. We'll bring the periscope down the starboard side so you can get your snaps.'

'Take a final target set up when you are ready and update all the plots and then we will go deep.'

Ian gave the set up on the unknown submarine and the frigate and then the periscope down and said, "3 down. Keep 100 feet." We quickly slipped deeper below the surface and were now dependent on sonar.

However, twelve fathoms was not a sensible operating depth. Indeed, at periscope depth we would be aground! And, at the back of every submarine CO's mind, is the need to have the safety of being able to go to a safe depth [your own height, keel to top of fin, plus the most likely depth of the largest target, and then a margin – your call what that is - so that the target could sail straight over you without any risk of a collision.

That safe depth depends on circumstances, but is seldom less than

120 feet (20 fathoms). To operate with no safe depth margin and with no margin to the sea bed was stupid and could result in us grounding or, worse still, collision with the sea bed. If we could not get our pictures within 7500 yards and the 12 fathom line (72 feet!), we would have to abort. And you had to decide how much you trusted the charts and the survey that resulted in it being produced along with all the other myriad of variables.

We continued to gain on the Soviet boat, but very slowly. This type of intelligence gathering is a controlled manoeuver and needs to be done with full concentration by everyone. I did not want to approach too quickly as it was important to get as much information as we moved closer.

Speak calmly I think to myself, but not feeling very calm. Show that you are in control of the situation.

I picked up the microphone and switched on the main broadcast. 'Do you hear there, this is the Captain speaking. We are close to a large unknown Soviet submarine on the surface and we think it is a new boat. We are going in for an underwater look, but we do not have much time as the water shallows quickly and we may have to bail out in a hurry. So stay with it. Max concentration please. That's all.'

I then ordered, '7 knots.' Behind the closed tunnel doors, John Davis, Chris Gillooly and the Engineer Officer of the Watch, Mike Potter, watched and tweaked and increased the steam feed to the turbines. That was not much of a closing speed differential, but it was enough. Reports were coming in thick and fast now from the navigation plot, the sound room and the target motion analysis computer operators. '5000 yards. Mark the plot.'

'Target bearing steady. Still on the surface. No change'

'Course unchanged. Speed now 3 knots – 4000 yards. Mark the plot.'

'Target bearing moving very slowly left. No change to attitude.'

I altered our own course slightly as I wanted a virtual, steady bearing. Not too much –   this was a time for small changes – refining the move of the boat towards the target. I scanned the dials on the ship control and everything looked fine. Roger Colborne was a picture of concentration on the planes.

'3000 yards.'

'Target bearing steady. Still on the surface. No change'

'Course unchanged. Speed dropped to 2 knots.'

And then the boat started to sink a little. The Officer of the Watch on Ship Control Jeff Thomas was on it in a flash and, in fairness, so was the planes man. The OOW resisted adjusting the trim of the boat. This was not the time and we did not want any pumps running that were not required.

'2000 yards. Mark the plot.'

'Target bearing steady. Still on the surface. No change. Course unchanged. Target Speed now 3 knots.'

I conferred with Ian. 'Time to go up,' I said.

He nodded, still scanning all the information being presented intensely. Now was the time to get up closer.

I ordered, 'Eighty feet, then flat and level. Stay within three feet of eighty feet. Maximum concentration everyone.'

This was submarine efficiency at its best.

Reports were coming in quietly and efficiently, being assessed and yet only those who needed to speak were doing so. A quiet control room is an efficient one.

'At eighty feet,' came the report.

The control room was silent except for the slow whisper of the fans at slow speed. The reports were still coming and I was listening intently as we crept up behind the target to get a good look at the starboard side. The Officer of the Watch, Jeff Thomas, was listening intently too and watching ship control and the movement of the boat, ready to react to any unusual movement.

At a depth of 80 feet we could see nothing, but Ian Mackenzie was calling out the distance until we were at the right range.

'1500 yards. Mark the plot.'

From sonar and then the Tactical System operator, 'Target bearing steady. Still on the surface. No change.'

'Course unchanged. Target Speed now 3 knots.'

Alex Peters came over the intercom and said, 'No more transmissions, no change to target.'

Ian Mackenzie was crouched over his plot and watching the small dot of light under the chart indicating our position.

'30 seconds to periscope. Mark.'

'Target bearing steady. Still on the surface. No change. Course unchanged. Target Speed 3 knots.'

'10 seconds to periscope. Mark,' said Ian Mackenzie and continued the countdown.

I leaned forward and touched Roger Colborne on the shoulder, showing my confidence in him and making sure he knew we were with him. The reports from Sonar intensified and, as we got closer, the bearings will move around a lot more [as you get closer the bearings will move as there is more sensitivity to each report], but we all had to hold our nerve. We had had a reasonable distance to run in and the quality of the sonar information was good. Our approach had gone well and we would be very unlucky if we were not in exactly the right place and attitude. I just hoped that we had enough light and that the Soviet submarine stayed on the surface until we had finished and withdrawn.

'3, 2, 1. Mark,' said the navigator, indicating we were in position to raise the periscope for underwater photography.

Instantaneously I ordered 'Up periscope,' and Ian crouched down on the deck to meet the handles as they came clear of the periscope well. He turned the scope to the right bearing being reported from the plot and sonar almost continuously and moved back and forward across 10 or 20° either side. I could see him straining to see and then he said, 'Nothing in sight. Estimate visibility 100 feet.'

I cursed under my breath. Had I gone deep too early? Was the run in not as accurate as I thought?

I might have been disappointed but did not show it and resisted the temptation to get on the periscope myself.

Instead, I said, 'Keep looking. Have a look in low power.' [This is a different level of magnification of the periscope picture.]

We waited and the reports indicated we must be very close. Ian continued to search and I looked intensely at the remote screen indicating what Ian was seeing.

By now, if our calculations were right, and sonar was telling us we were, we should be seeing things. Where is this boat?

It seemed an age and my mind was racing with alternatives – the "what ifs." I was beginning to doubt myself.

Then Ian almost shouted, 'VISUAL.' Followed shortly by, 'Got it. Switching to high power.'

I was watching the periscope video repeat from the periscope window and could just about make out the dark shape in the middle of the screen.

I could see Ian's finger working the shutter – multiple single shots per second as well as video. His view would be better than mine on the remote.

We sat in our little cramped room, our nose under the new boat's tail. We moved ahead slowly. Our speed looked alright and we were slowly overtaking the Soviet and all the indications were that she was still doing 3 knots.

The reports continued and I listened intently, looking for the unusual. Sonar continued to report and comparisons were being made all the time. There was a lot to take in but we were getting the required info and sucking it in – visual and acoustic. Ian started to talk faster and give a running commentary, explaining what he was seeing in as much graphic detail as he could. This was being recorded at the same time so we could put the whole picture together afterwards. I was looking at the video and was pleased with what I was seeing – clear definition of the hull and all its opening and protuberances, although exactly what they were was not clear. That would come later.

I estimated that we were forty feet away from the Soviet's reactor and our sensor system in HMS SPLENDID, both machines and humans, were in overdrive sucking everything in we could.

I thought that we must now be beneath their control room, manned by people exactly like us, except they were our enemies.

And then: 'Someone hammering,' said the Jeff Matthews from the sound room. 'Hell of a racket.'

'Something's stuck,' said Alex Peters. 'I guess it's a missile door stuck.'

It was certainly deafening and I was tensed up myself as the noise was very loud and was distracting. However, a small, dangerous feeling of smugness grew in me, but I was alert too and the tension and apprehension was there in everyone in the control room.

The periscope would be passing the torpedo room, now, the sonar array on the bow: always interesting, the sonar array. Then we would be clear. Ian had been giving a running commentary and was being recorded and this would be correlated later with all the other information.

'It's very big,' said Ian. 'Bloody enormous. Never seen anything like it. It must be an SSBN. It is too big for an SSN.'

'Give us all the detail you can Ian,' I said.

'Closing territorial waters,' said the navigator, in a quiet and measured voice. 'Shoaling.'

'Periscope clear of bow,' said Ian. 'Swinging round to look aft.' We had got enough and it was time to get out here!

'Down periscope, come right slowly 20°,' I ordered. 'Shoaling fast,' said the navigator. 'Seventeen fathoms.'

'Stopped banging,' said Sonar.

'Four knots,' said the navigator. 'Seventeen fathoms.'

The depth of water was now 102 feet and we were at 70 feet. So there was very little water under us now and a great big SSBN on top of us and an anti-submarine frigate alongside him. And we were right on the edge of Soviet territorial waters.

This was the stuff of a full blown international incident, or worse, if anything were to go wrong now. We had to get out of here and fast, but the depth of water was against us and I had to move slower than I would have liked.

In this situation the Soviets would be fully entitled to blow us out of the water and we knew how aggressive they could be. We had done our stuff, but we could be in trouble if we did not get out of this situation in an orderly manner.

I sensed that there was sweat on my brow, but ignored it. I could feel the tension in the control room and from the reports from the sound room. They felt the tension too. But we needed to go on, so the towed array could do its stuff, right under the new boat's belly. And we needed to give the array as much time as possible close to the target to suck in the whole spectrum of noises and frequencies: all invaluable information.

I considered whether to break off more quickly and whether I could come back again later, but the chance may not be there again. In submarine terms: "attack what you see, not what you think might be there." At that moment that was not an option. We had to go on. Six knots meant a mile every ten minutes. Six minutes to bring the full length of the towed array right under the Soviet boat as we turned away. But I did not have sufficient water under the keel to do that and I would have to break contact earlier than I would like.

'Wait,' said Jeff Matthews in the sound room. Pause. Then, loudly, 'Main vent opening.'

The Soviet boat was opening its main vents and diving and although we were starting to bear away we were still right underneath!

'Abort, abort,' I said. 'Abort, abort. Starboard 30. Speed 10 knots Down all masts.' I watched as these orders were put into action as my mind raced and tried to keep the mental picture I had of the physical interaction between HMS SPLENDID, the towed array, the Soviet submarine and the sea bed. The control room was still quiet, but the tension had visibly increased and the strain was showing on people's faces. I tried to hide mine.

On top of us, a very big submarine was starting to dive.

Half a mile ahead of us, water shallow enough to force us onto the surface.

HMS SPLENDID heeled into a starboard (right hand) turn, the deck pushing hard against our feet. 'Let's get out of here,' I said.

Ian gave me a nervous but relieved smile.

The boat kept turning and I could see Ian, like me, having moved from the periscope and was watching Roger Colborne wrestling with the turn and keeping on depth – not an easy task as turning hard to starboard tends to drop the stern as the large rudder acts as a hydroplane.

This was hairy!

The stern dipped a couple of feet but Roger Colborne was ahead of the change and had already corrected it. Slowly we reversed our course 180 degrees and slowed down to 8 knots still listening intently to the sonar reports which confirmed that the Soviet was indeed in the middle of her dive. But no longer on top of us. The bearings were in our stern arcs now and were not so accurate and were not giving us the good picture we had enjoyed for the last 45 minutes or so.

Sonar reported that the towed array, although not optimized, was providing multiple frequencies. But this was not the time to be analysing this. It would have to wait until we got home. And I was now concerned that the array, stretched several hundred yards behind us, could be ripped off as the Soviet submarine dived onto it. 'Navigator, how long before the towed array is clear?' I barked a little louder than I should have.

'Standby,' said Ian Mackenzie.

I estimated it would take the Soviet boat around 6 to 8 minutes to get down and she was unlikely to alter course in that diving movement.

But the sonar reports were important and continued to confirm what we thought and hoped was happening, which was that HMS SPLENDID was turning inexorably away from the diving Soviet boat. The bow sonar reports indicated that there was nothing close ahead of us as the boat turned her nose towards the open sea.

'Estimate 4 minutes before the towed array is clear,' said Ian Mackenzie at the chart table.

'Very loud,' said Jeff Matthews from the sound room as we slanted away from the new boat, which was now descending in an enormous roar of bubbles and hydroplane noise.

'Captain, Sir,' said Alex 'I wonder ... Is this an exercise or something else?'

I took in his comment, but was not interested in what he might be doing at that moment and I had no evidence it was anything more than what we thought it was: a controlled dive. But I said to Alex, 'If it is not an exercise, what is it?'

'I'm not sure,' said Alex. 'But I'll keep listening.'

We moved away and then Ian Mackenzie said, to the relief of all, 'Towed array should be clear now.'

Sound room is the towed array working as expected?'

Petty Officer Roger Crafts came back immediately, 'Towed array working fine Sir.'

I felt relieved again and, now that the towed array was clear, we could slow down to 6 knots and, as the depth of water increased, move the boat down in increments to 235 feet (50 metres + 70 feet) and slink back through Piccadilly Circus to the vastness of the open sea.

We remained at Diving Stations for another half hour and until we had done another full sonar check to make sure we were not being followed. The water beneath us deepened and, after about 40 minutes, I discussed with Ian that we should retreat and take stock. I decided it was time to go back to the watch. So I ordered the Officer of the Watch to fall out the Ships' Company from Action Stations, went back to the watch and we started to get back to a normal watch routine.

I went to the main broadcast again and said: 'Do you hear there, Captain speaking. It looks as though we completed a good underwater look on what may be a new Soviet SSBN. It will take some time to analyze all the information we have gained, but I think it looks pretty good. It was a bit tight in there and you all did very well. I am not sure what comes next, but we will retreat for a while and will be assessing our options in the next few hours and decide what to do then. Well done everyone. That's all.'

Typhoon by the seaside!

CHAPTER NINE

MISSILE FIRING

We moved out to sea for about 90 minutes and then the sound room reported that the tugs towing the target barges were still going but were moving more slowly to the North West. I looked at the chart and decided it was worth investigating. I spoke to Ian and he agreed it was worth having a look. I called Alex Peters into the control room and we studied the chart together.

'What do you think Alex?' I said 'Is there anything to suggest the target barges are positioning for a missile launch?'

'Could be,' replied Alex. 'It would seem logical that they are not out here for nothing and if we got closer we might be able to get in position to monitor a missile firing. I will keep an ear out for any communication chatter that might give us some better information.'

'Okay' I said 'we will get over there and see what is going on.

'Tactical Desk, what is the range of the target barges now? I asked.

'14000 yards,' came the reply, 'tracking northwest at 4 knots.'

'Officer of the Watch come right to course 320° speed 10 knots.'

I had another look at the chart and looked at where we should be close to target barges. I did not want to get closer than 2000 yards from the target barges. If there was a missile shoot then I did not want to be the target! And as long as the barges were still attached to the tugs we could follow them and it sounded as if they were. I reckoned on about 42 minutes at 10 knots but I also wanted to be at periscope depth not only to watch and record any missile firing but also to let Alex listen to any Soviet tactical communications. But I had to be wary as this was still an area where the presence of Soviet submarines was a high probability and I did not want to give away a detection opportunity. 10 knots was a compromise between good listening conditions for sonar and covering the ground.

After 30 minutes at 10 knots I got nervous and wanted to be slower and also get to periscope depth. In any case the tugs were still heading northwest at 4 knots and as we got closer there was plenty of noise from the target barges being towed. We had covered 10000 yards and had closed to within 5000 yards of the tugs and target barges.

We slowed down and did careful sonar check. There was nothing else around that we could hear so we came back slowly to periscope depth and I took the attack periscope as it broke surface. One all-round look confirmed that the only things in sight were the two tugs and they were indeed towing a target barge each. They were around 500 yards apart both on a course of 320° speed 4 knots and the nearest one was 4300 yards away. I gave a visual set up to the plot and then put the attack periscope down and the search up. There was a bit of ECM but it was weak. I handed over the periscope to the OOW with a clear brief and told him to get no closer than n 2 miles from the tugs and barges.

I then went to see Alex Peters and had a conversation with him asking him to clarify what we would hear in advance of a missile firing from a shooting vessel and what notice we would get of a firing. This was "teaching granny to suck eggs" as he did not really need me to tell him what to do but it was good for me to say it anyway. He nodded in understanding and went back to work in the comms room to start listening.

About an hour later the tugs stopped and a small boat left one of the tugs with a group of men on board. By now the cloud had lifted a bit and the visibility was getting much better. I reckoned we could see around 12000 yards (6 miles) from the search periscope. I went to the chart and saw that the depth of water where the tugs were was around 35 fathoms on a small bank about 1 mile across. Around it the depth of water was in excess of 50 fathoms.

The OOW on the periscope was now the Doc – Chris Kalman – and I watched him as he gave a running commentary as the small boat went alongside the first barge and started moving around. 10 minutes later there was a very loud noise that sonar immediately recognized as the barges letting out their chain anchors. Chris reported this too and as soon as that had happened and the noise ceased he saw the men break the chain tow between the barge and the tug.

It was not long before they were all back in their boat and were on their way to the other barge. The procedure was repeated and the other barge was anchored and broken free of the tug. The men got back on the boat and it returned to one of the tugs.

Jimmy Fergusson the 2nd OOW was on the plot and noticed that the course for the tugs to return to harbour was right across our track and told Tiny that we needed to get off track. Tiny took another visual set up of both tugs and we fixed the two target barges in the tactical system and on the chart as datums. Chris Kalman ordered 'Come left to course 280° Speed 6 knots' I went to the chart and satisfied myself that this would get us off track enough to keep out of the way of the two tugs. Five minutes later both tugs turned to a course of 130° and speeded up to 8 knots in clouds of thick black smoke.

We let the two tugs go by and then returned to a position about 2000 yards from the first target barge. They were only about 50 metres apart and if we assumed that the missile would be fired from the south east to the northwest then we needed to ensure we were in a good position to capture any telemetry from the missile coming towards the barges.

Meanwhile Alex had been combing the voice frequencies try to pick up any snippets of information that would tell us if a missile firing was going to happen and if possible when. We waited and kept a good sonar search on at the same time and hoped that we would get some tactical information to ensure we were training the periscope on the right direction. We were not interested in the launch just the missile coming towards us so we could intercept any electronic details and with a bit of luck photograph it. Another 3 hours past and it was getting dark. Would this happen today? I thought not and suspected it would be tomorrow but we had no idea as yet.

It was now dark and as I was drinking coffee in my cabin it was becoming clearer that any firing was unlikely to be done today but it was not beyond the possibilities that a night firing could be on. Ian, and I spent a good hour discussing the best position for the submarine to be in to monitor any firing and we decided that we needed to be offset from the likely track (good decision!) and about 2500 yards from the two barges.

So we set up a patrol line about 2 miles long that would ensure that we could clear our stern arcs and have an all-round sonar search just in case a Soviet submarine was sent to do the same as us or to check out that there was nobody watching. You have to be alert to Soviet submarines in this part of the world as they could be anywhere. I decided to stay at periscope depth so I could monitor electronic warfare in particular Soviet aircraft and mainly in the hope that we might pick up some tactical communications to help us know what was going on. We spent the next six hours in this mode with no close contacts on sonar and a small amount of air activity but clearly some way away from us.

The tactical comms picture was more confusing and at about 0230 Alex came up and said that there was an increase in voice communications but no real indication of a missile firing or who it was from.

I was dozing in my cabin, eyes shut but really listening to everything – sonar reports, reports from the Engineer Officer of the Watch, the hum of the ventilation and air conditioning fans and the light chatter from the tactical system operators on their displays right outside my cabin door. I drifted off and thought of Roisin and what she might be doing. I speculated but was probably wrong.

Then, at 0430 Alex came back with a report that had me wide awake and indicated that 'The firing will take place at 0800 and will be from a Charlie class submarine – probably a Charlie II' he said. How he had worked this out I was not sure and I was not about to ask him but I was happy to go with it. I went into the control room and sat in the Captain's chair and started going through all our crib sheets to see what type of missile was likely and thus where we should be and what we would expect to see or hear.

By 0730 we were in position on our patrol line with the aim of being 2500 yards from the target barge at 0800. More communications had been heard during the last few hours and we become more confident that a firing would take place.

Soviet Charlie Class Submarine

The Charlie class submarines were first built at the Krasnove Sormovo shipyard at Gorkiy in 1967 and another 10 being built over the next 5 years. The Charlie I had two banks of four missile tubes outside the pressure hull angled upwards on each side of the bow. The tubes had large outer doors and were designed to fire the P-120 Malakhit (SS-N-9 Siren) medium range anti-ship missile. There had been delays to the development of the SS-N-9 Siren missile and it was substituted with the short range Ametist (SS-N-7 Starbright) missile.

The class was designed specifically to counter United States Navy battle groups and their tactic was to sit about 25 miles astern of a battle group and track them until they were ready to fire. This would allow the Charlie to surprise the Battle Group and fire from the relatively short range of 25 miles. This led to a whole new approach to Battle Group defence with friendly SSNs stationed astern of the Battle Group to counter this threat which was taken very seriously by the USN. Indeed I had been involved in NATO exercises where we had taken on the role of the Charlie and tried to get into a firing position.

Between 1972 and 1979 six improved Charlie IIs were built with improved electronics and launch systems for targeting and firing of the SS-N-9 anti-ship missile as well as the more standard secondary armament of torpedoes for ant-submarine warfare. So the Charlie class was no pushover.

The SS-N-9 was developed as a "universal" anti-ship missile for submarines and surface ships. And was designed to have a shorter range to reduce the flight time of the missile and eliminated the need for mid-course guidance. This allowed a "fire and forget" submerged launch and removed the requirement for guidance radar on the submarine. The SS-N-9 when it has left its launch tube uses a solid-fueled rocket and then moves to a turbo-jet powered cruise, flying at around 100m altitude. It then switches on its active radar seeker to acquire its target and attacks with a steep terminal dive. On contact it detonates a 400kg fragmentation warhead, which is sufficient to disable a frigate or seriously harm a US Navy aircraft carrier.

We were ready by 0745 with both periscopes up and manned and with all our sensors ready to record what we could. Alex had reported more chatter on the voice communications networks but had not managed to pick up a firing count down as yet. I decided that Ian should be on the search periscope and would try to pick up the missile visually and follow it. I had Jeff Thomas and Toby Spreckley rotating on the attack periscope for ship safety and continuous all round looks. There was nothing close on sonar and we had done another careful search over the last 15 minutes to make sure before we got into this mode of concentrating on the missile firing.

0800 passed. 0810 passed and I started to think this was not going to happen. Then from Alex 'Just picked up firing in 5 minutes.' There is a countdown ongoing but it is difficult to follow.

'Let me know if you can tell when it has been fired,' I replied to Alex followed by 'Any idea of the firing position?' I had assumed that the missile would be coming from the south east and that is where Ian was looking but it could come from anywhere but I doubted we would be able to get a firing position. But it would be good to know the missile was in the air.

'No idea, Sir,' replied Alex.

Tiny Holmes was in the control room checking that everyone was ready and recorders of all sorts were on. The tape recorder above Ian Richard's head attached to the bulkhead above the search periscope was switched on so we could record everything Ian said. The video cameras on the search periscope were switched on to record and the 35 mm still camera attached to the periscope was also ready. This was pre modern digital cameras and we had 35 mm cameras that took 3 frames a second. It gave a good series of pictures but ran out after 250 although that was good for the time.

It was 0815 and I was waiting for a prompt from Alex. 0816. Nothing. 0817. 'Missile fired,' came the shout from Alex and I could see Ian tense and start sweeping 15° either side of south east.

'No idea of launch position' said Alex quickly.

Tiny repeated the information to the sound room. The mood in the control changed discernibly. They were used to waiting but when something was happening everyone sat up a little more and the concentration from everyone was there.

Ian was searching down the expected bearing and looking for a white trail. The missile had less than 60 miles to travel to the target barge at its maximum range and it would be going at 700 miles per hour so it was going to be here any second.

Then suddenly came 'Mark,' shouted by Ian from the search periscope 'missile on THAT bearing as he cut through to the plot.

He was following the missile trail cutting bearings continuously to the tactical systems and commentating what he could see which was not much more than a vapour trail of the missile at a speed of 700 mph.

'Are we off track,' I rather naively asked as if we could move away any further in that time.

Ian replied 'Looks alright at present.'

Then up came ECM with a report 'Missile mid guidance radar

detected – recording.' These reports continued but there was nothing further from Alex and the communications side but then I did not expect any.

Then from the sound room came an alarming sound. 'Possible sonobuoys in the water – no bearing yet.'

The Officer of the Watch on the attack periscope had seen nothing but was he looking properly? It was too late to worry about that now. There was an aircraft up there dropping sonobuoys. Were they here to monitor the missile splash or had they found us. I did not want to find out. We were very quiet in this mode but if they were either passive or active buoys we did not want to be near them.

Ian's commentary continued and he then said 'missile dropping fast – homing in on target.'

Within 10 seconds there was a loud bang on underwater telephone followed by a 'Wow,' from Ian as the missile hit one of the target barges fair and square. 'Missile has hit the target barge – plenty of debris and smoke.'

Ian had managed to follow the trail all the way down to the target barge which is not easy as at the speed the missile was going it is difficult to keep the periscope on it. But he had done it.

That was fine but my attention was more with the sonar buoys.

'Sound room report sonobuoys – do we have any bearing and are they active or passive?'

There was nothing on ELINT so the aircraft was not using radar which was a relief and I would have expected an alarm on our own intercept sonar PARIS if the sonobuoys had been active. PARIS is the code name for the intercept sonar that is enclosed in a protuberance on the forward casing. It detects active sonar transmissions from a ship or, more alarmingly, from a submarine and provides a frequency bearing and an intensity which can give a rough indication of range. 'Any sign of an aircraft visual?' I asked Jeff on the attack periscope. If these were sonobuoys then someone had to have dropped them and that had to be an aircraft. He scanned the air again and said 'nothing in sight.'

I went over to Ian at the search periscope and he was just checking that all the recording equipment was switched off. 'I think we have got enough – it is time to get out of here.'

'I agree,' he said followed by 'down search and the panel watch keeper pressed the lever which operated the search periscope.

'Sound room – do you have any bearing of the sonobuoys?' I

needed to know which way to go.

'They were only splashes so they are likely to be passive and they have not gone active yet'

I looked at the chart and decided to go deep and alter course to the south east and then do a granny's footsteps (old submarine phrase indicating a careful retreat) back round to the west.

As I was deciding this there were two reports almost simultaneously.

From ECM 'Racket dangerous Racket dangerous bearing 340°!' and in the control room the PARIS active sonar interceptor alarmed bearing 330°!

The situation was clear – we had an aircraft on top of us and it was using its radar and dropping sonobuoys including active ones. It must have had a sniff of us or it could have been monitoring the missile test but what would an active sonobuoy gain – not a lot.

'OOW down all masts - Come right steer 130° speed 8 knots keep 235 feet ECM report the racket.'

The reply came quickly 'No PRF (Pulse Repetition Frequency) captured but very loud.'

So what were we dealing with here. It was almost certainly a Bear Foxtrot or Tupolev Tu-142 to give it its Russian name. The Bear F is a Long Range Maritime Patrol [LRMP] reconnaissance and anti-submarine warfare (ASW) aircraft derived from the Tu-95 turboprop strategic bomber. It did patrol as far down the North Atlantic as west of UK but it was also used closer to home. It was the only aircraft that was likely to be dropping sonobuoys.

We crept away and slowly worked our way round to the west. The sonobuoy transmissions were much weaker and there did not seem to be any more. After another hour we had lost them altogether. Ian, Tiny and I went into the sound room for a discussion with Danny Fisher and Jeff Matthews. We agreed that it was most unlikely that they had been dropped in response to our periscope exposure as we had had detected no radar until after the sonobuoys had been detected. It was possible that the drop had been something to do with the missile firing but we were not sure. It was something the analysis boys back in UK would need to look at when we got home. I did not think we had been detected but it was worth moving some distance away from this area for the time being just in case.

Russia's new ballistic missile submarine

OLD
Typhoon class
16 x SLBM's
557 ft 9in

NEW
Borei class
20 x SLBM's
574 ft 2in

Yury Dolgoruky First Borei-class submarine is undergoing sea trials, two others are being built

Royal Navy
Vanguard class
16 x SLBM's
491 ft 10in

CHAPTER TEN

SHOTGUN SSN

We had been fortunate with the Charlie missile firing and also to find that SSBN and even more fortunate that it had chosen to surface and make a lot of noise, thus enabling us to do an underwater look. These opportunities do not come up very often on a dived submarine and they have to be grasped when you come across them.

They are inherently dangerous, but we would hope that the amount of information gained, when everything was analysed back in UK, will provide either confirmation of what we already know or give us new information and an insight into how we can utilize it to our best ability. I would expect that analysis to massively add to our knowledge of the characteristics of the SSBN we had found. If we could correlate it with other information and establish which boat it was that would be even better.

Apart from underwater photographs and noise characteristics at just about every angle, it was very satisfying to complete one of the more challenging intelligence gathering events and bring home some important information.

We spent the next 48 hours searching and listening, trying to pick out a likely target or opportunity, but the weather had deteriorated. It was blowing hard and there was a heavy sea which increased the background noise considerably.

We were now about 50 miles from Piccadilly Circus and moving around at 4 knots, listening and looking for further traffic. I had decided to wait a while before going back in as I wanted to see if any contacts moved further out to sea and might provide an interesting option to garner more information.

I was having supper in the wardroom with a number of the officers and John Davis was entertaining us with another succession of stories and jokes. Submariners always remember past successes and failures and as time goes on they tend to be embellished a considerable amount. David Crothers and Paul Slemon were discussing some weapon issue and Mike Potter was joining in with his usual shrewd and amusing comments.

Meal times are a good time to discuss both professional subjects and the more trivial. There were no contacts and all was continuing normally. Supper had consisted of one of my favourites – Cheese Ush with chips! Cheese Ush is really a quiche – yes, submariners do eat quiche – and I was on my post supper coffee when I heard a loud report on the intercom from back aft saying, 'Hydraulic Burst in After Hydraulic plant.'

John Davis moved first and disappeared out of the wardroom as Ian and I made it to the control room.

The OOW on ship control – Jimmy Fergusson – had hit the general alarm and was on main broadcast as I got to the control room. 'Emergency Stations. Emergency Stations. Hydraulic burst in the After Plant.'

I could hear people moving and waited for a further report. I could hear the damage control HQ being manned in the wardroom and all the paraphernalia which was stowed in lockers in the wardoom being brought out. Intercom systems, damage control boards with detailed diagrams of the boat's systems, training aid books and status boards would all be deployed. The off watch engineers would man the wardroom ready to analyse and take control of the incident.

The engine room lower level stoker, Marine Engineering Mechanic Johnno Johnson, had discovered it and correctly rushed to the Main engine platform to raise the alarm to the Engineer Officer of the Watch – Lieutenant Commander Chris Gillooly – the Engineer Officer of the Watch [EOOW] in the manoeuvring room.

He had informed the OOW in the control room.

The TG Tiff – Marine Engine Artificer Jim Knight – incidentally the brother of Weapons Electrical Artificer Neil Knight – was nearby and was conducting Steam Generator chemistry at the Health Physics Sampling Sink and he met Johnno legging it away on the port side as Jim investigated the noise.

Jim Knight explained later what happened as follows. 'The burst had occurred on a pipe coupling immediately in front of the hydraulic plant by-pass valve on the aft dome. The Panel watch keeper in the control room would have stopped the pumps but, with pressure in the accumulators, the bypass had to be opened as soon as possible to flatten the system. There was no hand wheel fitted to these valves so I pulled out my trusty shifter (an adjustable spanner is a key submarine tool), took a deep breath and walked into the oily spray to open the by-pass and depressurize the accumulators. In the process I became temporarily blinded by the oil and couldn't help ingesting some as well. I managed to open the valve, guided by touch alone.

With the pressure gone, the leak stopped and the emergency stations attack party was now on the scene so I was able to go forward and get cleaned up.'

The big danger with a hydraulic burst is that a fine oily spray getting onto hot equipment can quickly lead to a fire and hydraulic fires tend to start and spread quickly as there is plenty to fuel them. In the engine room it is hot and this is a real danger even after the pressure has been flattened. The attack party got on top of the situation and found the source of the leak and repaired it in short time and I thanked God for all those many hours of fire training we had carried out and continued to carry out.

Jim Knight continued 'Chief Petty Officer Medical Technician Ian Fraser took charge of me and I was made to drink several pints of UHT milk to neutralise the oil in my stomach. Then I had the pleasure of vinegar eyebaths to clean my eyes. What really cheesed me off though was I had just dhobeyed (washed) my other overalls, so I had to go back and finish the watch in my No 8s (standard daily dress of trousers and shirt).'

Subsequently, the after hydraulic plants on all boats were fitted with remotely operated fire isolation valves which would shut off the supply to the system and direct accumulator pressure to the replenishment tank to flatten the plant and system. Also dry powder extinguishers were placed nearby to enable the oil mist to be brought down.

The loss of the new Soviet Mike class SSN Komsomolets in 1989, when a fire started in the after end of the submarine due to a hydraulic burst and progressed forward, indicated the danger of these types of incidents. If it had not been for the quick thinking and bravery of Jim Knight and the training of the crew, that could have been HMS SPLENDID that sank instead. I always say that fire is the biggest danger in a submarine, not flooding or a plane failure.

Jim Knight remarked later 'I often think back to the hydraulic burst on SPLENDID and thank my lucky stars that all the electrical panels in the after ends of the boat were well sealed. Of all the dangerous events I experienced in my career, including bumps, fires, depth excursions and even Soviet scare charges, this was the only thing that still makes me literally shudder to think about it.'

Hydraulic pressure was restored and, just as this was being reported, I was called to the sound room by Petty Officer Danny Fisher. He said 'I am not sure what we have got here, Sir, but it looks as though there are probably two boats moving to the northwest. I can't give precise classifications at present, but there are definitely two of them.' I told Danny to keep working on it and pass 30 second bearings on both to the Tactical Systems in the control room. I then went into the control room and spoke to the OOW, Tiny Holmes, and the TS Operators, Leading Seaman John Boddy and Leading Seaman Pip Cox.

The reports started to come in and, although they were intermittent and faint, there was sufficient to be able to make some reasonable estimation of course and speed. I was still keeping an ant-metric depth so was happy enough with that, but it soon became clear that the nearest one was about 8000 yards away and the other around 15000 yards away.

Ian Richards appeared in the control room again and we discussed what these might be. They certainly looked like submarines and much of the frequency analysis indicated that, but we still did not know what there were or what they were doing. We both moved over to the navigational plot and looked at the chart where the dot of light showed our position relative to the navigational aspects.

Tiny Holmes came across and said, 'Could be a bomber and his shotgun deploying.' I considered this as a distinct possibility and went back to the sound room to see if they were any closer to a classification.

Leading Seaman Nick Slide was looking at the waterfall displays intently and had his hands holding his headphones on. The concentration on his face was very evident. He did not look up as I arrived at the sound room door. Petty Officer Danny Fisher held up his hand as I looked at him as if to say wait a minute. He too was listening hard.

I had to wait about a minute when Danny said, 'it is definitely two contacts and they are quite close together, but the right hand one seems to be getting weaker.'

Then Nick Slide looked up and said, 'There is a one contact bearing 030°. Classified SSBN and the second contact, bearing 019°, is a submarine classified, "probable SSN". The SSBN is getting weaker and the other contact is stable.

'What do you think Danny?' I asked, trying not to put words into his mouth.

'It looks like an SSBN and shotgun SSN, but we will do some more analysis to be sure.'

'Well done, keep at it,' I say as I return to the control room about 10 feet away.

I look at the Tactical Screens and note that the current best solution on the SSBN puts him on a northerly course at 8 knots at a range of 15000 yards. Are we really able to hold him at 15,000 yards I wonder? The other contact's solution is showing a similar northerly course at 4 knots at 10,000 yards.

We need some more information and more bearings to refine these solutions and these will come in the next ten minutes or so.

I go over to the chart again and have a long look at where we are, where the two boats are relative navigationally to SPLENDID, and where they could go. There is plenty of space to the north, northwest and northeast and before possible encountering the ice cap. The reports continue to come in and, after about 8 minutes, Nick Slide reports that the SSBN is now intermittent. I look at the Tactical screens and see that the range is estimated at 21,000 yards. I would expect to lose an SSBN at that range. Indeed, I would expect to lose one even earlier. I told the Leading Seaman John Boddy to let that track at 8 knots. The other contact was now bearing 020°, still on a northerly course, but the range was 8500 yards at 5 knots.

I was taking this in when Petty Officer Danny Fisher came over the intercom and said, 'Contact 45. Classified nuclear submarine and it seems to be changing aspect. Possible stern arc clearance.'

So it probably is a shotgun SSN searching behind the SSBN to make sure no one is following it. So I have to be careful not to get in his way, but at the same time try to hold on to the SSBN.

'OOW. Slow to 4 knots. Change course to 020°.'

If I point at him and slow down I will reduce my profile to him and there is less chance of him detecting me when he turns round to clear his stern arcs. My bow sonar is at the best aspect to maximize detection and information, although the towed array is compromised a bit as it does not really look right ahead very well, but I felt comfortable with this approach for the present.

The bearings continue to come in and I go and sit in the Captain's chair so that I can watch the screens in front of me. Lieutenant Commander David Crothers is on watch in the control room with Tiny

Holmes. David is standing next to me and I ask him 'What do you think?'

David – positive as always – says, 'It looks like a shotgun SSN alright. But what is he going to do?'

At that moment, Danny Fisher reports that the SSN has speeded up and is closing. I look at the plots and watch intently. Shades of my past in HMS CONQUEROR and that terrifying near miss began to come out of my subconscious. I don't want a close quarter's situation in these waters.

The bearings continue to come in and they are moving very slowly left:

020°, 019°, 019°, 018°, 017°. But, by now the range was down to 6500 yards. I did not want him to come any closer when he was clearly in search mode. Tiny Holmes had already gone to the search quiet state. I needed to decide whether to bear off to starboard and increase the bearing rate or to stay as we were and hope that he would turn round again and return to his northerly course. I was conscious that he did not want to lose the SSBN either, as he was supposed to be protecting it, and I knew that his sonar detection ranges were worse than mine.

Ian Richards had arrived back in the control room from the sound room and, together with David Crothers, we discussed options. I decided to stay as we were for another 3 minutes and see what the target did. The Tactical Screens were a mass of bearings coming in at 15 second intervals, but the computer was doing its job and we had a good solution on the target that made it abundantly clear that he had turned round and was closing our position. I estimated he would spend around 4-5 minutes on a southerly course before turning back again, but there was no way of really knowing. The Distance off Track [DOT] was now about 800 yards if things stayed as they were. The Distance Off Track is the separation between his course and your course and is a key mental calculation submarine Captains do as a matter of course on just about every contact, whether surfaced or dived.

The reports were still coming in:

'Bearing 017°. Range 5000 yards. Classified Victor III. Bearing 016°. Range 4500 yards.'

'Bearing 016°. Range 4000 yards. Target Course still 180°. Best speed 6 knots,' from Sean Runham on the Tactical plot.

So what did we have here? The Soviet Victor III SSN entered service in 1979 and 25 were produced until 1991.They were much quieter than previous Soviet submarines, and had 2 tubes for launching SS-N-21 or SS-N-15 missiles and Type 53 torpedoes, plus another 4 tubes for launching SS-N-16 missiles and Type 65 torpedoes. They could carry 24 tube-launched weapons.

Soviet Victor III

The Victor-III caused a minor furore in NATO intelligence agencies at its introduction because of the distinctive pod on the upper rudder. Speculation immediately mounted that the pod was the housing for some sort of new exotic silent propulsion system, possibly a magneto hydrodynamic drive unit. Another theory proposed that it was some sort of weapon system. In the end, the Victor-III's pod was identified as a hydrodynamic housing for a reel-able towed passive sonar array. The Victor III class was continuously improved during construction and late production models have a superior acoustic performance. I was aware that they were quieter and had better sonar and that made him a very dangerous opponent.

I decided that it was time for him to turn and 4000 yards was close enough. 'Sound room. Has he started to turn yet?' I asked optimistically to receive an immediate reply of, 'Negative, no indication yet.'

I could not stay here, but what was the best action? If I stayed on this course, although providing the shallowest profile to him, I was likely to be counter detected. Altering to port was turning in towards him and was closing the range significantly and presenting a broader profile. Turning to starboard would give a broader profile as well as turn my noisy parts of the boat towards him.

I had really left it too late and should have moved earlier! But I was in this position now and had to decide.

I continued to listen to the bearings as they continued to steady up. 'Bearing 016°. Range 3300 yards –

'Bearing 016°. Range 3300 yards.'

He was on a steady bearing and that meant collision! I had to move and do it now.

Ian Richards jumped in, 'We should come right 30 degrees and increase our distance off track.'

He was right, but I did not want to speed up and make more noise. I HAD to be within his detection range by now. He MUST have heard me?

I ordered, 'OOW. Come right to 050°. Stay at 4 knots. No use of the trim or ballast system... Pass to all compartments, quietly, that we are in a close quarters situation.' But the reports continued to come in.

'Bearing 016°. Range 3000 yards –

'Bearing 015°. Range 2800 yards –

'Bearing 014°. Range 2600 yards.'

The bearing rate was left, but he had still not turned. What was he doing? Had he detected me and what would be his action?

We reached the new course of 050° and remained at 4 knots.

Then the bearing started going left again. Had he turned to port as I thought? 'Bearing 015°. Range 2600 yards.'

'Bearing 014°. Range 2600 yards –

'Bearing 013°. Range 2500 yards.'

Oh dear! He was turning back to port and coming right across in front of me. I had turned the wrong way. His speed was still around 5 knots according to the computer and I was right in his bow arcs.

'Bearing 013°. Range 2500 yards –

'Bearing 012°. Range 2500 yards –

'Bearing 011°. Range 2400 yards.'

Do I hold my nerve or turn away? If I do I will give him and even better detection opportunity.

And then Danny Fisher came over the intercom 'Target speeding up, still turning to port.'

Had he detected me and was reacting, or was he just increasing speed in his turn having completed his search and was returning to his northerly course?

'Bearing 008°. Range 2400 yards. Target speed increased to 10 knots,' came the report from the sound room.

I waited and watched.

It was too late to turn HMS SPLENDID further to starboard and I just needed to sit this one out as much as I did not like it. Surely at this range he would have detected me?

'Bearing 006°. Range 2500 yards –

'Bearing 005°. Range 2500 yards. Target speed still 10 knots'

'Bearing 004°. Range 2600 yards –

'Bearing 002°. Range 2700 yards.'

I watched intently. Ian said quietly, 'I think he is going away.' I nodded and said, 'I think you may be right.'

'Bearing 002°. Range 2800 yards –

'Bearing 001°. Range 2900 yards –

'Possible cavitation on the target. Bearing 001°. Range 3000 yards, increasing speed,' came the report from Danny Fisher.

He was speeding up even more and had not put the revolutions on in a controlled manner and had given himself away by cavitating. He was trying to catch up the SSBN.

We had got away with it, but it had been closer than I liked. Thank goodness for all the time we spent on noise reduction, both in the design and maintenance of the submarine, but also in how we operate it. I think going to the search quiet state and staying at 4 knots had been crucial in remaining undetected.

He was clearly going away.

'OOW come left to North and speed up to 6 knots,' I ordered. I would try to follow him at a more circumspect range and see if he would lead me to the Bomber.

'Bearing North Range 3300 yards.'

The plot was indicating he was doing 15 knots and I would need to watch how quickly he opened to ensure that I did not lose him. Ian and I went to the chart. Tiny Holmes had plotted the positions of the SSBN, and the Victor III. It indicated that if the SSBN had continued at 8 knots then the Victor III, at 15 knots, would catch him up fairly quickly.

For now we would let the range open a bit and follow on behind him. I did not want to do this at 15 knots, so I hoped he would slow down fairly soon. He would probably station himself around 5000 yards from the bomber. We had all sorts of intelligence that speculated on the range a Soviet shotgun SSN would station himself from the boat he was protecting, but no one really knew. So this was an opportunity to find out and it would make perfect sense to try to do that. 'Still Bearing North. Range 5000 yards,' came the report from the sound room.

'OOW. Speed 8 knots,' I ordered.

After a further 10 minutes the report was, 'Bearing 358. Range 6000 yards. Target slowing down.'

I ordered, 'OOW. Speed 6 Knots.'

I would adjust my speed to keep him no closer than 6000 yards, but I did not want to lose him.

'Bearing 358°. Range 6500 yards. Target slowed to 6 knots.'

That was fine. I could keep station and see how the situation developed. We went back to the Patrol Quiet State and I wondered whether that was a good idea. But he had not detected me and I was astern of him now, I could change quickly if I needed to.

I needed a cup of coffee so went to the wardroom and sat down to reflect on the current position and what I considered was a close shave.

Soviet Victor III Submarine

Soviet Victor III Submarine

CHAPTER ELEVEN

IS THIS THE START OF WORLD WAR III?

In a hunter killer nuclear submarine [SSN] intelligence gathering never stops. We had been 'up north' for about 10 days and were at periscope depth in the dark in dreadful weather – rain rough seas and poor visibility with masts up monitoring Soviet communications trying to get an snippet of what was going on and what might be about to happen. There was faint surface activity on sonar and were following behind a Soviet SSN at around 12000 yards, holding him comfortably on passive sonar. We were confident he had not detected us.

Half an hour later and with little new information from COMINT, ELINT or SIGINT we were deep again and sonar reported an interesting and as yet unidentified contact. I went to the sound room door. The Executive Officer [XO] my second in command and a qualified submarine commanding officer in his own right, Lieutenant Commander Ian Richards was huddled over a sonar waterfall display with Leading Seaman (Sonar) Nick Slide with headphones on and were discussing what they were hearing.

After about 30 seconds Nick Slide looked up in my direction and said, 'It's a bit faint, but it sounds like another submarine.'

'Any classification?' Ian said. 'And where is it relative to the Victor III?'

'Not yet. But we should get more soon. It is definitely getting closer and the towed array has some good information. It is to the right of the Victor III.'

'Start sending the bearings through to the control room,' I said and Ian and I went back into the control room.

We watched the screens and listened to the reports and it was not long before the operator on the Tactical Analysis Computer [DCB] System had come up with a selection of solutions ranging from 6000 to 14000 yards.

We continued to watch. It was clear that the bearing was starting to move right, but very slowly. Nick Slide came on the intercom and reported 'I am pretty sure it is the same SSBN we held earlier – all the comparisons in the data library point to a Delta III.'

Soviet Delta III Ballistic Missile Submarine

'How sure are you of that classification?' Ian asked.

Nick Slide replied, 'Well, it is definitely a submarine and all the clues point to a Delta III.'

'Okay,' I said. 'Let's start getting in a good position to follow him and keep out of the way of the Victor III.'

Ian reminded me that the SSBN might be better at detection than the Victor III and we must be careful to remain outside his potential detection range of us. He checked on one of the cribs hanging by my chair. I had a collection of cards covered in clear polythene envelopes with all sorts of information on them - mostly intelligence stuff on various submarines and the key details of their various characteristics. This included likely counter detection ranges based on other submarine's experiences and they were always useful. Many were in the form of graphs when you could put in one or two parameters and read off another.

'Officer of the Watch [OOW],' I said. 'Go to the Search Quiet State and let's have a good listen to him.'

'Aye, Aye, Sir', replied the OOW and set things in train.

Over the next hour we maneuvered to get on his quarter, on the opposite side of the Delta III to the Victor III, which we still held comfortably at 12000 yards. A sensible distance to ensure we were able to track him comfortably and yet stay out of both their sonar detection ranges.

I went to the sound room door again and Nick Slide looked up and said, 'I am pretty sure this is a Delta III. All the information we are getting confirms this.'

I returned to the control room and Ian and I started discussing what we were going to do and how we should react if the Delta or the Victor turned round or got a sniff of us. We looked at the navigation situation and the depth of water around us and went through how we should react in different situations. The "what ifs" are a vital part of submarine command and you must always be ready for predicted and unpredictable circumstances.

The Delta-III class submarine is a large ballistic missile submarine operated by the Soviet Navy. Like other previous Delta class submarines, the Delta III is a double hulled design, with a thin, low magnetic steel outer hull wrapped around a thicker, inner pressure hull. The Delta III's are significantly quieter and have a higher missile section for new longer missiles. They have two pressurized water reactors with two steam turbines, giving 60,000 shaft horse power to two, five-bladed, fixed-pitch shrouded propellers. They have 16 tubes fitted with Strategic Launch Ballistic Missiles.

The submarines have four 533mm bow torpedo tubes and carry sixteen torpedoes of types SET-65, SAET-60M, 53-65K, 53-65M, or any combination thereof. The Delta III submarines which served in the Northern fleet formed a division and were based in the port of Sayda in the Yagyelnaya bay and in Olyenya port. On the Delta were sixteen Submarine Launched Ballistic Missiles (SLBM), each with Multiple Independent Re-entry Vehicles (MIRV) targeted at the cities of 'Who Knows' - New York, Washington DC, London, Paris, Beijing?

We followed the Delta and glued SPLENDID's nose onto his tail. Well, on his port quarter but at a safe distance. The Victor III – acting as an escort or shotgun - seemed to be keeping station on his starboard beam, which suited me fine. We lost him briefly and then regained him, but it was clear that he was going somewhere.

His course suggested that he could be going on patrol, but he might be taking a circuitous route to somewhere else. HMS SPLENDID was keeping anti-metric depths - to avoid being at the same depth as the Soviets who keep depth in metres as we do in feet - and we could stay deep as the sonar conditions were satisfactory for doing so. HMS SPLENDID, like the Delta, was sliding through very cold black water.

We spent the next 10 hours tracking the Delta and Victor and, apart from a false alarm that the Victor was turning back, I was conscious that we were closing the edge of the Arctic ice pack.

I wanted a navigational fix to confirm the SINS II position and to take the broadcast routine. We are supposed to read the broadcast at least every 9 hours – every 12 hours maximum – and the signals for us are rerun every 3 hours for 12 hours to ensure we have every opportunity to receive them. This is also important to those in CTF 311 at Northwood – submarine centralized operational control headquarters - so they have some idea of what we should have received. They do not expect a reply and I would not give one unless it was extremely important. I decided that we really did have to go up to periscope depth to get a fix in such hostile water and read the broadcast.

We came back to periscope depth very slowly and very quietly and I was relieved that we had managed to retain sonar contact on both the Delta and Victor. I made sure that everyone was alert as we were changing our profile and there was more to think about at periscope depth as well as keeping contact. It was at these sort of times that concentration could be lost.

The sea had freshened further and it was blowing around force 6, with a sharp sea state. We got our satellite fix to reset the Ships Inertial Navigation Systems [SINS] and I was dismayed to hear the report from the Wireless Office that there were 12 signals on the broadcast and SPLENDID's signals were 11th and 12th on the list. That was inevitable I suppose as we had been 12 hours without receiving a broadcast and there would be other submarines reading the same routine.

We would have to wait and we could be at periscope depth for around 40 minutes which was too long in this situation. The night was dark but I was pleased to hear that there was little ELINT of any significance. We could use all our sensors at periscope depth, but it seemed an eternity until the signal was in and we could glide back under the waves to continue our trail. The signals were interesting and had been worth the wait. There was intelligence that a Delta III had sailed 36 hours earlier, but it was not clear whether she was going on patrol or not. Additionally there was a very good weather forecast and an estimation of the arctic ice pack and where the edge was expected to be. I needed that information badly and I looked at the chart and I realised that we were less than 30 miles from the predicted edge. That could cause a problem if we ended up under the ice trailing two Soviet submarines. We would find it very difficult to come to periscope depth if we needed to.

The edge of the ice pack is very dangerous, particularly if you want to operate at periscope depth. In bad visibility, which is a regular occurrence, it is easy to come across a large piece of ice and hit it with one of your masts without ever seeing it or realizing it was there. Were that to happen there is no doubt who will come off best and to lose the capability of one of your masts would be very serious indeed.

The sound room team had done very well and had managed to retain contact through this excursion and we started to change our relative position a bit further up on the Delta III's port quarter but not too far as I wanted to make sure I could also still hold the Victor. He had not moved from the Delta's starboard beam which was a surprise, unless he thought his stern arc clearance earlier had removed the possibility of anyone trailing either the Delta or him.

I moved up slowly and then back again to get as much sonar data and specific noises on the Delta as I could. I would need all the information on him that I could get as that would allow us to continue to assess what our exact aspect was to the Delta.

I was becoming increasingly worried that neither the Delta nor the Victor had appeared to change course for some significant time and this was not something that I would consider usual. The Soviet submarines also have a bit of a blind spot in their stern arcs and it had been normal practice to clear stern arcs at reasonably frequent intervals. The "Crazy Ivan" of Hunt for Red October fame. The Delta's speed was 7 knots which indicated transit rather than a settled patrol, when his speed would be more like 4 knots. The Victor was matching his speed.

About 5,000 yards away, detectable on passive sonar - mainly by a piece of identifiable machinery – a specific pump - and checked on our computer database was a noise that confirmed our classification of this contact as a Delta.

We were efficient, hungry and, to an extent, fairly aggressive people who, given the right hint, would hunt and if necessary kill. When ashore, SSN people like us tended to like fast machines, work hard and play hard, and had a tendency to walk towards a fight. SSBN crews were picked for the opposite reasons. SSBN people were quiet and shy. Ashore, they drove regularly-serviced cars well within the speed limit.

Faced with a fight, they would fade discreetly into the background. They had a pathological dislike of being noticed. This was just as well, since their job was to carry the British nuclear deterrent to places on the planet where no-one would ever look for it or, more importantly, find it. On an SSBN the navigator sat in his own cubby-hole, and only he and the captain knew which hemisphere the boat was in.

I did three patrols on a Polaris missile boat in the very early days of the British nuclear deterrent. I was in the Commissioning crew of HMS REVENGE (Starboard). SSBN's have two crews – port and starboard – to ensure that the submarine can remain at sea for as long as possible.

I suppose my character was not really suited to this job. A Polaris, and later Trident submarine, has three aims:

1. To remain undetected (staying away from all contact)
2. To remain in constant communications and
3. To be at immediate readiness to fire.

Sure, it is a great tactical and technical challenge and the submarine and its weapons systems are awesome, but it was not what I wanted. That said, there is no doubt whatsoever that the Continuous At Sea Deterrent has helped keep the peace (of sorts) since we started in 1968. It is a great tribute to all those who served in them, and the Submarine Service as a whole, that we had kept a submarine on patrol, undetected and at immediate notice to fire, since May 1968.

On an SSN things could not have been more different. People walked past the chart table in the middle of the control room at will and would regularly stop to have a look. And when something interesting was happening, a trail or an attack, we patched the sonar operators into the internal intercom, so the people by the manoeuvring room and in the machinery spaces would not feel left out. This was not a noisy operation, but was vital for that feeling of belonging and being all of one company.

'He's turning to starboard,' said Nick Slide. I looked at my watch. Soviet SSBNs often changed course according to a series of random numbers generated on the boat, not some pre-ordained plan. This was to retain an element of unpredictability and frustrate the likes of me who might be following him.

I had had several hours to get to know this Delta-class submarine and, perhaps, something of the man driving it. Perhaps he thought he was manoeuvring at random. He wasn't. There was a pattern and we had been working it out for a while. Patience provides its own rewards.

'Delta turning to starboard,' said the report from the sonar sound room at the noise in the control room.

'Quiet,' I said a little irritated.

According to our assessment of the pattern, a sort of long-phase zigzag, he should be turning to port.

We waited. Down on my left, the target analysis operators battered their keyboards, plotting the Delta's range and bearing.

'Target bearing 031°,' Course 211°. Range 5900 yards,' came the report. This meant he was heading straight towards us!

'Where is the Victor? 'I said impatient for an answer, asking about the second SSN, escorting the ballistic Delta.

'Target remaining out to starboard. Bearing 085°. Range 9500 yards. Still on a course of 010°. Speed 7 knots,' came the reply.

'Keep a close eye on him and tell me if anything changes,' I replied.

Target analysis will give you a range and a bearing, but it cannot tell you the depth of the target. Soviets like to be at round numbers of metres. Therefore I always preferred a depth in feet that did not translate into a round number of metres – for example 100, 150 or 200 metres and the sort of depth a Russian commander would order. By doing this I minimised the chances of an underwater collision.

There was sweat on my palms. Deciding what depth to keep was always tinged with risk.

This manoeuvre could be leading to evasive action by the Delta. It could even be that he had detected us and wished to play silly buggers, though this was not normal SSBN behaviour. Not this SSBN anyway, from what I knew of him. Or, it could be that he was breaking off from his accompanying Victor riding shotgun for him. Or, it could be that there was another shotgun as well as the Victor. A shotgun that had perhaps been there all along, following us (the sweat now turned cold and my stomach turned over) and we had not realised this. The Delta could be trying to draw us off towards the other shotgun SSN, who would then play much sillier buggers with us while the SSBN faded into one of the underwater so called 'safe areas' where the Soviet submarines can retreat to if they need to do so.

We do not know whether they have special protection provisions in these areas, but they do like going under the ice and, in later years, there was a great deal of evidence that they were using these areas more often. We are always trying to establish where these potential safe havens are and how they are used.

'Turning to starboard,' came from sonar. 'Target bearing 049°. Course 039°. Range 3500 yards.'

He had been clearing his stern arcs – to check if anyone is hiding in his wake, a potential blind spot – looking for any followers and that was probably all. He was not reacting as though he had detected us.

I decided that I needed to have a good look around, just in case there was a third submarine in the area. Three Soviet boats and one Brit could make for a very lively encounter, but I was hoping to avoid that.

We cleared our own stern arcs carefully – very carefully – and returned to the trail. Instinct told me that I need to get another navigational fix and read the communication broadcast from Northwood HQ as I may be down here for a while.

With the Delta and Victor both moving to the northeast at 6 knots now, and both being held well at a range of around 8000 yards, we could safely go to periscope depth and return as quickly as we could.

We came up to periscope depth slowly, got the fix and the latest single signal for us on the broadcast. This was not a good place to be if you did not know where you were accurately. How glad I was that I did not have to rely on Loran C and how glad was I that satellite navigation had made so much difference.

We were about to go deep again when there was another report from the sound room. 'He's altering course,' followed by, 'to port.'

I sat in my Captain's chair and let that one sink in. Turning to port was not part of his pattern, either. I was about to order the submarine deep again when there came an unexpected report 'Traffic for the target,' from the team listening to all the communications we could from their miniscule office on the next deck down under my feet. There was traffic all the time, but there was something in his voice that made me think this might be different.

Alexander Peters, the Russian-speaking specialist communications technician, came into the control room in a rush and came straight to me. 'I stumbled across this frequency by chance,' he said. 'I am pretty certain that these signals are for this Delta. I think he is up to something – he's just received twelve groups.'

That meant he'd received a signal that may indicate some form of drill or tactical instruction for the Delta, but I wondered what it really meant. The Delta was either at periscope depth, and we had not realised that, or he was receiving this message by some other means – a trailing wire?

'He's slowing down,' came from the sound room. 'Three knots. I can hear his planes,' said Nick Slide.

'He's going up. He's using his upward-looking echo sounder.' So the Delta was returning to periscope depth and had either been alerted by this signal or he had a pre-arranged rendezvous to receive it. I looked at the clock – it was almost exactly 1558 – two minutes to 1600. What did this mean? What should I do? Have I missed any clues here?

I ordered the submarine back to a deep anti-metric depth and took stock of the situation. Ian Richards and I reviewed the situation carefully and mulled over what we knew and what we did not.

We still held both the Delta and the Victor at 10000 yards and I was very confident that if there was somebody else around I would have heard them and hold them on sonar.

Twelve groups was clearly a significant signal – but what did it mean? Had the Delta received it already or was he on his way up to receive it at a pre-arranged time – like 1600? And what would he do when, and if, it was for him? I suddenly had a strong feeling of foreboding and was struggling to make sense of what was really happening here. Why would a Delta SSBN and a Victor SSN, acting as a shotgun escort, be doing this and was it just routine or something else.

My knowledge of a twelve group signal was that this was a probably part, or all, of a firing signal and could either be an exercise or – God forbid – a tactical launch. But I had no idea which one it was. I was really worried! – What was going on here?

Ian Richards and I went to the chart table and started to review all the options on a piece of paper. He had the national rules of engagement with him and reminded me of the new clauses that we had received about 3 weeks ago. I had read them cursorily then but now I was reading them intently. The rules directed that in the event of a Soviet SSBN preparing to fire its nuclear missiles, I was ordered to open fire when I heard him open his second pair of missile doors. The first set of doors could be a test, but the second could only mean he was going to launch.

Oh dear! This was very serious stuff and as the words on the page starting to sink in I had a real feeling of apprehension and physical tension. I could feel the same from Ian and he started to speak quietly saying 'You know what this means don't you?'

'I do,' I replied downheartedly, 'we may have to fire here,' and picked up the intercom.

'Wireless Office, this is the Captain. Was there anything startling on the last BBC World Service news?'

'No sir. Only the football results. Dumbarton lost. Again.'

It is at times like this that training helps. The training meant that I did not have a picture in my mind of that great steel slug drifting upwards towards the white screen of the ice pack; the training meant I was not thinking of a signalman taking the Russian captain the message which, although in code, was looking awfully like a firing signal. Or envisage the captain fetching the first lieutenant or the political officer. The two men following protocol and using their keys to open the safe with the firing codes, walking quickly to the panel in the missile control centre, taking out the keys on the chains round their necks, turning them, starting the sequence that would burn the US eastern seaboard, the UK, Faslane or wherever together with its men and women and children. It did not bear thinking about.

Instead, I was thinking about what came next. What I might have to do and what might happen.

'He's settled,' said the report from sonar.

'He's slowed right down,' said the tactical displays operator.

'Sound room? Is the Delta at periscope depth? Ian asked.

'Could be going into the hover at 120 feet,' came the reply.

Oh My God! He was going into a launch sequence. Of course it could just be an exercise, I convinced myself. Ian came over and said 'I am not sure whether this is an exercise or not. I will talk to Alex again and see if he is sticking to his story and what he intercepted.'

'Good idea,' I replied rather unconvincingly. Bracing myself, I said,' 'Officer of the Watch. Go to the Search Quiet State and Action Stations. Slow down to 4 knots.'

Having the Victor as shotgun was now beginning to hold more credence and, if this Soviet SSBN was getting ready to fire his missiles, he would be relying on the shotgun Victor to keep anyone away.

But the Victor had not done anything alarming and had only slowed down to keep in station on the Delta's starboard beam. It was a strange place to be, but then I did not know the reason.

We had been watching carefully, tensed to react to any unforeseen movement that could indicate that he knew we were there. But we had been staying outside the Delta's counter detection range so we could hear him, but he had not been able to hear us – we hoped!

We had been concentrating on the ballistic boat. Perhaps too hard!

What was the Victor going to do? If he was doing his job properly he would have got a sniff of us and would know we would be readying our torpedoes if we suspected a missile firing. And he would be readying torpedoes of his own. Was he preparing to fire at us without us knowing it?

'Officer of the Watch – systematic all round sonar search; Sonar – have a really good listen. I need to know exactly what is going on and if there is another shotgun with us,' I said.

'Keep reporting the Delta and the Victor as well,' I said, perhaps a little too tersely. I must not show my tension to the control room team. If I am calm, they will be calm. But I was not calm inside. Ian was repeating what we knew, and my mind was racing with all the possibilities and how I should react to each. Dismissing some options and favouring others and at the same time trying not to kid myself into thinking what I wanted to believe.

The reports came in. 'Delta. Bearing 015°. Range 7600 yards. Course North. Speed 3 knots.'

'Victor. Bearing 034°. Range 8200 yards. Course North. Speed 4 knots.'

I looked at the tactical display and took that in. Ian, over my shoulder, said reassuringly that we were well positioned on the Delta's port quarter at 7600 yards and there were no torpedoes coming at us. That was comforting – of sorts.

After 7 minutes we had completed the sonar search and resumed our position. I had not dwelled on the clearing course for long – just enough to get a decent sonar picture, but it was enough to get the all clear from sonar.

No other submarine was a good sign. Normally, we thought that the Soviet ballistic subs had shotgun nuclear subs glued to their tails but we did not really know that this was their modus operandi. Particularly if there was going to be a live firing – or worse a tactical launch!

I knew where the Victor was and I felt we were in control of the situation. I prayed that I was right. Action Stations were closed up and Ian made a brief pipe on the turned-down main broadcast to tell the Ship's Company what was going on and how important that we remained alert and quiet.

It takes around ten minutes for any NATO ballistic submarine to move from orders received to missile launch. It would take a Soviet boat about the same. There were a long series of actions to come, each of them easily audible. We would follow the sequence and we knew what it was likely to be. Intelligence, while always very useful, is no substitute for having heard the real thing. And US and UK submarines had heard the Soviets firing their missiles often enough to know what to listen for.

That meant the opening of his missile hatches could be eight minutes away. Was this a non-firing drill, a test firing or tactical launch? We needed to be ready for anything and be prepared to fire if we thought it was the latter.

I rushed to my cabin and opened my safe and pulled out the latest procedure from intelligence to read again. Eight minutes was as good as a lifetime. The preliminaries would be in full swing. The Soviet missile ratings would be in what we called "Sherwood Forest" – among the missile tubes. Pairs of men would be taking the firing keys to the tubes. They would be sorting out the electronics. They would be hitting the switches that ran up the gyros that worked the missiles' inertial navigators.

'Sounds like a gyro running up,' said Nick Slide from the sound room.

I acknowledged, indicating my understanding, 'Roger.'

Out there, in the dark, that huge tin can would be taking measures to make itself a stable platform for launch. If a ballistic missile does not know where exactly it started from, it can have absolutely no idea where it is going to end up.

Then, 'Going into the hover,' said Nick Slide.

To keep 13,000 tons of submarine dead still in the water there is a big tank and a big valve and a huge, high-revving pump. These are computer controlled by sensitive sensors that measure and anticipate the movement of the submarine up and down and bow down or bow up. In essence, they allow the boat to hover in the water, the same way as a helicopter does in air. This provides the perfect stable platform from which to launch ballistic missiles.

This was not looking good. Not good at all.

I whispered to Ian, 'Do you think he is going to launch?' This was more in hope that he would say no. Ian replied, 'All the signs are there but it could be a drill but we are ready for both.'

The training is still there, though. Our torpedoes were loaded and the tubes were flooded.

I was looking intently at the picture in front of me on the DCB – we were in the centre and the Delta and Victor were clearly there but nothing else. I watched as the new bearings kept coming in and continued to confirm what were now very good course, speed and range solutions on both boats. I was transfixed and totally focused, waiting for the next thing to happen.

I had asked for the latest fire control solutions and had them in front of me and my mouth was certainly a lot drier than it ought to be. Because the 'what-ifs' were running through my mind again and again and I was rehearsing my reaction. The biggest ones were: 'Is he going to conduct a tactical launch?' and, 'Is the Victor going to move and, if so, where?' Towards me, I wondered. I must be prepared for that. And had the Victor actually detected us, and was he waiting to fire at us, lulling us into a false sense of security? Was there a torpedo running, racing towards us right now, and we had not heard it?

I dismissed all that because I wanted to, but there was no real evidence either way. Ian had been to the sound room and came back into the control room and whispered that Alex was certain of what he heard so that was that. Ian and I went over the possibilities again quickly and how we could or should react.

'Nitrogen,' said Nick Slide from the sound room. This was the one certainty that the missile tubes were being readied. This was bad news and had my mind working overtime.

Before a ballistic submarine opens its missile hatches, it is necessary to equalise the pressure in the tube with the pressure of the water outside. Nitrogen is pumped into the tube to do this. As the submarine hovers, it makes tiny movements in the water. The nitrogen pumps compensate for each one, to keep the pressure in the tube and in the water outside equal. The sound is distinctive: a random series of hisses, like a big animal sniffing.

I look to Ian. 'Let's refine these fire control solutions again. Are we ready to shoot?' I asked.

'Re-computing target parameter again, and affirmative. Ready to fire,' replies Ian.

'Missile hatches opening,' said Nick Slide. 'One ... two. We were now two minutes away from ... something.

Two minutes at most. One more hatch open, and our rules of engagement permitted us to engage and, as soon as we fired a torpedo at him, he would know we were there. One touch of a button by either of us. And what was to be my escape route? I took in everything in front of me again but could not resist a nervous three step walk to the chart table to confirm our navigational position and get a mental picture of the chart, depth of water and possible routes clearly in my brain.

'Open 4 tube bow cap,' I said, knowing that this would make a noise and, although unlikely if we were detected this could be seen as a provocative act. I did not know as I did not hold a copy of Soviet Rules of Engagement! But we had no choice. But I should have thought of this situation earlier and opened bow caps when I was a safe distance away. But it was too late now.

The bow caps are the torpedo tube covers. There is no way of opening them quietly. The sound of bow caps opening will probably get the Delta III and the Victor CO's immediate and undivided attention if they are on the ball but we have done a great deal over the years to make sure this procedure is as quiet as we can make it.

Surprise in any type of warfare is a key element to have in your favour.

I winced as I waited to hear the bow cap open. Had I made the wrong or the right calls here? I would soon find out that was for sure. The sound constitutes the broadest kind of hint that, within seconds, there will be a torpedo in the water directed at his boat, which is lumbering around in the hover, unable to take countermeasures of any kind.

Have I left this too late? Should I have fired by now? Will the torpedo get there on time? Will the torpedo work? All these questions were running around my mind and in fairness David Crothers the Weapons Engineer Officer had been prompting me to open the bow caps earlier but I had resisted. At this moment I cursed myself for not taking his advice and probably should have done but ... Should I fire straight away? Was the target fire control solution good enough?

And then...

'Hatches,' said Nick Slide and then more urgently 'Hatches ... Hatches – they are shutting. One...'

'Belay open bow caps,' I shouted loudly. The order is acknowledged in the nick of time.

'Two. Hatches closed.' Another pause. 'Nitrogen draining down. Coming off the hover.'

Ian said 'didn't expect that' and gave a wry smile. 'Any reaction from the Victor? 'I ask nervously.

'Victor Bearing 040°. Range 7000 yards. Course North. Speed 4 knots.' Then I lean back in my chair. Let the eye travel discreetly round the room. A couple of them grinning. George Elwood the Outside Wrecker on the Panel, impassive, as usual.

'He's putting on revs,' said Nick Slide from the sound room.

'Bearing 016°,' came from the DCB operator, clearing his throat to remove the croak from his voice. 'Course 022°. Range 4500 yards. Speed four, now five knots.

'Opening slowly.'

I had crept up a bit closer than I had realized, but now it looked as though this little episode might be over and not what I dreaded it might be. That was close and I was not sure what it all meant but there would be plenty of tapes and records to pour over back in the Ministry of Defence when we returned and to pull out anything we had missed during the last few hours. That was good as it would lead to better intelligence.

It was time to back off now but keep alert.

'OOW Let's drop back to 8000 yards and match the Delta's course and speed.' 'Aye, Aye, Sir,' came the reply.

We had been within ninety seconds of a potential start to the Third World War. Not that that has anything to do with anything.

After half an hour we had dropped to 12000 yards and were still holding both the Delta and the Victor but they had turned away from the ice edge and were going east again. We slowly followed them round retaining a distance to close enough to trail them. It looked as though they were going home again.

I asked Ian to draft a report to send back to Northwood at the next opportunity and reflected on this episode. It was sobering and exciting all at the same time. The consequences could have been awful and I put those to the back of my mind. It appears we have been lucky enough to witness a training exercise. We have done what we are here for, and we will carry on doing it.'

'OOW Fall out Actions Stations go to the watch,' I ordered then gave got on the intercom and gave the Ship's Company a resume of the last few hours. I said well done and was grateful that all our training has resulted in a harmonious focused team effort. They would be pleased that we had outwitted the Soviets.

And at that I filled my pipe with St Bruno flake tobacco and struck a Swan Vestas match and puffed away contentedly. It is times like this that I am really glad that I smoke a pipe!

Later, I went for a walk round the boat and chatted to several people. Everyone had done very well indeed, and everybody knew it. We were very, very good at our job. But it is always good to hear the Captain tell you. That breeds confidence. Not that we could not get better. I had gone to the Weapons Compartment and there was the stalwart of the department Steve Hogg. 'Pity we couldn't fire Sir – We were all ready and right behind you – damn Soviets!'

I explained to him how close we had come and he understood completely. We talked about the state of the weapons and he said that he really wanted to see if the Tigerfish would really work.

I thought to myself that I was glad I had not been forced to do a torpedo trial just to see if it worked. But Steve was right in some ways – we had never fired Tigerfish in anger and there was some doubt as to how good it was. I never let myself think that it would not work. When I got back to my cabin I reflected on the last few hours. I had been very close to firing a torpedo and I was in no doubt that I would have done it. But did I wait too long before opening bow caps? Should I have opened them before I was this close?

I was certainly thinking hard about my justification as events were unfolding and I re- read the Rules of Engagement to satisfy myself again that I had read and responded to the situation correctly. My training had kicked in, but I was still thinking of the consequences of what I was doing. I had been through the 'what ifs' a thousand times, and I had a pre-prepared scenario in this case.

I would have fired.

Well, I say that now, but at the time all I can say is that I was ready and mentally clear that I could and should fire. Would we have been able to deal with the consequences? I don't know.

I did not expect anyone to disagree with my actions as, certainly, the officers and senior rates are more than aware from numerous exercises that this is how we would respond. But reality had struck and I was very much aware that the situation was tense and I did not want to make it more difficult. But then a submarine Commanding Officer has to weigh up these situations carefully.

The control room team carried on as usual, but the situation created a tense but controlled atmosphere in the control room. The sound room reports were coming through in the same tone and speed as if it were an exercise.

We spent the next 4 hours following the Delta and the Victor when suddenly the Victor peeled off to starboard increased speed to 16 knots and disappeared to the south east. We were initially alarmed by this as we thought he had detected us and was coming in our direction but after a tense 3 minutes to see what he would do we were content to see him move away.

The Delta continued to the east still at 4 knots and we dropped back and turned in behind him. We were able to stay with him at a range of 14,000 yards which surprised me but we had been with it for a while and the sonar team was very clued up on this particular submarine. After another 4 hours it began to be clear that the Delta was moving back to port and I decided this was a good time to go to periscope depth for a navigation fix and a broadcast routine.

When we were back at periscope depth we sent our report and amongst the incoming signals there was one signal for us. We had been re-tasked to move back into the northwest approaches to the UK as there was concern that there was a Soviet submarine in the area there somewhere. So we broke off from the Delta and followed my directions from CTF 311 to conduct a 15 knot passage back south of the Iceland-Faeroes-UK Gap to pick up another Soviet submarine transiting north from the Mediterranean. I reflected on the last few days and decided that it had been hard work tense but very rewarding and I only hoped that the intelligence take proved to be good. On to the next target!

PART TWO

HMS SPLENDID IN THE FALKLANDS WAR 1982

CHAPTER TWELVE

PROCEED WITH ALL DISPATCH

30th March 1982

As far as I was concerned I was at war – the Cold War – and it was a war even though there were no bullets flying about. Below the chill waters of the north-western approaches to Scotland my nuclear powered hunter-killer submarine was on the front line of the Cold War. HMS SPLENDID was the newest attack boat in the fleet and we had yet another mission to find and track a Soviet submarine. The control room and the sound room adjacent to it was focused on collecting and checking every small piece of information, every piece of intelligence and every sound.

Collecting this information for later analysis but also trying to understand what it meant and how it could be used for tactical advantage.

Driving a submarine is as much an art as a science – nearly everything is subjective. The control room was tightly packed with mechanical and electronic machinery, displays and screens, repeats of all sorts, valves, gauges and pipes. There were around fifteen or sixteen people squeezed in, each with his own area of responsibility; ship and system control, navigation, tactical information and analysis computers and fire control. Central in the control room were the two periscopes side by side. The attack periscope was monocular and longer and thinner to reduce exposure above the surface. The search periscope was thicker and shorter and was binocular but fitted with electronic countermeasures, aerials for satellite navigation and communication.

The control room is an intense claustrophobic environment in which everybody knew their job. There were no secrets in the control room of a nuclear submarine.

For me, the Cold War was personal and that's the way I wanted it. Stuck on the bulkhead of the mast well of the boat's control room were pictures of Soviet submarine commanders.

I learnt very early on in my submarine career that I was not trying to outwit or fight an enemy boat, but it was the Captain in the other boat that was the foe and I had to ensure my team and myself were better than him.

SPLENDID had been at sea continuously now for three months. We had had our moments and here we were again in the front line of the Cold War. For the last twenty four hours or so we had been assisted in finding the Soviet boat by RAF Nimrods vectoring us in to the target from its own sonobuoys. We had over the years reduced the time of detection by the Nimrod to around 13 minutes the details having been sent to Northwood, turned round and transmitted again on the submarine broadcast. Real time information today may be almost instant but in 1982 this was quick.

We were deep and in contact with the Soviet boat and were stationed around 2 miles off her port quarter, continuing to refine her solution and suck in intelligence. We were still trying to classify her exactly. We had plenty of time and there were indications that this was a Victor III, an Akula or something new. We were good at this and the massive training both individually and collectively was evident as everyone went about their various tasks with energy, diligence and quiet efficiency.

I was concerned that if this was going to be a long trail I needed to be very clear of my navigational position and, although the new Mark 2 Ships Inertial Navigation System [SINS] was good I wanted that extra confidence. I also wanted to see if there was any further intelligence available and so I decided to return to periscope depth without breaking or losing contact.

As we arrived at periscope depth to take a satellite fix the VLF broadcast started to be received and I was alerted by the Radio Operator on watch in the Wireless Office that "there is a Blue Key message for you." I was really surprised by this as these type of signals are extremely rare although I have a safe in my cabin crammed full of crypto key cards that change at regular intervals. But a Blue Key signal had to be deciphered by me personally.

Reluctantly in this situation I handed over the boat to the Executive Officer, Ian Richards, opened my safe and pulled out the current crypto and started down the ladders to three deck where the Wireless Office was located my mind racing with annoyance at being distracted and inquisitiveness as to what this was all about.

I was met by the Chief Radio Supervisor Martin a very amiable and professional man who I trusted implicitly. 'Come on Chief you are going to have to help me with this.' Fifteen minutes later I looked at the message in disbelief. I was to break off contact and return to Faslane in radio silence and store for war. Was this a joke or some bureaucratic exercise? I had no idea and so went back up to the control room and showed the signal to Ian Richards. We speculated and then decided that we had to do this however unpalatable it seemed.

I took the main broadcast microphone and said: 'Do you hear there, Captain speaking. We have just received a signal ordering us to return to Faslane and store for war. We have no more information other than this is clearly important. I am sorry but we will have to break off, withdraw and return to Faslane as quickly as we can. We will probably get there around 1500 tomorrow when we will find out some more. In the meantime we need to switch our minds to what we need to do to store for war. I will keep you informed as soon as I have some more news. That's all.'

This signal was personal from the First Sea Lord Admiral Sir Henry Leach and had ordered me to "Proceed with all dispatch." That is a rare order to receive and part of me was very excited to have received that signal. In Royal Navy terms "To proceed with dispatch" means act with speed. "To proceed with all dispatch" effectively means act with speed but at your own discretion. In essence this means you can do what you wish to complete the task. I had to let that sink in as we broke trail and reversed course and started back to Faslane. By the next afternoon we were tied up at No 1 berth.

SPLENDID had left Devonport, her home port, on 12th February 1982 and was close to the end of her running period expecting to return to Devonport for maintenance and leave on early April. The next 18 hours was intense as we fixed minor defects, loaded everything from torpedoes to toilet rolls, sausages to lubricating oil.

Lieutenant Commander David Crothers the WEO remembers that:

"In March 1982 the MOD was subject to a moratorium on spares contracts, so stocks in stores were very low. When we were ordered to Store for War, I was impressed by the efficiency of DGST (N) – Director General Stores and Transport (Naval). Items were released from store throughout the UK, or obtained by store rob, aircraft were on standby at the southern bases and everything we asked for, ordered on arrival at about 1630ish appeared by 0800 the next morning. As well as that, we were carrying a minimal weapon outload, and the necessary weapons to complete our full outload were waiting for us in two barges when we arrived alongside. As we finished loading weapons at 0100 the local contracted greengrocer turned up on the jetty. The stores support was first class.

Lieutenant Paul Slemon, the Deputy Weapons Engineer Officer remembers that he found it very odd that when he went up to the Faslane film library to change the reel to reel 16mm feature films that he could have his pick of the entire catalogues – this was normally only reserved for SSBNs! Films were important as this was before videos and DVDs. Each film was in a metal box around 2 feet by 8 inches with two or three reels for showing on a 16mm projector.

The whole of the support team at Faslane were fantastic and the Commodore at the Clyde Submarine Base – George Vallings – had made it clear on my arrival that I could ask for anything I wanted. It was also a difficult period for the Ship's Company as I had to ensure that they understood why they could not telephone home. No one really knew what we were in for, where we were actually going – although the rumour mill was in full swing and this type of uncertainty always makes submariners nervous. It is to the credit of the whole support team and the Ship's Company that we sailed without a single store demand outstanding – an amazing response.

I had been on the secure telephone with Northwood my Captain (SM) and Commander (SM) in Devonport and had a good idea of where we were going but no one was really clear as to what we would be required to do. We would have to wait for that. I discussed the state of the submarine and I said that I did not think a towed array was appropriate and did not want to take one. There was some heated discussion about this but I got my way in the end. I had assessed that if we were going to be travelling fast for long periods it could prove to be a burden and although I might have liked it to find Argentine submarines this was a risk I was prepared to take.

TG Tiff Jim Knight remembers and wrote to me as follows:

'Quite by chance I wrote a diary recording the events as we saw them. The entries began towards the end of March as we were searching for the Victor sneaking around the Western approaches. I had no idea at the time that it would turn into a record of the Falklands patrol. I had never kept a diary before nor have I been inclined to start one since, and it was prompted by the fact that I had only married in the previous December and was feeling depressed at not having seen my bride since leaving Devonport in the January. Little did I know as I put pen to paper, that it would be June before we would be together again. It may have been a harsh introduction for her, to the life of a submariner's wife, but she took it in her stride and we have been happily married ever since.'

MEA Jim Knight continues:

'I can remember, during a brief break from the last minute preparations in Faslane, 'phoning the wife to explain that I would not be coming home on leave as planned. Although I did not tell her where we were going she had already worked it out from the television reports about events down south; in fact she seemed to know more about the situation than I did.'

Jim Knight continues:

'The diary barely paints the true picture of the confusion and frantic repairs as we hurriedly prepared to leave Faslane for the South Atlantic. It was probably not too much different to the preparations for a standard patrol "Up North" but there was sense that this was something special and we all gave it 100%. I didn't sleep for two days. With all the extra spares and tools we loaded there was no doubt we would be able to dive the boat. The only question was would we be able to surface again? I remember the store keepers in Faslane were shocked when their precious Polaris stores were laid open before us. We struggled back to the boat with all manner of nice shiny things most of which we didn't really need!

One of the back aft Stoker Petty Officer Jacko Jackson was tasked with finding some bails of rags. Everyone else had failed up to a point but Jacko, being an ex Faslane rating knew just where to look. It was only when we were at sea that the bails were opened up to reveal a complete set of freshly laundered bunk curtains, mattress and cushion covers (in the famed submarine budgie pattern) for a Polaris boat in Assisted Maintenance Period. Anyway they certainly soaked up oil!'

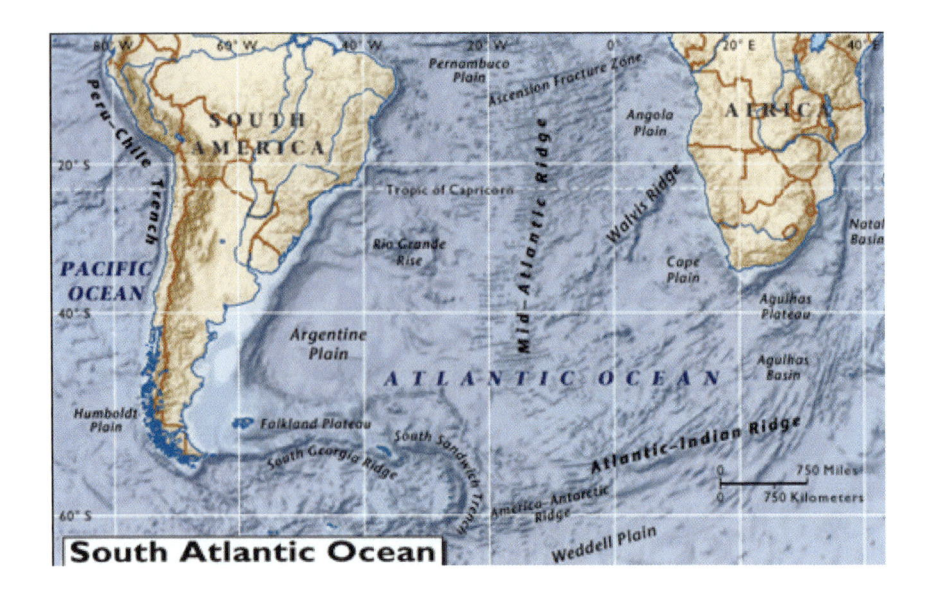

Argentine Commanders 1982

CHAPTER THIRTEEN
TRANSIT TO SOUTH ATLANTIC

Thursday 1st April 1982 – Day 1

<u>Falklands War Timeline</u>: HMS SPLENDID *sailed from Faslane and HMS SPARTAN sailed from GIBRALTAR.*

SPLENDID Sailed from No 1 Berth Faslane at 1300 fully stored for war in full radio silence making for the Falkland Islands and we expected to get there around 16th April. I spoke to the Ship's Company and having thanked them for their hard work in the previous 18 hours gave them a brief assessment of where we were going and the probable reason why.

Remember at this stage there was no official or press report that Argentina had landed on the Islands. I decided to remain on the surface overnight and progress as far south as possible down the Irish Sea before diving for a check trim.

Friday 2nd April 1982 – Day 2

<u>Falklands War Timeline</u>: *Argentine forces invade the Falkland Islands, entering the capital Port Stanley early in the morning. The garrison of Royal Marines is outnumbered and outgunned and after some brief skirmishes the Governor Sir Rex Hunt orders them to lay down their arms and surrenders.*

0730 SPLENDID dived in the Irish Sea for a trim dive and surfaced again at 0910 with a defect on the snort muffler valve. While investigating we continued on the surface to make for the deep water south of Ireland. By 1645 having dived and surfaced again we had failed to solve the snort muffler valve problem. Bearing in mind that I had to "Proceed with All Dispatch" I decided that we had to live with this and crack on.

Marine Engineering Artificer Jim Knight in a letter to me said:

'You may recall the saga of the leaking Muffler Valve on the journey south. We had surfaced so that Mick Stoker (another of the TG Tiffs) and I could attempt a repair from the outside. This involved crawling under the casing, dragging a bucket of spanners etc back to the Hull Valve pen to remove the outboard section of Diesel Exhaust pipe to get at the offending seal. It was dark, wet and humid under the casing and we felt a bit vulnerable. With the usual attention to detail to avoid leaving noise shorts in our wake we made sure we didn't let nuts bolts or tools slip down into the wing bilges although I should point out that there were all manner of weird sea creatures flapping about in there and neither of us wanted to reach down to retrieve something. I'm sure that in the event of some emergency, we would not have been trapped up there during a rush dive but it was with considerable relief that we completed a repair and crawled back to the main access hatch. You can imagine our despair therefore when a check of the tools in the bucket revealed we were missing a torch. Back we went and searched without success where we had worked, even groping around the monsters lurking in the darkness. Eventually we deduced that the torch must have been left inside the exhaust system, potentially a worse scenario than it lying in the wing bilges. There was nothing else for it but to remove the section of exhaust pipe again and have a look. And there it was, standing upright on the valve lid, still switched on and shining brightly in our embarrassed faces!'

At 1700 I tuned in to the news bulletin on BBC Radio 4 when it was confirmed that Argentina had invaded the Falkland Islands and that the UK had broken off diplomatic relations with Argentina.

We thus proceeded as fast as we can for the depth of water available. The main limiting factor was the snort muffler valve which could be embarrassing later if we need to snort. If time and circumstances allow later on we may be able to repair it. But for now the main aim is to get to the South Atlantic as fast as possible.

Saturday 3rd April 1982 – Day 3

<u>Falklands War Timeline</u>: *UN Security Council condemns the invasion and demands the immediate withdrawal of Argentine forces.*

We spent the day on passage at maximum revolutions in the full power state. We heard today that Operation CORPORATE is underway.

Sunday 4th April 1982 – Day 4

Falklands War Timeline: HMS CONQUEROR sailed from Faslane. United Nations Resolution 502 called for Argentina to withdraw from the Falkland Islands.

Continuing south at speed and the Ships' Company are now coming to terms with the fact that we are going to war and there is much uncertainty of what we can expect or do. The information we need is sketchy and the only real detail we have about the Argentine fleet is what is in Jane's Fighting Ships. It is ironic that the Argentine destroyer HERCULES (a UK Type 42 destroyer) was built on the same slip in Barrow as SPLENDID.

The submarine threat is worrying as they have two German built 209 diesel boats and we have little knowledge about the weapons. We will have to get to grips with this. We are basically as near as any of us have been to war and we must prepare ourselves in every possible way to ensure that if we are required to defend ourselves or attack then we can do so effectively and survive.

Argentine German built 209 class submarines

The coming week will be a very busy time – training for weapon firings, recognition, surveillance, first aid, maintenance of equipment, noise checks and testing of every system and piece of equipment we have.

The submarine principles remain Float, Move, Fight in that order.

Argentine Destroyer HERCULES

Monday 5th April 1982 – Day 5

Falklands War Timeline: *British task force of more than 100 ships sets sail for Falklands, including aircraft carriers HMS Hermes and HMS Invincible. Lord Carrington, the Foreign Secretary, resigns over the invasion and is replaced by Francis Pym.*

HMS INVINCIBLE Leaves Portsmouth for the South Atlantic

It was a shock to hear that Lord Carrington had resigned as Foreign Secretary. He had been the Guest of Honour at Founders Day at Pangbourne College in 1963 and had presented me with HM Queen's

Gold Medal and had wished me well in my naval career.

This was the first real day of concentrated training with action stations and attack teams going well. John Davis has come up with and amended drill for snorting with the muffler problem and we will try that later. At this stage there was a great deal of work going on trying to prepare ourselves about the Argentine Navy but the information was still sketchy. I decided to get a selection of questions ready to send to CTF 311 at Northwood.

This also highlights that the UK Satellite Communications system SSIXS was due to come on stream on 1st April but we still had the US version and it was working well and it was clear that long range communications was going to be important and I did not wish to give up a working system for an untried one.

We also had a set of support messages which told us that the Task Force had sailed and that Rules of Engagement are still be worked on. It seemed strange to me that we had both NATO and National Rules of Engagement that we knew well and yet the National Rules did not appear to be suitable for this situation. Nothing new there then but it does indicate that this was an exceptional situation and we were all going into the unknown.

I held a HOD's meeting and we decided that we should do a deep dive to ensure that the boat was as tight as it should be. It would be better to find out any problems now than if we had to use depth as a tactical or evasive action later on.

We slowed down to 8 knots and spent an hour going in 100 foot steps down to our deep diving depth. We stayed there for about 10 minutes while every compartment did a series of checks to ensure that systems were working and there was no sign of any leaks or issues. As expected there were no none. I said a little thank you to the team at Vickers Shipbuilding in Barrow –they had, as always, done their job extremely well and I also thought of all those design engineers in Bath who had ensured that all the calculations had been done again and again to allow a submarine of this size and complexity to be under such extreme water pressure.

Tuesday 6th April 1982 – Day 6

We were closing on the Equator and it is traditional in all ships and certainly in the Royal Navy to invite King Neptune onboard and to initiate any member of the Ships' Company on "crossing the line."

This is not the right time to don this and we will see if there is another better opportunity on the way home. Steve Hogg decided that we should name the torpedoes and I thought this was a great idea and so we started a competition to see what names were suggested. I anticipated a very diverse set of options but this was a good distraction as proposals were made.

Easter is coming up at the weekend so we decided that we would hold church services on Good Friday and Easter Sunday. It is always difficult to judge the religious loyalty or interest in a Ship's Company. I have never met anyone in submarines who pushes his faith but at the same time there are a few who are very open about it. The majority don't get involved and yet it is striking how many have crucifixes on chains around their necks or tattoos in a similar vein.

We had no declared Muslims on board – this was a time when there were very few in the Royal Navy yet alone in submarines so having to provide the bearing of Mecca on a regular basis was never required. However, there were many closet Christians of various persuasions and I would be very surprised if the majority at some stage did not pray for family and their survival. Religion in submarines has always been observed officially as the Commanding Officer is required by Queen's Regulations and Admiralty Instructions to hold an ecumenical service at regular intervals.

Generally there are a few officers doing their duty, a couple of senior rates and one or two junior rates. But I suspect we may have a bumper congregation over Easter as natural fears and apprehension kick in.

Wednesday 7th April 1982 – Day 7

A frustrating day as the support signals we have received have not really answered many of our questions. I need to know so many things.

What is the state of the Argentine submarines? Are they operational?

Are their German submarines still using German torpedoes? What is the current capability of the French A69 frigates?

Do they any effective ASW capability?

Have the British built Type 42 destroyers any updated ASW capability? What is the Argentinian airborne ASW capability?

What about the carrier and the Belgrano – do they have any ASW weapons capability?

So with lots of questions still unanswered I decided to send an updated Sitrep [situation report] and a shopping list for information. We were still relying on the BBC World Service for the best overall information but it is clear to me that diplomatic options are running out and the only options is to fight and kick the Argentinians out of British territory.

We are still working through Zone time changes working towards local Argentinian time and we have nearly finished doing routine planned maintenance on just about everything so that we are ahead of the game as we do not expect to have much opportunity to conduct maintenance once we are on station.

Marine Engineering Artificer or TG Tiff Jim Knight remembers:

'Charging south at full speed meant that the temperature in the engine room was oppressive, such was the flow of steam through the ranges. To even think of lifting a spanner to conduct a repair brought on a sweat, although at that speed the steam pressure was relatively low and leaks were therefore unlikely. My diary recorded all the breakdowns we endured and fixed, although the frequency and variety of problems were little different to a trip up north. The notion of a boat stopper, requiring a return to port, was never entertained or countenanced.'

Thursday 8th April 1982 – Day 8

We now have a lot more intelligence information and more explicit detail on the Rules of Engagement. This is good and we will have to spend some time ensuring that we understand the implications for SPLENDID.

Around 1930 I was in the control room looking at the chart when a loud report came from back aft.

'Fire, Fire, Fire. Fire in the Electrolyser space.'

The Officer of the Watch pressed the general alarm and rebroadcast the report throughout the submarine and everyone went straight into action.

It took less than 5 minutes before the report was received that the fire was out. Swift action by the guys back aft but I needed to know the cause and whether the Electrolyser was damaged in any way as this was our main source of Oxygen. I awaited a full report from John Davis and I did not rush him as I knew he would come and speak to me when he had more information.

As you can imagine, Fire, after flooding is a massive issue in a submarine. We spend a great deal of time training for all types of fires with a structured approach and a Damage Control HQ being set up in the wardroom. We have all the required information and communications stored in wardroom cupboards ready for immediate use. Obviously fire prevention and training in dealing with fires is very important and is taken very seriously. On average there is a serious fire in a submarine about once per year and smaller ones once per month. Most are extinguished very quickly and the training and equipment to deal with fires is state of the art and regularly checked. But with so much electrical equipment, mechanical failures, galley malfunctions and human error have often combined to spark a blaze.

John Davis came to see me and explained what had happened and that the repairs were underway and would take a few hours.

At sunset I decided to surface as we needed to see if we could repair the snort muffler valve and we need to check the WT mast insulator. It was a warm dry evening and there was a light swell and 20% cloud cover. There were no contacts on sonar and there was nothing visible for 8 miles through the periscope.

So I ordered. 'Officer of the Watch, prepare to surface,' and Ina Mackenzie went through the process and ensured that the people going into the fin were ready in the control room and had all the right safety and repair equipment.

When he was happy he reported to me 'Ready to Surface,' and I replied 'Officer of the Watch, Surface the submarine.'

Ian ordered 'Speed 5, 10 up, Blow main ballast.'

Suddenly there was this roar as high pressure air at 4000 pounds per square inch was rushing out of the High Pressure Air Reservoirs and forcing its way into the main ballast tanks at a tremendous rate. We all watched as the boat rose out of the depths and after about 10 seconds Ian shut off the main ballast blows. The boat lurched up the surface and bobbed for a bit before settling. In practice, when a submarine surfaces, it doesn't use a lot of air from its high pressure air tanks to "blow the ballast tanks" because it takes a long time to replenish the high pressure air tanks again with compressors. What happens is that all the ballast tanks are given a "good shot" of high pressure air (a few seconds), and then the planes are used in conjunction with the speed of the boat to actually drive a submarine to the surface. Once there, the Low Pressure blower system can be used to finish blowing the ballast tanks (while the high pressure air compressors are running to replenish the tanks.

Once the Officer of the Watch was happy that the boat was stable and had enough buoyancy he ordered 'Open Up.'

Toby Spreckley was in the conning tower [this is a tube from the pressure hull up into the fin] he pulled out the pins in the two clips and opened one clip at a time. 'Pressure in the boat,' said Ian to Toby. This ensured that Toby knew that when he took off the second clip the hatch would be likely to open quickly as the pressure in the boat was greater than outside.

Toby took off the second clip and the hatch sprung open with a rush of air from the submarine escaping into the fin. 'Upper lid open,' shouted Toby and he started to scramble to the bridge followed by the lookout, Able Seaman Curran carrying a plug in microphone and binoculars around his neck.

When Toby got to the bridge he unclipped the bridge covers and swung them open before climbing onto the bridge followed by Curran. He had a quick look around and shouted down the voicepipe 'Officer of the Watch on the bridge.' The planesman had opened the voice pipe cock next to his position in the control room and had a bucket ready to catch any water coming down the voicepipe. There was always some!

Ian and both looked through the periscope and agreed that is calm enough to open the main access hatch to speed up the process of getting people onto and then under the casing and conduct the repairs. This meant having a permanent sentry on the Main Access Hatch as it was much closer to the water than the conning tower.

We slowed to 4 knots to ease any possible wash over, sent the team of 3 up and set them to work. 20 minutes later they were back down below, the Main Access Hatch was shut and we prepared to dive again.

No Commanding Officer likes having any of his team outside the submarine at sea and we go to extremes to ensure every safety issue is addressed.

When I hear the report that the Main Access Hatch is shut and everyone is below I breathe a sigh of relief and order Toby Spreckley on the bridge.

'Officer of the Watch, Dive the Submarine,' Toby repeats the order and we go through the opposite process again of getting Toby and AB Curran down from the bridge and shutting, clipping and pinning the upper lid before Ian MacKenzie opens main vents and we dive again to our proper home under the waves.

The repairs seem to have gone well but the proof will be in whether the snort muffler valve will work as it should.

It has been a busy few hours as we continue our passage south and cross the Equator later that evening. Several of the Ships Company were observed trying to see water ran out of the basin plugs the opposite way!

Friday 9th April 1982 – Day 9

<u>Falklands War Timeline</u>: *'Canberra' sailed from Southampton with 3 Para, 40, 42 and 45 Royal Marine Commandos on board.*

It is clear that from the signals we are receiving there are plenty of people who are not on Easter weekend. We received more support traffic and more information but unfortunately for us the snort muffler still leaks and we will have to use the amended snorting procedure still. John Davis Ian Richards and I discussed this and decided that we would try the amended snorting drill over the weekend.

Canberra in the Falklands

We had something different today when we conducted a Postbox routine with an RAF Nimrod long range maritime patrol aircraft flying out of Ascension Island. Two Nimrod MR.1 of 42(TB) Squadron from St. Mawgan were the first to patrol Ascension waters and act as links with the nuclear submarines. This was a procedure which was used greatly in the Cold War and allowed for Nimrod aircraft and nuclear submarines to talk to each other via secure UHF radio either by voice or teletype. It was used extensively for prosecuting Soviet submarines and allowed immediate updates to be made between units working on the same mission. In the Cold War it was often the quickest and most effective way for a nuclear submarine to be vectored onto a Soviet submarine that had been detected or was being tracked by a Nimrod using sonobuoys.

RAF Nimrod Maritime Patrol Aircraft

For SPLENDID today it had two aims – first to prove that the system worked in the current environment and to enable Sitreps to be passed both ways quickly. An added advantage was being able to receive a link picture of activity and contacts over a wide area. Submarines had always worked well with maritime aircraft even when the submarines were diesel electric and the aircraft was a Shackleton – the predecessor of the Nimrod. But it was in the Cold War that the relationship became stronger and much more effective. There were a lot of similarities between sonar analysis equipment in Nimrods and Submarines and a great deal of post patrol analysis work was conducted at the combined analysis centres using both RAF and Royal Navy personnel. We did regular exchange visits and I remember very well two 12-hour sorties I did in a Nimrod in the Norwegian Sea with a visit to the US Naval Base at Keflavik in Iceland where the US P3 Long Range Maritime Patrol aircraft were based. So despite the investable RAF/RN rivalry we had worked well together operationally for many years. One of the signals received was to tell us that the Rules of Engagement allowed us to shoot inside the Maritime Exclusion Zone. So what was the Maritime Exclusion Zone? It is explained in this British Government Statement:

> "In announcing the establishment of a Maritime Exclusion Zone around the Falkland Islands, Her Majesty's Government made it clear that this measure was without prejudice to the right of the United Kingdom to take whatever additional measures may be needed in the exercise of its right of self-defence under Article 51 of the United Nations Charter. In this connection Her Majesty's Government now wishes to make clear that any approach on the part of Argentine warships, including submarines, naval auxiliaries or military aircraft, which could amount to a threat to interfere with the mission of British Forces in the South Atlantic will encounter the appropriate response. All Argentine aircraft, including civil aircraft engaged in surveillance of these British forces, will be regarded as hostile and are liable to be dealt with accordingly."

I also received a personal signal from Vice Admiral Peter Herbert the Flag Officer Submarines which read as follows:

> "Your quick preparation and deployment for operations off the Falklands was magnificent. As the spearhead of the UK response your impressively fast passage is being monitored with great interest at the highest level. Your actions will be vital to a successful outcome for the UK and your sensitivity to political directives even more so. Your families are being kept in the picture as much as we can and I will continue to monitor. God speed and good luck."

Saturday 10th April 1982 – Day 10

Everyone is upbeat today for some reason and I believe it is because we have crammed in so much preparation and training that there is a confidence that we can do whatever is required. We continue to train and most people are responding well but just can't wait to get on with the "war." We now know the surface ship plans and it is likely that not a lot will happen until we have been in are for several days. Our speed of advance is still around 21 knots which is excellent considering everything we have to do.

The European Economic Community today backed trade sanctions against Argentina.

Sunday 11th April 1982 – Day 11

At 0500 SPLENDID returned to periscope depth and prepared to snort.

To run a diesel engine in a submarine there is a requirement to bring air from outside the submarine into the boat and to eject the diesel exhaust to outside the boat. In SPLENDID we had a diesel which could be run to charge the battery which was required to start or restart the reactor plant if needed but also to provide emergency propulsion via an electric motor.

The snorkel system was originally designed by James Richardson, an Assistant Manager at Scotts Shipbuilding at Greenock in the 1920s but it was not developed properly until the Dutch and then the Germans moved things forward in the Second World War. There are some key parts of the system. First, the induction mast is a long hollow tube that is located in the fin outside the pressure hull. Air is sucked into the submarine through this tube which must be drained down prior to starting the diesel generator in a very precise procedure. On top of the mast is a large ball shaped box almost a metre wide called the snort head. It has two openings to allow the air in and inside the snort head is a flap or float. In normal operation when the snort head is above the water the flap drops down allowing air into the induction mast and then to the inside of the submarine. If the water completely covers the snort head [for example if the submarine loses depth] then the flap will move up and this will stop any water coming into the induction mast. This of course stops the air too entering the submarine until the snort head is clear of the water again.

In essence when you open the Snort induction hull valve to the elements you are opening a huge hole in the submarine where water can come down. At the bottom end is another very important valve called the Snort Induction Hull Valve and this is the biggest valve in the submarine.

Second is the snort exhaust mast which is located at the back of the fin and can be raised a few feet. Since this is an exhaust it can be operated very close to the surface and the volume and pressure of the exhaust gases will not allow any water back down the mast. At the bottom of the mast is a muffler valve which does what its name implies – it muffles the exhaust noise as it moves from the generator through the exhaust mast.

We completed the trial run with the new snort muffler procedure and although it was not easy at least it worked satisfactorily. While snorting we were able to change the controlling rod group on the reactor. It is good to have done that before we arrive on station. The Rules of Engagement have changed again and we are now in surveillance mode. The naval blockade starts at 0400 tomorrow and we are now in Argentine time.

We had a church service as it was Easter Sunday and I was not surprised to see that the congregation had swelled considerably. Sailors may not be overtly religious but they are superstitious and if here is an opportunity to arrange for some extra comfort or luck they will take it.

There was definitely a sombre mood amongst the congregation but also a steely determination to do everything right.

We completed a calorimetric on the reactor system following the rod group change which meant going up to maximum revolutions in the full power state for several hours. This is measuring technique which is based on heat flux sensors that are located on the wall of the reactor pressure vessel. The measurement is independent of temperature as the sensors measure directly the heat across the reactor wall.

Heat flow as well as heat transfer information are obtained immediately and allow a clear picture of system performance.

Monday 12th April 1982 – Day 12

We are still travelling at a speed of advance of over 22 knots despite coming to periscope depth to fix the submarine's position by GPS, check our inertial navigation system and take in new signals from Northwood, the weather and listen to the world service. Intelligence signals suggest that Argentine naval forces are all in harbour but I find that difficult to believe. Is this the quality of intelligence we are going to get?

The UK Government today announced a 200-mile Exclusion Zone around the Falkland Islands. The destroyer 'Antrim', the frigate 'Plymouth' with M Company, 42 Commando, sailed from Ascension to recapture South Georgia.

HMS ANTRIM and HMS PLYMOUTH

Tuesday 13th April 1982 – Day 13

At 0800 we were 600 miles east of Montevideo in Uruguay and continuing to transit at speed. We may be entering possible air cover now but there does not seem to be any indications of that. Ian Richards, John Davis, David Crothers and I decided that we need to do a few more emergency drills and give the planesman some high speed manoeuvring and torpedo evasion practice. This was always good fun and the planesman took it in turns to practice their skills. After couple of hours I was very happy with their performance. We did another fire drill and made sure that we were on top form in this area too. All this while continuing to do recognition training for those who would be using the periscope and more studying of the intelligence information by the sound room team as well.

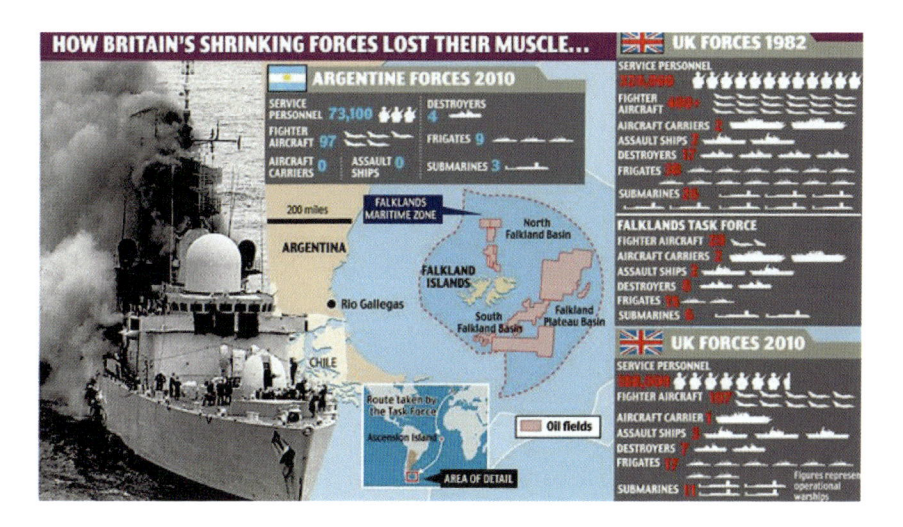

CHAPTER FOURTEEN
ON STATION

Wednesday 14th April 1982 – Day 14

<u>Falklands War Timeline</u>: *The South Georgia Task Force rendezvous with HMS ENDURANCE already in the vicinity.*

We are approaching our first patrol area to the west of the Falkland Islands and up threat towards Argentina. We have slowed down to sonar limiting speed and have conducted the final "exercises" before setting up our patrol. Quiet states, torpedo evasion routines and actions stations have all been exercised satisfactorily. It is vitally important that all the Officer of the Watches understand the torpedo evasion drill and have a chance to practice it. They are the front line of the submarine in this situation and they may have to act before either Ian or I can get to the control room. So we talked through the options and the key things that have to be done and in which order. But of course no situation is the same and the OOW has to be ready to use his initiative and "attack what you see not what you think." We then spent a good 90 minutes giving each OOW a chance to practice the drill for real. This also meant understanding what types of torpedoes could be fired against us from what kind of vehicle (submarine or helicopter) and the characteristics of each weapon. I felt more confident after this and stressed to the OOWs that they had to be ready for this at a moment's notice and that their initial actions were critical. The Rules of Engagement now in force currently only allow surveillance which is a bit disappointing.

I planned to start patrolling where the shipping lanes between Puerto Belgrano Naval Base and Puerto Deseado to Port Stanley cross. Puerto Belgrano is the largest naval base in Argentina and is situated close to Punta Alta near Bahia Blanca about 430 miles south of Buenos Aries. It is the home of the Argentinean Fleet and is the home port to all the major ships and support facilities. It is also close to the Marine Camp Baterias and the Naval Aviation's base at Comandante Espora.

We have done as much as we can in preparing both equipment and people. We seem to be on top of things although the intelligence picture is a bit thin and I suspect we will have to use our own assessments of where the best place to patrol is within our allocated area.

There is so much that is unknown in this situation that I am feeling pretty apprehensive and nervous but must not show it. It is vital that the Ship's Company have confidence in me and my decisions. I have started daily and sometimes twice daily meetings with the officers, key senior rates and a representative from each junior rates mess. At these meetings I explain what we know from intelligence and our own sensors and I explain my intentions and ask if there are any questions.

There sometimes are and I try to answer them but there are still a great many imponderables. That does not matter as this is an important part of keeping the Ship's Company informed. I see the submarine as a large safe and when you are at war it does not make sense to keep things from your team. This routine is going down well and I am pleased that I am getting plenty of engagement from the whole boat.

Thursday 15th April 1982 – Day 15

This was our first proper day of patrol and it was very quiet. We did detect some radar transmissions from a Hercules to the South and West but it was pretty intermittent but is probably a supply trip. We spent most of the day at periscope depth at 4 knots so that we could use all our sensors. That was quite a change for Ship Control and it took each watch an hour or so to settle in.

The Rules of Engagement have given us approval to engage any submarine contact which is comforting. I needed that and it took a long time to come!

Which brings me to my partner in crime – Commander Jim Taylor in HMS SPARTAN. Having broken off Exercise Springtrain and sailed from Gibraltar earlier than I left Faslane he was a good two days ahead of me. He has been off Port Stanley and Northwood have dived the area around the Falklands to East and West with a dividing line. We have sent each other signals via SSIXS and have dubbed ourselves COMSUBFALKEAST (HMS SPARTAN) and COMSUBFALKWEST (HMS SPLENDID). We did not appreciate until later that the signals we thought we were sending to each other using the satellite communications system were all being read in Northwood! We were not very complimentary about the intelligence information we were receiving and it was quite clear from some of the yo-ho signals that we had received that back in Northwood they had not really tuned into our mood which was deadly serious.

Argentine Submarine Santa Fe sunk at South Georgia

CHAPTER FIFTEEN
TORPEDO EVASION

It is 2330 and I am in the wardroom talking to Ian Richards and suddenly I hear PARIS alarm. PARIS is the code name for the intercept sonar that is enclosed in a protuberance on the forward casing. It detects active sonar transmissions from a ship or more alarmingly from a submarine and provides a frequency bearing and an intensity which can give a rough indication of range.

By the time we both reached the control room the Officer of the Watch has already started to take action. The issue is that an active transmission from a submarine could indicate an attempt to gain a final range to fire a torpedo. We can't take any chances here and we have to believe that this is coming from a submarine and the frequency of 6.4 KHz being shouted out by the sonar operator was close to the expected active ranging transmission from an Argentine German built submarine.

'What is the bearing?' I yelled as I arrived in the middle of the control room and went straight away to the PARIS display. Full evasion drill was called for.

'Bearing 290,' came the reply and I quickly looked to see that our course was 180. The best copybook tactical advice was as follows:

a. If the bearing was aft of the beam, we were meant to turn 20deg beyond the reciprocal, increase to max possible speed and climb above the layer/cross the layer and try to outrun the weapon's endurance.
b. If the weapon was coming in from the bow, we should turn towards minus 20 degrees, full speed and cross the layer again.

So with a bearing of 290 and our course being 180 the transmission was coming from abaft the beam the reciprocal of 290 was 110 so I ordered 'Port 30 course 110 maximum revolutions.'

The Officer of the Watch had gone to Action Stations and the navigator had appeared in the control room and as I saw him running to his plot I shouted 'Pilot, what is the depth of water here?'

Very quickly Ian MacKenzie replied 85 fathoms.

I calculated quickly – 80 fathoms equals 480 feet so followed up with '10 down keep 350 feet' [10 down means the angle you require to increase the pitch of the submarine as you change depth up or down.]

These orders were repeated and the transmission came again and the PARIS operator shouted out 'Bearing Frequency 6.4 Bearing 290 loud.'

Ian Richards came back quickly 'Layer at 100 feet.'

I watched as the boat turned, started to go deeper and speeded up. We quickly went to 15 knots and were changing depth fast.

There was a clear tension in the control room and my mind was in overdrive. Ian was watching Ship Control intently and was giving advice to the Petty Officer Cook Barnard who was on the planes and although CPO Coxswain Roger Colborne had arrive in the control room in response to the Action Stations this was not the time for him to take over. So he got behind the PO Cook and also provided advice as we spiralled down and off to the reciprocal bearing.

'OOW tell manoeuvring that this is NOT a good time to cavitate.' I said followed by 'what's our speed?' Quickly came back the reply '28 knots still increasing.'

There had been no more transmissions for 1 minute now and we were levelling out at 350 feet and were almost on course 110. The speed was continuing to increase and we were now at 18 knots.

I went to the plot and said to the Navigator – 'where are now?' He pointed to the dot of light on the table that was taking gyro compass and log information to generate a dead reckoning position matched to the scale of the chart. I put my hand on the tracing paper over the chart so I could see the depth information on the chart where we were and also where we were going on a course of 110. It suggested an average depth of between 80 and 100 fathoms and Ian Mackenzie said 'there is nothing shallower within 20 miles.'

That was reassuring and I went back to the PARIS display.

We had not had any further transmissions for 2 minutes now but I did not want to slow down. I was clearing the area quickly and if it was a torpedo it would be still transmitting. But there was nothing.

5 minutes, 10 minutes and 15 minutes passed with no further contact so I decided to slow down but stay deep and do a really good sonar search. We needed that as we had been at speed for a while.

We cleared stern arcs and then reversed course again. Ian Richards had been doing some detective work and with Tony Rowe the AMEO had come to the conclusion that the transmission had come from the Ballast Pump Hull Valve! What an own goal!

We fell out Actions Stations went to watch and came back to 200 feet and started to clear the area while continuing to search.

This may have been a false alarm but the Ship's Company reaction to Action Stations had been very good and this served as a further reminder that we could not be complacent about anything. Maximum alertness was required at all times. I was pleased with the sonar reports that I received and the Officer of the Watch had reacted correctly and swiftly. We would remember this if it happened again. Later we operated the ballast pump hull valve in a controlled test to see if we could recreate the PARIS alarm. On the 4th attempt it did alarm PARIS at 6.4KHz so this was confirmation of the situation.

Friday 16th April 1982 – Day 16

By 0100 we were moving away from the datum of the transmissions but by then we had established that the transmission was caused by the Ballast Pump Hull Valve. Whether it shut harder than usual or what it certainly gave a big scare and we will now be prepared if it happens again. But what it has done is bring home to everyone the severity of the situation we are in and if anyone onboard felt this was another exercise that illusion has been dispelled once and for all!

We stayed deep for most of the night and came back to periscope depth around 0830 to find a fine day with a slight sea and visibility of around 6 miles. We started to move northwest to see if any Argentinean surface units were heading along the coast. They have two options after sailing from Puerto Belgrano. They can head south east to extend air cover to South Georgia and north east of there or they can head south along the coast and the boundary of the Maritime Exclusion Zone [MEZ]. The former seems the most likely but nowhere near us as we are restricted by our water allocation. We can only cover the westerly option or the current unlikely event of surface units coming south into the MEZ. However, we can only shadow them and report as we do not have Rules of Engagement to sink surface units at present. I am not sure why but can only assume that these restrictions are based on ensuring that while diplomatic efforts are continuing that whenever Mr Pym, General Haig or Senor Perez de Cuellar are in the UK, USA or Argentina. This is frustrating but we have to live with it. I can understand Margaret Thatcher's desire not to be seen as the aggressor while such efforts are ongoing.

But all in all it turned out to be a quiet day.

Saturday 17th April 1982 – Day 17

Having taken a broadcast routine at 0800 there were indications that the Argentinean aircraft carrier (the 25th De Mayo) a cruiser (General Belgrano?) and a Type 42 destroyer are heading our way so we decide to stay in the northwest corner of our area where we are in the best position to detect them if they are moving down the coast.

By 1800 we had nothing – very disappointing as we were all up for some action – so decided to move further south.

The starboard turbo generator is sparking badly so has been taken down for maintenance – I hope this is not a long term problem.

It appears that General Haig has put together a proposal that included a five point peace plan. The plan calls for the withdrawal of Argentine troops from the Falklands in return for the departure of the British Task Force. A provisional administration of the Falklands by Britain, Argentina and the United States would be set up to last until December 1982. Then there would be fresh talks on the way ahead including a say for the Falkland islanders. I read this on a signal and it seemed to me that as it did not mention the word "sovereignty" I had my doubts that this was a proposal that the HM Government and in particular Margaret Thatcher would accept.

Sunday 18th April 1982 – Day 18

<u>Falklands War Timeline</u>: *Task Force sails from Ascension.*

We moved south overnight and by 0430 we had intelligence that the Argentine Carrier Group may be preparing to run the blockade and perhaps try to get their carrier into the Falklands Sound. This news prompted me to seek a change to the Rules of Engagement as I did not want to come across the Group and be able to do nothing. Surely they realise this is Northwood!? This hits my confidence that they really understand what we are doing and how we are operating and responding to intelligence reports they are sending.

However by 0840 we had a Rules of Engagement change and we can now fire at Argentine warships in the MEZ. Great news! This also makes me believe that the view at home is that the Carrier Group might try to come through and so we continue to move south a little faster towards the entrance to the Falklands Sound.

We have also heard that Local Overseas Allowance is £1 per person per day!

We clearly need to get to this choke point at the entrance to Falklands Sound as quick as we can but we are very wary that there may be an Argentine submarine hovering in that area and we must be on full alert for this. This is very worrying and I decide to open 3 and 4 torpedo tube bow caps with weapons loaded. This will speed things up if needed and more to the point will mean that we will not have to make the noise in opening them if we end up in close quarters with another submarine. Ian and I studied the chart and as both of us a previous diesel submarine Commanding Officers we considered where we would set up patrol off the northern entrance to the Sound. After an hour of discussion we deduced the most likely area in shallower water and decided to steer clear of it for the time being.

Twenty four hours ago it looked as if some form of engagement was inevitable today. As time has passed it seems more and more unlikely. The Mk 24 torpedoes in Tubes 3 and 4 remain equalised with bow caps open in case we come across the Argentine submarines SAN LUIS or SANTE FE. General Haig is staying in Buenos Aries until tomorrow so it seems unlikely that they will "have a go" when he is in Argentina.

This situation is typical for a submarine captain. Long periods of waiting, searching and looking for targets with woolly intelligence.

This was readily apparent in World War II when submarines of both sides endured hours and days of waiting for 15 minutes of extreme action usually followed by depth charging. I was reminded of the brilliant film "Das Boot" where this waiting frayed nerves and strained all on board. It was ever thus!

CHAPTER SIXTEEN

DO WE GO INSIDE THE FALKLAND SOUND?

Monday 19th April 1982 – Day 19

<u>Falklands War Timeline</u>: *US Secretary of State Alexander Haig attempts to mediate with the Argentine military junta, travelling between London and Buenos Aires to negotiate. His proposals include calls for Argentina to withdraw and for an interim administration on the islands. However, the junta rejects the proposals and signals its insistence on adding guarantees for eventual Argentine sovereignty. The talks are effectively over.*

0030. This was a long dull and very dark night mainly at periscope depth trying to suck in everything we can through ACINT [Acoustic intelligence – from sonar], ELINT [Electronic Intelligence] and COMINT [Communication Intelligence]. We searched for the Carrier and his escorts really hard and spent a great deal of time working out whether we would better inside or outside Falkland Sound. If we went inside we would have potentially more than one chance of attacking the Carrier but our only route out was south down the Sound. And getting in there involved a dangerous passage through the gap for part of which we would have to surface. The map below demonstrates the problem.

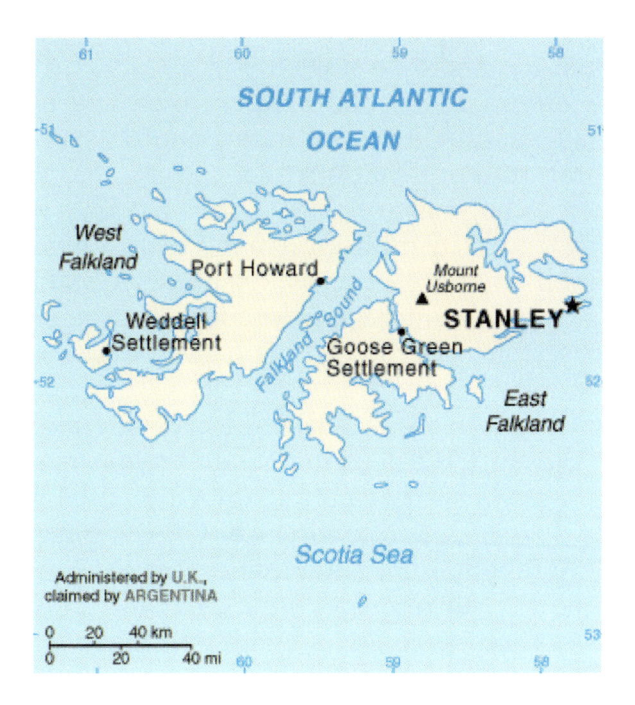

If we stayed to the north of the Sound entrance we would be able to get into a better position to fire but we may find Argentine submarines waiting in the area for us. We would probably only have one chance and would have to escape to the north.

Neither options were particularly palatable but in the end I decided to remain outside the Sound.

Not very happy to receive in a war zone with SSKs probably about, a signal saying that two of the Mk 24 torpedoes loaded in Faslane may have a depth keeping modification problem! Fortunately the two weapons loaded into 3 and 4 tubes seem to be okay – just as well really!

It does, however, make me wonder what else we have not been told?

We strained through the night but there was absolutely nothing. Until there was a loud call from the PARIS Operator 'Bearing 230. 7.2KHz transmissions – loud."

Jeff Thomas was the Officer of the Watch and immediately pressed the general Alarm and broadcast 'Action Stations, Action Stations.'

He went into the Torpedo Evasion maneuvers straight away and by the time I reached the control the speed was already coming on and we were altering course. We settled down at 450 feet and ran at speed for about 20 minutes and then slowed down again and turned back. There was no other contact and as there was only one transmission and we had responded we conducted another careful all round search remaining at Action Stations and on high alert but there was nothing further and no passive sonar contact at all. This frequency was not one we expected from an Argentinean submarine and we started looking at alternative causes. Eventually became convinced that this was not an Argentinean submarine but the either biologically caused or the Port Turbo Generator which was running up at the time.

Notwithstanding, these spurious PARIS detections are beginning to cause some concern. We need to have confidence that PARIS will detect an Argentinean submarine transmission and a series of spurious contacts does little for confidence. On the positive side it is providing live Action Stations situations and is allowing us all to be familiar with the Torpedo Evasion procedure.

I returned to periscope depth and with nothing in sight or on any other sensor I fell out Action Stations.

As there was nothing visual or on sonar or other sensors I decided that it was wise to clear the datum at 240 feet which is beneath the temperature layer which is currently at around 200 feet. Moved to the North North East for about an hour at 10 knots and came back to periscope depth for another all sensor search. There was nothing so we can only surmise that the Argentine carrier is not coming this way to the Falkland Sound despite the "clear intelligence" we have received. This is very frustrating and again makes me wonder just where this intelligence is coming from and what credibility we give it? I suspect that Northwood has the same issues and is trying to give us everything they have got however tenuous. The Ships Company have responded well, are in good form and the last 24 hours has produced an atmosphere – particularly amongst the junior rates – of spoiling for a fight!

Tuesday 20th April 1982 – Day 20

During the night we moved east and then slowly worked our way south and towards Port Stanley. The aim was to continue to cover the Falkland Sound option and be able to respond to any updated intelligence. The Rules of Engagement remain unchanged and we can fire at any Argentinean warship in the Maritime Exclusion Zone.

HMS CONQUEROR is now off South Georgia and the initial surface force is due to arrive later today. We also heard that the British Government is not happy with the proposed peace plan put forward by General Haig although we do not have too many details as yet.

0900 we are at periscope depth and ELINT has detected faint and intermittent rackets (this is the name used for contacts in ELINT parlance). It was difficult to classify these but they could be surface or air contacts but decided to cancel the immediate intention to move to the North East. After some more work we decide that the rackets were probably AN/APS 29 fitted to Hercules aircraft.

We have been given a rough idea of an area where the San Luis submarine may be operating. Again it is difficult to establish the credibility of this but it is worth investigating. There has been nothing of note for a while and decided that we must go towards the Port Stanley area. I am mindful that although the Rules of Engagement allow, an attack on any Argentine unit may not help negotiations but I will need to decide if we find one. Adrenalin must have run high in SPARTAN today when an Argentine merchantmen went past him – but frustrating too as we do not have the Rules of engagement to sink that type of vessel.

At present I have come to the conclusion that the Argentine surface forces will not come into the MEZ. They must know that we have nuclear submarines down here and they would be stupid to ignore that. Intend running in towards the 100 fathom line off Stanley.

Argentine German 209 Class submarines
SALTA and SAN LUIS

CHAPTER SEVENTEEN

IS THIS THE ARGENTINE CARRIER TASK GROUP?

Wednesday 21st April 1982 – Day 21

<u>Falklands War Timeline</u>: *HMS ANTRIM arrives off South Georgia, but a reconnaissance operation by the SAS on Fortuna Glacier almost ends in disaster after two helicopters crash in severe weather conditions. A third helicopter manages to extract the SAS men.*

Hoped to get a good update on the state of diplomatic negotiations on the World Service but reception very poor and did not manage to get much information. As far as I am concerned it is far too late for that and the only way to deal with this situation is to kick the Argentineans out of the Falklands. I don't underestimate the task in hand but I am confident in the British Armed Forces to handle this but it may take a while.

We should be off Stanley by 1600 but by then we were in position in the middle of a violent westerly gale which is making life difficult at periscope depth. No contacts on any sensor. Just after this we received new instructions to move to the North West off the Argentinean coast. Full details and reasons are not yet clear as we are missing a signal or two. Communications, communications!

Every time we have started to get close to the Falkland Islands things have changed and we still have not been close enough to see land.

Started to move NW and clear San Luis possible area and decided that we would shut 3 and 4 tube bow caps for the time being as the submarine threat seemed to have reduced. I hope this is the right decision?

1840 It is now clear from the latest reports that the Argentine Carrier may be operating to the North West closer to the Argentine coast. Once we have got well clear of the San Luis possible area we will speed up and get over there as soon as we can. After about two hours careful searching and working our way towards the North West we speeded up to 24 knots. However, having to take one broadcast routine in two to ensure we have the latest intelligence information is slowing down our average speed of advance but do not want to push it any further.

Thursday 22nd April 1982 – Day 22

Having spent the night moving North West towards an area east of Ponta Delgarda by 1040 [Sunrise] we had slowed down and detected three contacts to the west and northwest of us. Initial classification was 2 shafts 4 blades and blade flutter which despite the early morning mist and visibility of 3000 yards nothing was visual. It was difficult to give a firm classification and it could be a fishing vessel or something else.

That is one of the fascinations of submarine warfare. With only passive information to go on it is often difficult unless you get other information from visual to ELINT you cannot be sure. But these contacts were sufficiently interesting to close them. So we chose an intercept course to the south west and speeded up to close the range as quickly as we dared.

1100 The two contacts are now around 14000 yards away and seem to be tracking south at around 10-12 knots. I suspect that one of them is a merchantman heading for Deseado and after another detailed assessment Chief Ops Turner indicates that they are almost certainly both merchantmen. We still have not seen anything and the visibility is not in our favour. We are content that they are not warships. And so it is better to move towards the area that might provide better trade.

1400 At periscope depth and picked up a Echo/Foxtrot band radar transmission to northwest which was much more interesting as this is an indicator that the transmitter could be a warship as not many merchantmen or fishing vessels have that type of radar. By 1700 the racket was alarming the ELINT system but the visibility was still only 3-4000 yards. However this does indicate activity in our area – designated CARLOS. There was no point in staying at periscope depth if we could not see much so decided to go deep for a few hours and close the coast. We are optimistic that this will lead us to potential targets.

But frustrated again at 2100 when we were back at periscope depth and had another racket to the north that had the parameters of THE

Argentinean British built Type 42 destroyer radar Type 996/992 Q 3-D. If this is right then we could be close to either the HERCULES or SANTISSIMA TRINIDAD. It is fascinating to think that these two ships were built in Barrow in Furness just like SPLENDID – irony indeed!

We took the latest routine only to be told that we were now instructed to keep away from the Carrier Group as the Foreign Secretary Mr Pym was in Washington DC talking to General Haig. An incident now would be politically unacceptable.

This is really frustrating and I was as angry as hell that there seemed to be no real plan for us and I was concerned that we would be pushed from pillar to post chasing intelligence shadows and never actually finding anything. Northwood must have known when Mr Pym was going to be in Washington so why were we sent over to the coast in the first place. I have to admit to be losing confidence on what is going on in Northwood and some of the decisions coming my way. I can't help thinking that maybe Admiral Sandy Woodward is right and we should be under his tactical command in theatre where we would be able to respond to his 'in theatre intelligence' picture. This goes against my personal background of centralised operational control from CTF 311 in Northwood as I know from my experience how hard it is to put themselves in your shoes and anticipate your requirements. We are now going back to an area west of the Falklands.

And to add to the frustration the starboard turbo generator [TG] is sparking badly and has been shut down for repairs and is likely to be down for about 48 hours.

Friday 23rd April 1982 – Day 23

Having worked our way back towards an area northwest of the Falklands we can still hear sonar contacts to the west and southwest. Range estimates are around 40,000 yards and sonar conditions indicate we could be getting a convergence zone detection. A convergence zone is where sound coming from a ship is only detected a considerable distance from the submarine. They are only likely to occur in deep water and when there is a strong sound channel well below the surface. The sound is bent upwards towards the surface and extends the range in which it can be heard.

This afternoon we did see a ship when we came across a Soviet Fish Factory ship with a trawler alongside. It was white and was moving east at around 6 knots. It was not what I wanted to see!

Continued to the south towards the West Falklands areas and set up patrol on the northern edge of the area putting me in an intercept position between the main Argentine naval ports and the Falklands.

CONQUEROR is moving southeast towards South Georgia and SPARTAN is covering Port Stanley. By now the Argentineans will be aware of the advance task force off South Georgia and may get a bit excited about it. They may not have realised that this will involve the SAS/SBS but then who knows what they will be getting up to?! So now we are in the northern segment of the MEZ and must await developments.

Saturday 24th April 1982 – Day 24

An all too quiet night with a few fishing vessels around but not causing any issue. By 0900 we had be asked to move further north towards the best intelligence of where the Carrier group was likely to be operating.

A signal update indicated that CONQUEROR has been switched to target the Guppy class submarine SANTE FE which is now thought to be off South Georgia.

SPARTAN continues to guard the entrance to Port Stanley while we go north to find the Carrier group. The Rules of Engagement are still for surveillance only and I really hope that we can get some contact soon. The Ships Company are performing well but I think they are as frustrated as me.

So another day with little activity apart from a few fishing vessels but it looks as though the TG is fixed and we are close to area CARLOS again.

We have been told that the cruiser General BELGRANO is in Ushuaia right at the bottom of Argentina which is not a big surprise and it probably transited there inside the 12-mile territorial limit.

Sunday 25th April 1982 – Day 25

Falklands War Timeline: South Georgia is retaken by Royal Marines and SAS. Prime Minister Margaret Thatcher refuses to answer questions from the press on the operation, saying: "Just rejoice at that news and congratulate our forces and the Marines".

Royal Marines recapture South Georgia

Sunday means grapefruit segments and mushrooms for breakfast. It is upon such simple things that submariners register the passing of time.

And today we would be operating very close to the Argentine local areas – a sort of Argentine Portland (which is where UK ships work ups are conducted). In the middle of the night we started to intercept COMINT information on a number of frequencies but much of the transmissions were in five letter groups. This could be coming from shore but as we were in a regular naval operating area I think we were surprised there was little activity. We had closed the 100 fathom line and were closing the continental shelf. We stayed at periscope depth until around 1300 but with nothing to show for it I decided to run deep for a while and close the coast before returning to periscope depth for an all sensor search. By 1530 we were conducting an all sensor search and there are indications from intelligence signals that the Argentine Carrier Group may be operating East North East of us. We will move towards that and it seems there is confidence that the Argentine Carrier the "Veinticinco de Mayo" is due in our area at around 1200 tomorrow, so we will patrol the southeast of the area and wait developments. The Carrier would be a big prize and speculation was rife in the boat about how we would sink it and how long it would take to go down. Typical submarine thoughts from 100 men in a tin can under the water!

Argentine Aircraft Carrier "Veinticinco de Mayo"

But the Veinticinco de Mayo [this means 25th May which is the date of Argentina's May revolution in 1810.] is an aircraft carrier in the Argentine Navy and had come into service in 1969. Ironically the ship had previously served in the Royal Navy as HMS VENERABLE and even in the Dutch Navy as HNLMS KAREL DOORMAN. She had been involved in the dispute with Chile over the Beagle Channel in 1978 but had spent the greater part of her life in harbour. The ship was built during WW II at Cammell Laird Shipyard in Birkenhead as a Colossus class aircraft carrier and served in the Pacific but was transferred to the Dutch Navy 3 years later. The threat she poses comes from her aircraft and the ordnance they can deliver. The Argentine Navy bought 14 Super Etendards from France in 1980, after the USA put an embargo in place because of the so called 'Dirty War' and refused to supply spare parts for their A4 Skyhawk aircraft.

Argentine Super Etendard (left) and A4 Skyhawk (right)

The Super Etendards, armed with the French Exocet anti-ship missiles, were originally bought to operate off the Argentinean carrier and thus provide air power from the sea. But there were all sorts of problems as the flight deck was not strong enough to take the Super Etendards. This was fortunate for the UK as any extension from Argentina to the east, towards the Falkland Islands, could have extended the offensive range of Argentina and put the UK Task Force at severe risk. That has been tempered by the fact that there were 4 Royal Navy SSNs in theatre and the chance of the carrier being attacked and sunk was high. This led to the UK infiltration missions to raid the air base, aiming to destroy the Super Etendards on the ground to prevent their use.

The re-taking of South Georgia is good news and this may provoke some action in our area soon. I certainly hope so! At the moment I can only detect, identify, trail and report and of course I must not go inside the 12 mile limit. We have a received a possible rendezvous position for the Carrier Group but how reliable it is or what it is based on I have not been told. This is another example of why I need more information to establish the credibility of intelligence reports. This is important as it is a crucial part of any risk assessment. Notwithstanding we are closing the position while searching.

From SPLENDID's viewpoint the carrier and its fixed wing aircraft did not pose a real threat, but we did expect the carrier to have an escort of sorts – at least three A69 frigates as they did have an ASW capability. Moreover we did not know if the carrier would have ASW helicopters. If it did they would be a real threat to us.

We have received a possible rendezvous position for the Carrier Group, but how reliable it is or what it is based on I have not been told. This is another example of why I need more information to establish the credibility of intelligence reports. This is important as it is a crucial part of any risk assessment.

CHAPTER EIGHTEEN
CAN WE GET THE CARRIER?

Monday 26th April 1982 – Day 26

<u>Falklands War Timeline</u>: *Formal surrender of Argentine forces at South Georgia. 2 Para sailed from Hull on the 'Norland'.*

I decided that the submarine threat was now low and that if I was going to be a position to attack the Carrier I needed to change my weapon load to MK 8 torpedoes which would be more suitable against such a target. The WWII Mark 8 torpedo was designed as an anti-ship weapon and, if the main threat was now the Carrier, I would need to have fast moving shallow running torpedoes. So overnight the Mk 24 Tigerfish Torpedoes were withdrawn in favour of Mk 8s and by 0300 the reload was complete.

The irony of the fact that I was changing – in my very modern nuclear submarine – a so called modern torpedo for a WWII vintage, powered by a diesel engine was not lost on me! But it was my only choice.

We have warned the Ships Company that we may be at Action Stations for long periods tomorrow. I certainly hope we are.

By 1000 there was no sign of any activity and we had been in the vicinity of the RV position for around 3 hours conducting an all sensor search at periscope depth.

But as the morning went on we started to get rackets from ELINT classified as 992 Q radar and 2 shaft 5 bladed contacts on sonar. The tactical systems plotted their bearings and put the main contact into the fire control computers to continue to generate a solution. It became clear that this was a Type 42 destroyer at about 17000 yards though it is difficult to assess which one and it looks as though it is transiting south at about 12 knots possibly to join the Belgrano. That said she could have been waiting for the Carrier to catch her up and I did find it difficult to understand that the Argentine Navy would let the Carrier go anyway without at least one Type 42 as well as the

French built A69 frigates. Conditions for an all sensor search at periscope depth were far from ideal with a long swell on a balmy surface with visibility around 12000 yards. Too many seagulls for comfort around the periscope and it was providing a very marked feather at 5 knots. Some of the rackets reached danger level very quickly bbut I doubt if they ever came closer than 15000 yards despite closing them on an intercept course all the time. It would have been stupid to be detected at this stage and it is the Carrier I am after.

By 1600 the Type 42 had almost faded from sonar and the rackets had stopped. It was difficult to understand this as the last bearing did not register with any navigational point of interest. I wonder if the loss of the SANTA FE in South Georgia had made the Argentine Navy rethink their plans. I tried to put themselves in their place and come up with a plan from their perspective and it seemed to me that they had to risk a pincer movement with both the Carrier Group and the Belgrano Group although there is no indication of this at present. At 2000 I was notified by the navigator that we were exactly 10000 miles from Faslane!

So all we can do at present is keep looking and hope that the Carrier Group makes a move.

Tuesday 27th April 1982 – Day 27

0800 We are now about 150 miles from the Argentine coats trying to cover up threat from the Falklands in as big an arc as we can. This is not easy as we could do with three SSNs to do this properly but we are probably in the best position we can be.

Intelligence suggests that at least one of the 209 submarines remains in harbour – not sure if I want to believe that. By noon we had started to head southwest to an area off Cabo Raso where we have been told the tanker CAMPO DURAN is likely to patrol to top up Argentine surface ships. Again, I am not sure how accurate this intelligence or its credibility – but it is all we have got.

So we increased speed and went deep for a couple of hours to close the distance. But there is no sign of anything – another frustrating day.

Wednesday 28th April 1982 – Day 28

We are operating around 80 miles off the Argentine coast and the latest intelligence suggests that the Veinticinco de Mayo has a defect which has reduced its operating speed to 16 knots. The Carrier's associated tanker also has a defect which may cause some delays too but from all accounts we are waiting in the vicinity of their planned operating area. We have no idea where this information is coming from but must assume that there are agents or UK friendly people who are feeding back information to UK. It is extremely difficult to keep the movements of a large ship completely secret as there are just too many people who are in the know. In UK we try hard to keep information on a "need to know" basis and this has its advantages and drawbacks. In some cases it works well but it is still difficult.

There is an old story that when the Polaris submarines were running from Faslane you could always find out when a particular boat was returning from patrol from a very friendly butcher in Helensburgh! I don't know whether that is true or not but I suspect it is. Certainly the wives and families were not told until about 48 hours in advance but maybe they had their own intelligence network.

We will stay in this area and move slowly towards Cabo Raso and the possible rendezvous area tomorrow. We shall see if anything turns up.

1300 Three signals from UK leave little doubt as to UK plans over the next 24 hours. It would appear that the Carrier - Veinticinco de Mayo – sailed from Puerto Belgrano Naval Base [just south of Buenos Aries] a couple of hours ago and will almost certainly head south to re-embark her aircraft from Trelew airfield. Options open to SPLENDID are:

1. Head for Cabo Raso to try to find the CAMPO DURAN
2. Stay where we are where we believe the Type 42 and the A69 escorts are most likely to rendezvous
3. Head northeast to a position where we can intercept the Carrier as it head south.

As always as the Captain you have options. The trick is to pick the right one and that is not always based on logic. All submarine Captains have a "feeling in the water" and more often than not that instinct based on experience is the right choice. After a discussion with Ian Richards and a further reading of the intelligence signals I decide to go for option 3. This gives me a chance of finding the Carrier cold when it has only been at sea for a short time and before it meets its escorts. So we move north east for couple of hours deep and come up after about 3 hours for an all sensor search at periscope depth.

By 1700 we were back at periscope depth doing an all sensor search and well placed to cover the Carrier's movements and also to cover any attempt to move towards the MEZ. But yet again there is no contact and all we can do now is sit and wait.

Thursday 29th April 1982 – Day 29

We spent the night mainly deep but coming up to periscope depth every few hours. At 0200 we had a signal that indicates a possible rendezvous position for the Carrier and we are quite close. Our mission is still the same to detect, trail and report De Mayo.
At 0300 today the UK Task Force should arrive off the eastern edge of the Total Exclusion Zone which comes in to force at 1100Z on 30th April.

At 1300 we had sonar contact to the northeast that we estimated at 30,000 yards tracking south. Shortly afterwards we heard intermittent loud bangs which could possibly be gunfire. We have also intercepted strong morse code groups on 8MHz.

At 1400 more loud bangs were heard shortly afterwards and these were classified as gunfire about 25,000 yards away. This was followed by an ELINT report of a racket which was classified as Air/surface DRBV 51A Sentry radar which is one of the radars that the A69 frigates have. This was followed by a sonar report of diesel. At 1411 Ian Richards was on the search periscope when he exclaimed 'Ship visual bearing 309 – range about 14000 yards – looks like an A69 frigate' By the time he had given the angle on the bow we had a fire control solution on DCB [The tactical systems computer suite] of Course 206 Speed 15 knots at a range of 14000 yards.

At last – after all this waiting we had actually seen something tangible and possible target. There was a buzz in the control room and the message soon went throughout the boat. I was now really thinking that all this waiting had been worthwhile and we were in a good position but the Rules of Engagement meant that we could still only detect, trail and report.

By 1420 we had three A69 frigates visual and manoeuvring to the west of our position. All three were about 15,000 yards away and were doing 12 knots in a southerly direction. This was even batter as these three had to be the escorts and screen for the Carrier – but where was it?

Then at 1450 sonar picked up a 4 bladed contact doing 120 rpm to the northwest and this was soon classified as a Type 42 Destroyer. So they were here too. It was just not feasible that these should be together if they were not waiting for the Carrier.

For the next couple of hours we monitored the 4 ships and although we had not seen the Type 42 visually we were pretty sure it was there. We were losing visual contact at periscope depth as we were doing around 6 knots and the frigates were doing 12 knots. We could not go more than 7 knots at periscope depth for fear of damaging the periscope and so we went deep and closed the track and positions of the A69s.

Keeping contact with them was straightforward and the sonar operators were passing through accurate bearings of all three every 30 seconds so our fire control solution was good. But we could not fire!!!

By 1800 we were back at periscope depth and held all three at ranges of 9000, 14000 and 18000 yards. We also had two other contacts on sonar on a bearing of 330. Toby Spreckley now on the search periscope went to the bearing and reported in a loud voice 'Type 42 visual bearing 330 range 12000 yards.' Followed shortly afterwards by 'another warship close by but don't know what it is.' Ian was about to take over the periscope when Toby said 'I think it is the COMODORO PY.'

'Let me have a look' said Ian and took the periscope. He asked Ian MacKenzie who was at the chart table to show him the picture of the COMODORO PY from Jane's Fighting Ships. 'That's him' said Ian.

The COMODORO PY was the ex USS PERKINS – a Gearing class destroyer laid down in 1944 sold to the Argentine Navy in 1973. As well as guns she was capable of firing both torpedoes and depth charges.

By that stage reports were coming in thick and fast from sonar and ELINT and that helped us classify the Type 42 destroyer as the SANTISIMA TRINIDAD. This was a Type 42 alright but while the HERCULES had been built at Vickers in Barrow-in- Furness the SANTISIMA TRINIDAD had been built in Argentina although it did its work up and weapons trials in UK. Background intelligence indicated that she was probably the leading ship of the Argentine landings in the Falklands and was probably had the main task of co-ordinating air defence of the Carrier group.

None of them seemed to be in any hurry to go anywhere and so we remained at periscope depth watching through the attack periscope and showing as little mast as we could in what was a 4 to 6 foot sea from the north which provided good cover.

We spent the next hour continuing to monitor all the contacts we had both visual and on sonar and ELINT. We had a good handle on all of them and had fire control solutions which were being constantly updated.

By 2000 we had the HERCULES at 6000 yards and they were still milling around not apparently intent on going anywhere specific. They must be waiting for the Carrier – that is the only realistic option! Surely!

I decided to go deep again as we knew which contact was which ship on sonar and we would be more able to respond to speed changes from below periscope depth. To my surprise there was no indication of any active sonar transmissions from any of the argentine ships. That was not really surprising as they would probably not want to attract a Brit SSN by giving away their position and the two Type 42s were optimised for air defence not anti-submarine warfare. We were now tracking the COMODORO PY and the TRINIDAD SANTISSIMO moving south and leaving the HERCULES and the three A69s milling around. The depth of water was a limit for SPLENDID and we could not go faster than 12 knots in the area we were. By 2330 the COMODOR PY and the TRINIDAD SANTISSIMO seemed to be making for Comodoro Rivadavia and were about two hours ahead of the HERCULES/A69 group but we did need to close the range.

I sent an enemy /situation report to Northwood and Admiral Woodward explaining what I had found and said that I was convinced that they would lead me to the Carrier as these were the only units available as a screen. I felt there was an inevitability about this and talked to Ian Richards and David Crothers about the state of our weapons and whether there was anything else we should do to prepare. We came up with a few items and David went to carry those out.

I reflected on what had been a fascinating day with some real contact at last. I had prepared myself for firing at Argentinean ships and I was convinced that if I stayed with these ships I WOULD find the Carrier. I was calm, certain in my Ship's Company's ability and mentally prepared for sinking a major ship and had gone over in my mind how I would do it and get away afterwards. We just had to find the Carrier now.

Friday 30th April 1982 – Day 30

At 0800 as the Task Force arrived in the 200 mile exclusion zone surrounding the Falkland Islands, the Total Exclusion Zone came into force.

The Total Exclusion Zone (TEZ) was an area declared by the United Kingdom on 30 April 1982 covering a circle of 200 nautical miles (370 km; 230 mi) from the centre of the Falkland Islands. From now on any sea vessel or aircraft from any country entering the zone may be fired upon without further warning.

The TEZ was an extension of the Maritime Exclusion Zone (MEZ) declared on 12 April 1982 covering the same area. Any Argentine warship or naval auxiliary entering the MEZ could have been attacked by British nuclear-powered submarines (SSN).

On 23 April, the British Government clarified that any Argentine ship or aircraft that was considered to pose a threat to British forces would be attacked in a message that was passed via the Swiss Embassy in Buenos Aires to the Argentine government:

CONQUEROR is now south of the Falklands looking for the BELGRANO and SPARTAN is north of the Falklands and we are northwest of her.

Through the night we continued to track the Argentine group as they transited slowly south. Contact was intermittent but we still had a good enough handle on them. We came up to periscope depth at 0600 for a broadcast routine hoping for some more definitive intelligence on the Carrier. But there was no news.

Went deep again and up to 14 knots which is about the speed limit we could manage in this depth of water. We have a carefully constructed operating envelope which advises what the maximum speed is and depth an SSN can travel depending on the depth of water under the keel. This takes account of the recovery depth required in the event of a plane failure or other casualty situation. Even though this was war it made sense to operate as close to the limit as possible.

At 1115 came back to periscope depth and the COMODORO Y was visual at 12000 yards tracking northwest and the TRINIDAD SANTISSIMO is visual at 15000 yards tracking south east. They are both doing around 10 knots and do not seem to be going anywhere specific. We watched for another 2 hours and then decided to open to the east and clearing away from these two units who seem to be slowly moving in an easterly direction on north/south legs about 5 miles apart from each other. What are they doing? Are they waiting for someone?

At 1800 I sent another sitrep on the HERCULES and COMODORO PY who were about 12000 yards away but we are firmly in sonar and occasional visual contact. I plan to stay in the area and keep track of these two. The A69s seem to have continued south west.

Argentine Destroyer HERCULES

CHAPTER NINETEEN

BREAK CONTACT OR NELSONIAN BLIND EYE?

Then came the signal I did not want.

I have been ordered to break contact with these two units and move further southwest. I was told to move and pursue the Carrier which was apparently – from Chilean sources – supposedly to the north. I could not understand why they wanted me off the escorts when, by definition, in due course the Carrier would join them or vice versa. I was angry. I had already had Argentine units in my periscope cross wires without the authority to fire. This was Northwood's best intelligence on the Carrier.

I decided to ignore the order and stay with these two. We had been having some difficulty with communications anyway and had missed some signals. They all have sequence numbers so you know whether you have received everything or not.

That evening Ian Richards and I had a long discussion as to whether we should move or not and how soon we should respond to that order. It was intensely frustrating and most of that was caused by adherence to old submarine Commanding Officer's adage that "You attack what you see not what you think might be there." We could see the escorts, we could not see the Carrier and the intelligence we had received about it had been unreliable, to put it mildly, to date.

Eventually I decide that we will reluctantly have to move. Even though I think I am close I have not got contact with the Carrier and that must be the priority. The trouble is that there is a lot of, what appears to be from where I am, somewhat dodgy intelligence. I don't know how good or credible it is but, as much as I don't like it, I have to believe that Northwood have analysed what is the best option. Also I can only disobey a direct order for so long!

I was still deciding when to break off, and hoping like hell that the Carrier would come over the horizon, when a signal came in:

Personal for the Commanding Officer. It was from Vice admiral Sir

Peter Herbert Flag Officer Submarines and simply said:

"I understand. Go now"

That finally did it for me. I had to move away but at least I could comfort myself by the thought that Flag Officer Submarines understood the situation I was in. Later when I was FOSM I remembered that situation!

Saturday 1st May 1982 – Day 31

Falklands War Timeline: UK Task Force entered the Exclusion Zone. Vulcan bomber 'Black Buck' attacked the runway at Port Stanley. The mission is a logistical nightmare, involving several tanker aircraft refueling bombers during the 8,000-mile round trip from Ascension Island. First air attacks by Harriers on Argentinean positions on the Falklands. SAS and SBS landed on the islands.

0400. Just as we start to move south in response to the intelligence reports and instructions from Northwood we receive a signal that says that the Carrier can be sunk anywhere!

I have held several sonar contacts over the last few hours but most have been classified as merchant or fishing vessels but not the Carrier. Admiral Woodward is very keen that we find and attack the Carrier as soon as we can and I share his view. The problem is in large ocean I have to find him first! I have more water allocated and will be going towards Deseado.

By 0900 we had a few interesting rackets and I am now of the view that the Carrier is running inside the 12 mile territorial waters limit. That is frustrating but there is nothing I can do about it.

1000. Sonar has a contact at an assessed range of 7000 yards that has characteristics of a diesel submarine. I find it unlikely that there will be one in this area but we have had no information on the Argentine submarine SALTA for several days and we must be on our guard. This gives me a dilemma as I currently have Mk 8 torpedoes loaded – waiting for the Carrier – and I need to have Mk 24 Tigerfish to take on a submarine.

There are clear drawbacks associated with operating in shallow water with the Mk 24 Tigerfish so this was not the time to be changing weapon loads. There is a problem with some torpedoes including the Mk 24 that mean they are relatively useless in shallow water because they dive on discharge. This was always going to be a judgement but we did not have another anti-submarine torpedo at the time and we were only in the early development stage of the Tigerfish successor – Spearfish.

However keeping faith with the old Mk 8's brought its own set of unique problems too. Changing scenarios dictated changing weapons in tubes which resulted in numerous weapon movements in the Torpedo Compartment which had to be managed on the watch with the bare minimum of Tubes Crew – inevitably health and safety rules were compromised on more than one occasion. But that is the nature of the beast.

CHAPTER TWENTY

FALSE CONTACTS AND BELGRANO SUNK

1230. 'Bearing 288 unknown contact – possible submarine' comes from the Sound Room. I go in and speak to the team. They have what sounds to them like hydroplane noise or hydraulics. If this a submarine it is very close and I go back into the control room and ask the Tactical Systems operators 'Do you have a fire control solution on this contact?'

'Course 330 Speed 6 knots range 5500 yards.' This is getting too close and I all my senses are in overload. For some reason I think this could be the SALTA and I do not want to make it easy for him particularly when I cannot fire back!

'Let's get out of here' I say and then 'Officer of the Watch come to 140 and speed up slowly to 21 knots.' It is time to clear this datum just in case. I hate doing this but without the proper torpedoes loaded I cannot get into a close quarters situation where I cannot put a weapon in the water.

We move away and if there has been no obvious reaction to our increase in speed to get away from it. If it is a submarine I would have expected some reaction but it is possible that it did not detect us. It may be that is the SALTA – heading northwest but with noise problems.

1800 HMS CONQUEROR has her target in sight – the cruiser BELGRANO. I wish we were in the same position!

This was a significant day in that we are now permitted to take out the Carrier wherever we find it except in the Brazilian Exercise areas (as they have a Carrier that looks similar but they would be mad to have it at sea at the moment) or inside the Argentinean twelve mile territorial waters. Unfortunately we have had no further contact with the surface ships which is very frustrating and I still think we should have stayed with them and not chased intelligence shadows. The possible submarine contact is disturbing but I don't think the

SALTA is in our area. But this also highlights the lack of intelligence on Argentine submarine movements but it is difficult.

The BBC World Service continues to be an important and in some ways reassuring source of information for the Ship's Company. Despite Small speakers in each Mess they are huddling around the main receiver in the EMR/Amplifier Space on 3 deck as though they want to be as close to the actual information as they can. They sit on the ladder steps and the deck and as one leaves another takes his place.

Later in the day we heard that the Task Force have gone ahead with the strike on Port Stanley airfield but have no idea as yet if they have been successful.

Sunday 2nd May 1982 – Day 32

Argentine General Belgrano Sinking

<u>Falklands War Timeline</u>: *Argentine cruiser General Belgrano torpedoed and sunk by HMS Conqueror, killing more than 320 Argentine sailors – the single biggest loss of life in the war. Margaret Thatcher faces criticism over the sinking because the vessel was outside the 200-mile exclusion zone around the Falklands.*

We have spent the last few hours working our way into the Gulfo San Jorge and towards Deseado which is where the best intelligence has indicated we should go.

At 0630 we received a signal that indicated that the Argentine Carrier Group was heading southeast to attack the Task Force and thus there was little point in going to the Gulfo San Jorge. We have had a brief racket, possibly from the remains of the escorts so went deep for a couple of hours to close that area.

By 1800 we had received new area allocations and intelligence. It was becoming clear now that SPARTAN and SPLENDID were being positioned to try to stop any potential attack from mainland Argentina to the east and threaten the Task Force.

2300. We have detected what appears to be several ships to the southeast tracking to the west. From ELINT and sonar they look as though they are warships about 15000 yards away but I need to get closer and identify them if I can. I expect they are darkened and unfortunately the maintainers have been working on the Image Intensification system on the periscope. This system gives the ability to see in the dark – or at least gives you the capability to identify. I really need this at the moment but I don't think it is going to be available for a few hours yet.

After some more analysis it seems that these contacts could be the A69s a Type 42 and a heavy – perhaps a tanker. So we are closing but going deep at present to close. By 2300 the contacts were all continuing to the west/southwest and opening range and becoming fainter on sonar. These contacts are keeping quiet which means they are almost certainly warships.

We received a signal this evening confirming that HMS CONQUEROR had found, attacked and sunk the Argentine Cruiser GENERAL BELGRANO.

Well done Chris Wreford-Brown and team – a great achievement and the first time a nuclear submarine has sunk anything in anger.

I sent a signal to Chris congratulating him and although I am extremely professionally envious that he has done this I would just hope that I would have done it as professionally as he and his team clearly did. This has been great motivation for the SPLENDID Ship's Company and myself personally. We need to get a few breaks and find something to sink!

Monday 3rd May 1982 – Day 33

0100 Still have these contacts but I would really like to classify them with more confidence. So went deep and ran at 20 knots to close the range.

When we came back to periscope depth 90 minutes later there was no sign of them which means they may have turned around while we were at speed and sonar was less effective.

By 0700 we had searched north and east without contact. It could be that earlier on we were under ranging which may account for why we were unable to classify these contacts more precisely. More frustration but that is part and parcel of a submarine Captain's life.

1000 Received an intelligence report that they may have moved further southwest overnight when we thought they had turned back. So back to the southwest at speed for about three hours and towards Puerto Deseado.

After a few visits back to periscope depth during the move southwest by 2000 we were in contact with what sounds like a patrol vessel that seems to be patrolling north and south off Deseado at high speed. Not sure what it really is at present but will stay here for the moment and see how things develop.

We have also been told that the UK SSIX satellite communications broadcast will no longer be used but this does not affect us as we are reading all our traffic via the US/UK Bilateral SSIXS satellite. I am glad we are on that system which has been very good.

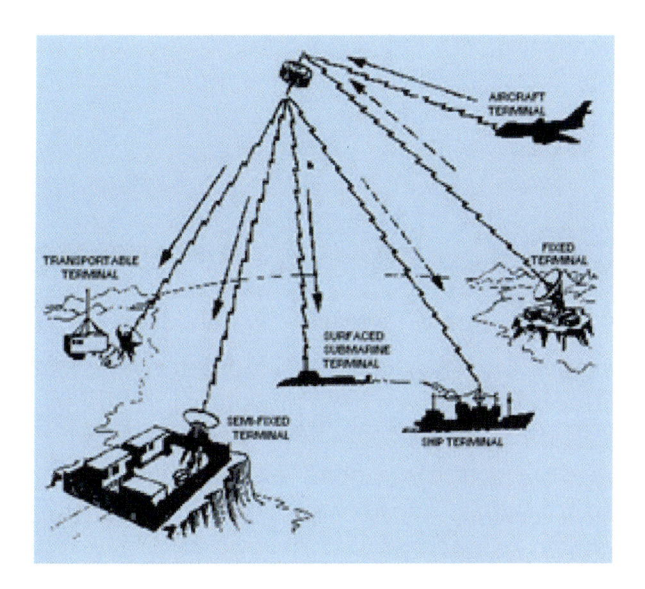

Satellite Communications

CHAPTER TWENTY-ONE
IS IT OUR TURN NOW?

Tuesday 4th May 1982 – Day 34

Falklands War Timeline: HMS SHEFFIELD hit by an Exocet missile and 20 men were killed.

The HMS SPLENDID Songbook is almost ready for publication and Chris Gillooly and Steve Hogg has put out a call to anyone who knows the words of "The Good Ship Venus" or "My Brother Sylvester" or any other suitable songs. The significance of these two are lost on me but it is clear that the songbook composition is proving a good diversion for some!

0300 Monitoring movements off Puerto Deseado and we now have 3 contacts on sonar but they are still too far away to obtain good characteristics or classify. I suspect that there may be some warships amongst them so I will stay in the deeper water about 8 miles from the Argentine twelve mile territorial waters – so I am about 20 miles from Puerto Deseado.

0700 At periscope depth and there are still numerous contacts off Puerto Deseado. This is not surprising as it is a port with some facilities. However, there is sufficient evidence to suggest that they may be warships. Ranging maneuvers indicate they may be outside the twelve mile limit.

0900 Still nothing visual but I now have no less than 6 contacts on sonar and there seems to be at least two A69s and possibly two Type 42s. At least four of them seem to be heading northwest towards Cabo Blanco. The question is now whether they are the escorts for the Carrier or not and where are they going. Sunrise is not until 1125 today – remember all the times I am providing are in GMT or Zulu time - So as I must visually identify any target before I can fire I will continue to trail them until I am in a position to identify them visually. But I will stay deep but outside the 30 fathom line until sunrise when we will close to identify and attack a selected target. It may be that they are forming into two groups but we will continue to look at all possibilities.

Ian Richards and I decide that we will go to Action Stations before returning to periscope depth at sunrise and be ready to attack. The Ship's Company have been kept informed and it is clear they are up for it. So much so that the reports on the intercom from the sound room, which we can all hear in the control room, have reached other parts of the boat. Somehow the manoeuvring room and the Engine Room have patched through the sonar reports so that they can hear them as well. There is intense interest and we also take the opportunity to check everything again – noise rounds, weapon readiness etc.

1030 'Officer of the Watch, go to Actions Stations' I order.

Ian leans over and whispers – 'No need sir, they are already there!' This simple fact gave me a boost and even more confidence that this was going to be our time.

The reports came in from all compartments thick and fast and within three minutes the Officer of the Watch Jeff Thomas reported that the submarine was at Actions Stations. We checked the various contacts yet again and by now we had fire control solutions on all of them but the procedure for returning to periscope depth is a well-worn path and it has to be done to return from deep to shallow safely.

We came to periscope depth and I was on the attack periscope as it broke surface and we steadied at 65 feet. It was just getting light as expected as I looked intently and did a quick all round look but could not believe my eyes. Visibility was about 6000 yards and there was NOTHING in sight! I was amazed as were the whole control room team. It seemed almost certain that we would have several ships in sight and this was a huge disappointment.

I now have no alternative but to close to the northwest and hope that the visibility will improve. Sonar tells me that we have two A69s and two Type 42s and the characteristics confirm that. The ranges vary from 13000 to 20000 yards and their courses still indicate a north westerly movement at varying speeds from 12 to 17 knots. I decide to close the distance off track and head for the deeper water to the northwest before turning and attacking.

A short burst deep at 20 knots and then back at periscope depth the visibility was poor – around 10000 yards in misty conditions and there was still nothing in sight. A further assessment and it seemed likely that all of these contacts were operating inside the twelve mile limit and therefore not available for attacking as yet. Not that it matters very much at the moment as I could not visually identify them in this visibility.

At 1200 I fell out Actions Stations with a warning that they may be required again at short notice. But 45 minutes later David Crothers on the search periscope saw what he thought was a possible warship to the south at 6000 yards.

Marine Engineering Artificer Jim Knight remembers:

'Another event, that will forever remain imprinted in my memory, was when we went to Action Stations for an attack on a group of vessels that included one of their Type 42s. Having just come off watch I was part of the damage control party and was standing by in the mess dressed in full breathing apparatus. The adrenalin was flowing and there was a mixture of excitement and anxiety amongst the party as we monitored the few scarps of information filtering down from the control room. I knew that Keith, as off watch planesman, had volunteered to be part of the "Action Reload" team in the bomb shop. After a while a "one all round (cigarette)" was authorised and Keith came up to the mess for a cuppa. Well, when he appeared before us dressed head to toe as a pirate, the tension in the mess immediately dissipated and we were able to relax a little. It was quite surreal, typical of the submariner's mentality and sense of humour I suppose!

Naturally we were all "up for it" and contemplated a successful attack, so it was disappointing not to have been allowed to sink something; it is interesting to note that today I can thank God that we didn't have to.

Ian went to the periscope to have a look but it was faint in the mist and immediately identified it as the FORMOSA which is a 12,762 ton cargo ship and could be classed as a blockade runner but was in essence a merchant ship and thus cannot be attacked. She was heading north at 11 knots.

Then a few minutes later we had another sonar contact as before exhibiting hydroplane and hydraulic noise and with a possible classification of the SALTA again. The analysis of this contact indicates that it may be as close as 15000 yards but I am not convinced but we do need to clear the area as quickly as possible just in case. I do not want to give him any opportunity if it is the SALTA. So we open to the northeast of Capo Blanco to cover any movement by the Argentine surface ships and clear away from the SALTA possibility.

1630 We came back to periscope depth having detected on sonar before coming up a contact that sounded like a large merchantmen but not the Carrier. It was identified visually as a very large tanker heading south close to the coast. This contact was at 20000 yards which has confirmed our thinking that sonar ranges are exceptional and are perhaps giving us detections that we think are closer than they actually are. It would seem that we have been severely under ranging in the last 24 hours and the contacts we held overnight may have been as much as 30000 yards from us which would have put them well inside the twelve mile limit and may explain why they were not detected visually.

2030. I am closing five sonar contacts to the southwest but all very faint and too little to classify and I think they are well into the twelve mile limit.

So this was another day of frustration. Sonar ranges have been so good today and we have been tracking numerous contacts well within the Argentine twelve mile limit. Cabo Blanco is, of course a choke point for coastal traffic from Deseado and Gulfo San Jorge. There is considerable evidence that some warships were around Deseado and it looks after further analysis onboard that they have probably come outside the twelve mile limit at some stage. Now by standing off to the east we should be better placed to detect the one that does try to do something out of the ordinary. I must not underestimate the effect of the sinking of the GENERAL BELGRANO would have had on the Argentine surface forces. If they were not clear before then now they certainly know that there are nuclear submarines around and they will be attacked. I think that is a key issue and should give me some advantage in the mind game stakes.

Wednesday 5th May 1982 – Day 35

0730 The latest intelligence report suggests that the warships held yesterday off Deseado have moved to the south towards the Bahia Grande, so I will move towards that area so that this option can be covered.

1230. We have picked up another sonar contact to the west that is exhibiting hydroplane noise, clicks and bangs and then ten minutes later rushing air, more clicks loud bangs and then a faint burst of diesel, compressed cavitation with harsh blade flutter. This looks like the possible submarine contact we had on 1st and 5th May. If it is the SALTA it may have been snorting but again there is no definitive classification although I pushed the sonar team hard to make one. They resisted my urge to make it something it may not have been.

We have now had faint contact with a possible submarine on four occasions. We have received an intelligence report that suggests that the SALTA may be patrolling off a naval base somewhere but this seems a strange use of a quiet submarine.

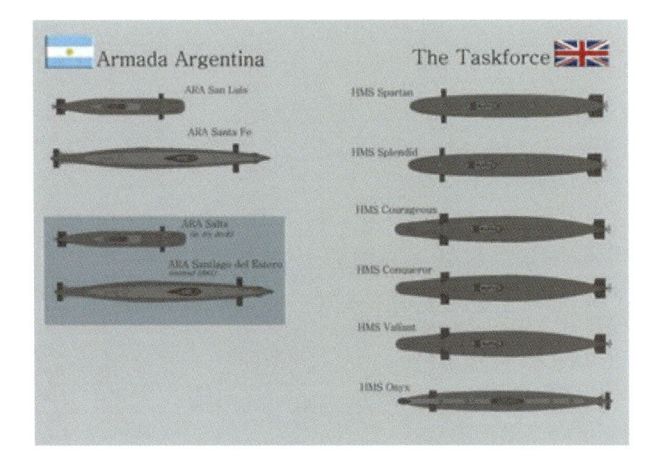

Armada Argentina	The Taskforce
ARA San Luis	HMS Spartan
ARA Santa Fe	HMS Splendid
ARA Salta (in re-refit)	HMS Courageous
ARA Santiago del Estero (non-op IMO)	HMS Conqueror
	HMS Valiant
	HMS Onyx

Maybe they have been tasked with protecting their ports or their surface ships but this has made me decide that I must have a weapon available to fire. So we are withdrawing the Mk8 from 3 tube and replacing it with a Mk 24 Tigerfish. If we get this contact again we will fire at it. On further analysis and reflection I now think that the contact we had at 120 was almost certainly a submarine but once again at very long range – maybe 15-16000 yards – perhaps even further. We reported this contact in detail at 1500.

We continued south towards the southern edge of our allocated area and at 2100 received new areas and we have been cleared to go down to the Santa Cruz area and continue our search for surface targets.

We have also been told today that HMS SHEFFIELD was attacked yesterday by Exocet missiles from an Argentine A4 Skyhawk and subsequently sunk with the loss of 20 men.

This is a real blow and has hit the Ships' Company hard and there is a sombre mood in the boat this evening. If they had not realised before they certainly know now that this is a real hot war. We have also lost the first harrier over Goose Green.

CHAPTER TWENTY-TWO

DEFECTS AND THEIR RECTIFICATION

Thursday 6th May 1982 – Day 36

0200 The Port TG Exciter is sparking badly and has been shut down for cleaning and further investigation/maintenance. We will stay where we are until it is fixed.

0900 A sitrep received from Northwood indicates that it seems likely that the Carrier was in the vicinity of Cabo Blanco inside the twelve mile limit but nobody seems to know where it is now.

This is getting increasingly difficult as we can't seem to get any definitive intelligence on this key unit and it would now seem that despite all the possibilities that it may be that the Argentinean have decided to keep it inside the twelve mile limit. I must not, of course, assume that. I must work on the principle that it will try to move towards the Falkland Islands in order to better launch aircraft to attack our Task Force.

We also have a report that the COMODOR PY was off Bahia Grande early morning and is now off Bahia Engano which would make it the fastest surface ship in the world!

The view from Northwood seems to be that the Carrier is up to the north of us and as a result SPARTAN is being stationed slightly further north in her area.

But our main issue at the moment is the Port TG and I need to retire to a quiet area to the east behind HMS SPARTAN to try to carry out repairs. I will also take this opportunity to deal with steam leaks on a couple of major valves. This will mean that we will have to snort and run the diesel at periscope depth while these repairs are carried out. Snorting is a noisy activity for any submarine and certainly in a war situation.

I held a Head of Department's meeting and discuss what we are going to do and what other precautions we need to take. I also reported these defects Northwood and have been given a water allocation for a transit further east and our own Total Exclusion Zone. SPARTAN is clearing out of our way to the north.

Friday 7th May 1982 – Day 37

Falklands War Timeline: On 7 May 1982, the Total Exclusion Zone was extended to within 12 nautical miles of the Argentine coast, meaning that any Argentine vessel or aircraft world-wide was liable to be attacked.

By the evening we had moved further to the east and work was still progressing on the Port TG but the armature is still not working correctly. After some discussion I agreed with John Davis's advice that we should rebuild the exciter and seek further advice from the MOD in Bath.

We have had no contacts on any sensor all day.

Saturday 8th May 1982 – Day 38

Still working on the repairs. In order to keep the steam pressure down on the two leaks means that we have to remain in the Half Power State. As this state infers it restricts us to half the power available from the propulsion plant and means that we are restricted if we need full speed for any reason.

It would seem from intelligence reports today that virtually all the Argentine Navy is off Puerto Belgrano well up to the North. No action has been reported for few days now except for an Argentine claim that it had attacked a British submarine yesterday. None of us were within at least 100 miles.

1400 Our areas have changed slightly and this has meant a reverse in course and a lane has been allocated taking us east along 48° South to 35° West. We have decided that it would be best to surface for the repairs despite the potential issues involved. I do not like this but it should speed up the ability to do the repairs. We will run the diesel so that the Starboard TG and secondary loop can be shut down for the steam leak repairs. The weather is clear and the sea state is only 1 foot with 30% cloud cover. Not ideal but we will have to live with it.

The alarming advice from the manufacturers of the Port TG (Lawrence Scott) is to skim (machine) the armature by about ¾ inch and try again. A spare is also being flown out but I am not sure how we are going to receive that.

Sunday 9th May 1982 – Day 39

1200 Conducted a one hours snort at periscope depth to test out the diesel and make sure that everything was working well before we surface tonight. The amended snort muffler procedure which is the result of a defect found on Day 2 worked well.

This also allowed us to have a good blow through the boat with fresh air which has given the atmosphere a new lease of life.

1930 I ordered 'Officer of the Watch, Stand By to surface.

We went through the process of preparing to open up and had a full watch on all sensors including the periscopes to augment the Officer of the Watch on the bridge together with ELINT, COMINT and sonar although this would be degraded on the surface.

I decided that we only wanted an Officer of the Watch and two lookouts on the bridge and Ian Richards made sure that Tiny Holmes who was going to be on the bridge was absolutely clear what he should do if a surface ship or aircraft was detected.

2000. At sunset we surfaced and started the diesel and prepared to change over the electrical loads. There were no contacts on any sensor.

The Ship's Company had made a Soviet ensign flag so that if any Argentinean aircraft came along they would think we were a Soviet. It wasn't appropriate but it amused the Ship's Company so I allowed the Soviet ensign to be taken to the bridge attached to a mop handle to be used if required.

2200 The attempt to repair the steam leaks in single steam generator mode with singe loop recovery had to be stopped when the motor generator loading became too high and essential electrical supplies were at risk. This is deeply disappointing and we will have to write a new procedure to try again. So the steam leak repairs have been delayed for the moment.

Unfortunately the Ship's Inertial Navigation System (SINS) has dropped off due to a sudden voltage surge during electrical changeovers and will now take some time to sort out including an at sea restart which is never ideal. I had come to rely on SINS a great deal and it had performed admirably and provided a very good positional information in open ocean and was constantly confirmed by satellite navigation fixes to be within 1.5 miles at maximum error.

The upside of the period on the surface has been the chance to ditch gash (cardboard in particular – all weighed down), clean the periscope windows and Wireless mast insulators and check the fin for noise shorts and the casing for any similar problems. There are none which is good news.

At 0300 we were still on the surface and have a new defect on the after planes emergency air changeover valve and will have to delay diving again until this is fixed. It took all night to deal with the various engineering sags that were thrown at us and it was not until 0900 that we were able to dive again.

That was an uncomfortable night. No submariner likes to be on the surface when the natural place for a submarine is below the surface. It would only have taken a chance encounter with an Argentine aircraft or surface unit and I would have had to scramble beneath the waves as quickly as possible. The sea might be vast, but it happens.

Monday 10th May 1982 – Day 40

We have told Northwood that the best area for transfer of a new TG would be off South Georgia and it seems that Northwood agrees.

The Port TG repair is a complex one. To skim ¾ inch off the armature is a big task to do at sea. The problem is that the lathe we have on board was designed for small items and not for an armature that is about 18 inches in diameter. The armature would not fit into the lathe even if we could move it there bearing in mind its weight. So John Davis and his team came up with an ingenious idea of taken the cutters in the lathe and rigging them inside the TG and skim the armature in place by putting steam on the TG. The problem will be that the normal speed of the TG is around 2500 rpm which means that accuracy of cut will be very difficult. So the 'jury rig' inside the TG would need to be carefully constructed so that the depth of cut on the copper armature could be controlled and the speed of turn of the TG be kept to as low a speed that was possible conducive with achieving the right result. It will take a while to manufacture the appropriate rig. The steam leaks have not deteriorated thank goodness and SINS is being restarted. The problem is that to restart SINS we need to be stable and slow while steam leaks prefer more speed to reduce the pressure.

At 2300 we went to deep and stopped and caught a stopped trim [i.e. achieving neutral buoyancy at zero speed] and we stayed in that state for approximately 5 hours to allow SINS to settle on start up.

Today has been difficult and is not what we want to be doing. We have to keep going and we have to fix these defects. I have every confidence in the engineering team and we are seeing a real togetherness and will to deliver amongst them all. John Davis is a rock and is always exuding optimism and confidence despite the setbacks. I sense that he is in his element – despite what engineers say they don't really like everything working correctly as they always need some taxing engineering problem to solve.

Tuesday 11th May 1982 – Day 41

0400. SINS seems to be working satisfactorily but we will not know for sure until we have had a series of fixes to compare. We broke the stopped trim which had been held extremely well by the Ship Control team and came back up to periscope depth for a fix and broadcast routine. It was very strange to be stopped for so long when we had been in perpetual motion since we left Faslane.

Preparation work on the Port TG continues. We have been told that its replacement is now in the MV STENA SEASPREAD and should arrive off South Georgia on Friday 14th May. HMS ENDURANCE is making arrangements for the transfer. For the moment we have been told to remain in the vicinity of our present area. This is probably so we can be redirected to the northwest if the military situation dictates.

It seems that HMS FEARLESS and HMS INTREPID the two assault ships are about 1200 miles away.

In the meantime SPLENDID is "loitering" as we endeavour to repair the Port TG and settle SINS. Work on preparing the machining rig for the Port TG is taking longer than expected but it is very complicated and risky. The aim is to start machining tonight.

Wednesday 12th May 1982 – Day 42

Falklands War Timeline: *The HMS HERMES/HMS INVINCIBLE Task Group are northeast of Port Stanley inside the TEZ. RFA REGENT, MV UGANDA (Hospital ship) and MV British ESK will join them today. The Fifth Army Brigade sailed from Southampton on the Queen Elizabeth 2. HMS Glasgow disabled by an Argentine bomb.*

A quiet day awaiting developments on the Port TG but we have managed a number of fixes today and SINS is looking good which is a relief. The work on the Port TG got underway tonight and the skimming has gone satisfactorily although I think it was pretty scary for the engineering team. At least the rig worked even if the skimming took place at high revs.

Thursday 13th May 1982 – Day 43

0300 The Port TG is looking good but intend to allow a further 24 hours for cutting back the mica and setting up for a further test tomorrow. Then hopefully we can repair the steam leaks and get back into the action. This is not what we should be doing and we are all frustrated that we are not involved at present.

0800. Received more intelligence and it is clear that we are wanted back on task as soon as possible as we are being allocated water away from South Georgia and it is obvious that any replacement TG Exciter will not be dropped for some time yet.

1300. Received a new Rule of Engagement which includes any ship or fishing vessel which may be engaged in resupply of the Falklands. If this had been in force earlier we could have attacked the COMMODORO PY but such is life!

We also intercepted Spanish voice on HF and the frequency but could not get a bearing. It was the same as that intercepted by HMS GLASGOW a few minutes later and is thought to be the SAN LUIS calling her base. But we have no real idea where she is or indeed if it is the SAN LUIS.

2100. Being moved back to the Cabo Blanco area again south of the Falkland Islands. The Port TG work is still progressing but there are still a few hours of work to be completed before it can be fully tested and loaded. Hopefully tomorrow morning we will be able to progress the steam leak repairs and maintenance of the Starboard TG. The operational requirement is for us to get back to Capo Blanco as soon as we can.

Friday 14th May 1982 – Day 44

Falklands War Timeline: The SAS have attacked Argentine forces on Pebble Island, a remote spot on the north coast of West Falkland, leaving six Argentine ground- attack Pucara aircraft destroyed on the airstrip. These were viewed as a major threat to a British landing.

The weather is not good today. It is very rough and overcast and the wind is around 25 knots from the northeast with a 12 foot sea and visibility of 8000 yards maximum. The Port TG has now been fully tested with the reactor plant in the Full Power State. The engineering team have done extremely well in trying conditions.

We now have to slowly shut down the starboard side in preparation for the steam leak repairs. These are the sort of things you have to deal with in a nuclear submarine. Despite being the most complex machine in the world – more so than the Space Shuttle or any other space craft there will always be defects. It is the training and determination to fix things regardless of the conditions that matter and ensure that the boat is ready for anything at any time.

1900 The steam leaks and maintenance of the Starboard TG are now complete. So now we have to snort and run the diesel to support the battery as we will have to conduct a Full Scram of the reactor and a fast recovery to get back into double loop again. The reactor provides pressurised hot water to two steam generators in the reactor compartment. Each one is in a separate loop so that you can operate in single loop – i.e. one steam generator or double loop – i.e. two steam generators.

Single loop does have a speed restriction as you can only provide half the amount of steam as in double loop. Sounds complicated but if you look at the nuclear plant diagram it will become clear. This is not going to be easy!

Pressurized-water Naval Nuclear Propulsion System

The weather has deteriorated further with the wind at 30 knots and a very rough sea from the northwest now at 20 feet. A full scale raging South Atlantic gale.

2000. We have started snorting four times in the last hour but it is becoming increasingly difficult to maintain the snort in such violent weather conditions. Depth keeping at periscope depth has been very difficult indeed and the snort induction mast which has a large float valve at the top has been immersed in water for periods which has resulted in the valve shutting for longer than we want. This means that the air coming into the submarine is severely restricted and with the amended snort muffler problem we have had since the Irish Sea has made it very difficult indeed and I have come to the conclusion that this is not going to work.

I discuss the situation with John Davis and Ian Richards and although we don't like it we are going to have to do the scram deep and hope there is enough in the battery to allow us to recover. In a normal situation there should not be enough in the battery to recover from a Full Scram without running the diesel to support the battery. But there is no option and we have to do it.

I ask John Davis to make the fast recovery after the Full Scram to be as efficient as possible as we will need to cut every corner possible to get the reactor critical and become self-sustaining again before the battery is flat!

Not a pleasant thought and a flat battery means we would be left with no option but to surface – not a pleasant thought in this weather - and re charge the battery and use some of that power to maintain essential electrical supplies. We would not be knocked over, but the submarine would roll and pitch violently and could be very unpleasant indeed.

Reluctantly I give the go ahead and start by reducing the electrical load to the minimum possible and then at 1940 we Full Scram. Fast recovery from a Partial Scram at sea is the normal procedure and this takes around 35 minutes. From a Full Scram this will take longer but we don't know how long. This will be a close thing and I am very apprehensive and nervous about this option. If this goes wrong we will be left with no electrical power and thus no way of running the numerous life supporting machines in the submarine. And, without the reactor being critical, we could not boil feed water and produce steam for the main engines and we would have no propulsion. We would be left wallowing on the surface with possibly no chance of having enough power to transmit for help. The consequences of failure are more severe and the more I think about it – and I couldn't think of anything else – the more I worried.

Then at 2010 to my amazement came the report that the reactor is critical again and I don't want to ask how we did that in 30 minutes. I sigh in partial relief and it takes another 30 minutes to get into double main engine drive again and the turbo generators producing electricity. And by 2100 all systems are restored.

I wait until John Davis comes back into the Control Room and hear his report and tell him that he and his team have done a great job. I do back to the manoeuvring room with John to tell the team back aft personally how well they have done. This is celebrated by a cup of back aft tea – which will beat any builder's tea anytime – and I spend around 15 minutes hearing how they did it and what a close run thing it was.

I ask if anyone knows the battery percentage and I am told that a reading is being taken as I speak. Two minutes later one of the team comes into the manoeuvring room and says that there is 4% left in the battery! That was a close run thing but worth the risk in the face of a very difficult situation. I go back to my cabin again and reflect on the severity of that situation and have only complete relief that we got through it.

The inability to hold the snort earlier has resulted in the boat being full of Carbon Monoxide (CO) and we will need to ventilate soon to get rid of it later this evening.

2250. We return to periscope depth and drain down the snort system again to allow fresh air into the submarine. We run fans and the LP blower – which is a very noisy machine – to suck out the air blow it into the ballast tanks. This is a slightly unusual procedure but it does the trick and by midnight we are back deep again to get away from the weather and conduct a careful sonar search. There were no contacts at periscope depth on any sensor but we did get a fix to confirm the settling of SINS and receive the broadcast.

We have been told to go to an area south of the Falklands – where CONQUEROR sank the GENERAL BELGRANO – and have been told that two frigates the HIPOLITO BOUCHARD and the PIEDRA BUENA – both ex US destroyers - are reported to have left Ushuaia yesterday.

This has been a very satisfying - if somewhat scary – and very successful engineering day and we can now head back to the action.

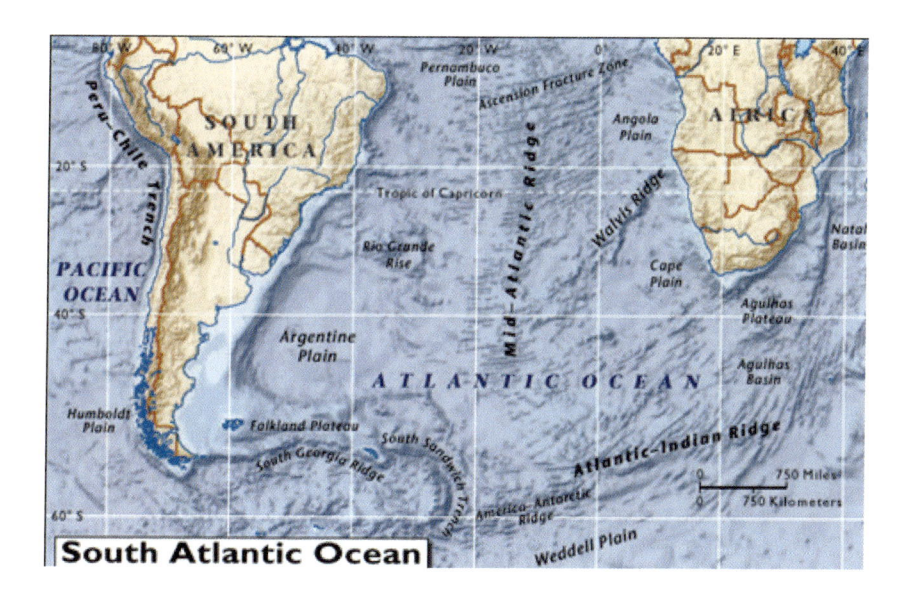

Royal Marines Yomping

Argentine Prisoners of War

CHAPTER TWENTY-THREE

BACK TO THE FRAY

Saturday 15th May 1982 – Day 45

0600. Continuing west at best speed in the ¾ power state heading for our new area south of the Falklands. It seems that HMS VALIANT under the command of Commander Tom Le Marchand has joined us now and with HMS SPARTAN and HMS CONQUEROR are all north of me patrolling between Puerto Belgrano and the Falklands. We are close to the TEZ south of the Falklands.

The transit to the west has continued but our original orders to going back to Deseado seems to have been cancelled and it looks as though we will now be covering the units at Ushuaia which currently intelligence indicates are HIPOLITO BOUCHARD, PIEDRA BUENA and the hospital ship BAHIA PARISO.

1200 We have now received a clear view of the area allocations for the four UK nuclear submarines and we have been provided with the code names for Argentine radars which is useful and the broad plan for re-invasion. It would seem from both reports from Northwood and the BBC World Service that the Argentine units on the Falkland Islands are very concerned about their plight and what is going to happen. The Type 42's and the A69s are still of Puerto Belgrano and not coming outside the twelve mile limit – I wonder whether they will again. I suppose it all depends on what the Carrier does.

Sunday 16th May 1982 – Day 46

0800 We are now patrolling South of the Falklands on the edge of the TEZ and are in a good position between Ushuaia and the Task Force to intercept anything that comes our way. The Ships Company are in good form but really want to get involved.

1600 Received a good update on the broadcast. There is a faint possibility that the Carrier is in Bahia Grande off Rio Gallegos so decided to head off to that area at best speed while we are still in deep water. It seems that water allocations will be changing again soon.

However, the reality is that there has been no positive intelligence as to the Carriers whereabouts for nearly two weeks. I find that very disappointing as I would have thought we would have found some way to get better information. If the Argentineans wanted us to believe that the Carrier was at Puerto Belgrano, so that any SSNs would be biased in that direction, then they have achieved their aim. The Carrier at Bahia Grande is well placed for shore based air support from Gallegos and Rio Grande air bases.

For some reason I have become concerned again about a possible Argentinean diesel boat threat in the area to the west of where intelligence thinks the Carrier may be and so I have opened 3 tube bowcap with a Tigerfish inside just in case.

By 2200 we had crossed the 100 fathom line and were approaching shallower water again tracking northwest towards the Carrier area of probability.

Monday 17th May 1982 – Day 47

0230 Several contacts have been detected to the north with loud banging but they do not sound like ship contacts. They sound like wellheads, buoys or bio or a combination of all three but we have no knowledge of oil exploration in that area.

We spent the day moving from deep to periscope depth to try to maximize long range detection but not miss any new intelligence coming over the broadcast.

By 1700 we were closing on the 30 fathom (180 feet) line and intend patrolling along that line. I am keen to have a good visual search before sunset at 2040.

At 2038 sonar detected a contact to the north which had one shaft five blades and was classified as a medium merchantman. By 2110 we had him visual at 13000 yards and he was tracking south east at 16 knots. Unfortunately we cannot attack as he is clearly not a blockade runner at the moment so we will track him to make sure he continues south and does not turn east for the Falklands.

After spending some hours evaluating some extraordinary noises which we eventually decided were biological, we have searched the datum for possible Carrier operations and have also patrolled within 30 miles of Gallegos. We have identified the merchantman as probably the BAO DE HORNOS and unless he turns east into the TEZ we cannot attack him.

Tuesday 18th May 1982 – Day 48

By 0100 we had watched the merchantman continue south and I decided we should move north again to search the Bahia Grande area. By 0600 we had become convinced that the Carrier was not operating in the Bahia Grande area and so will move a little further east to the edge of the TEZ.

1600 We have spent all day at periscope depth and had a lot of problems with SSIXS satellite communications. It looks as if these issues are at the shore side end not ours. By 1800 everything was back to normal but there was still no sign of the Carrier. I will continue the search moving slowly south to cover the southwest approaches to the Falklands.

Wednesday 19th May 1982 – Day 49

Falklands War Timeline: 22 British servicemen killed when helicopter transporting SAS soldiers ditches in the sea.

0200. The banging noises which have been annoying us over the last couple of days are continuing and certainly affecting sonar detection as they produce significant background noise. I think we have convinced ourselves that they are a combination of wellheads and biological but we do not really know.

1500 Still nothing and it looks as though there are going to be more area changes soon. It is difficult to get an overall picture of what is planned but I suspect that we will re-invade soon. Where and when

I have no idea.

We have had some rackets today which indicate aircraft activity but at 2100 we had a succession of dangerous rackets which was a possible AN/APS 88. AN/APS-88 is a light weight derivative of earlier AN/APS-80 with more compact size for smaller aircraft such as Grumman S-2 Tracker. But we can find no indication that the Argentineans have this. However, it does not make sense to stay in this area. I do not think we have been detected but it is better to move away just in case.

This was another day of searching but no surface warship contacts have been detected. There was clearly an aircraft close by presumably on a reconnaissance patrol. I intend to head slowly south and search out the western edge of the TEZ.

The latest UK/Argentinean proposals seem to at deadlock so one assumes that re- invasion is likely soon. There has been much speculation as to where it will be with Senior and Junior rates crawling over charts and starting a sweepstake on where it will be.

Thursday 20th May 1982 – Day 50

It does not seem like 50 days but it has gone quickly.

It looks as though we will be pulled off at some stage and return for a short maintenance period and personnel change before sailing again for another patrol. The planning for this has already started. Meanwhile in the real world we have moved now to patrol on the south western edge of the TEZ covering the approaches from Ushuaia.

1400 We have received a signal which gives us a firm steer to try to intercept BOUCHARD who is believed to be leaving Ushuaia and heading for Rio Grande to act as a radar picket. [A radar picket is a radar equipped ship, aircraft or submarine used to increase the detection range around a task force or collection of units to provide early warning from attack. Destroyers were used traditionally with specialist high power long range radar but any unit can do the task if it is suitably located and has appropriate radar equipment].Intend going south west as quickly as possible and then searching at periscope depth some 15 to 20 miles off the coast. The landing has the go-ahead for tonight so tomorrow may bring some reaction and we must remain fully alert.

1800 We have a serious problem with the WT Wireless Mast. The insulation on the mast has reached an all-time low and makes the mast almost useless. Hopefully a good drying out using desiccation will get it back up again. At present we can only receive UHF for Satellite navigation and communications on the stub aerial [called AVS] on the search periscope but cannot transmit UHF. I will go a little further north to dry the mast out and as the weather is very bad we are not getting much here anyway.

2300 The landing gets underway very shortly and we all wish them very luck in the world. My main concern is still the WT mast but I hope we can sort this out overnight.

CHAPTER TWENTY-FOUR

RE-INVASION STARTS

Friday 21st May 1982 – Day 51

Falklands War Timeline: First British landings begin at San Carlos Bay on East Falkland with 3000 men from the Royal Marines and Parachute Regiment along with commando artillery and engineer units and 1000 tons of supplies. HMS Ardent is sunk by Argentine aircraft, killing 22 sailors. HMS Argonaut and HMS Antrim are hit by Argentine bombs that fail to explode and two sailors are killed. Fifteen Argentine aircraft are shot down.

0200 We are off Rio Grande as BOUCHARD is believed to be operating in this area as a radar picket. We managed to send a sitrep on the WT mast and it seems that desiccation has worked which is good news.

1200 There does not seem to be anything here and no contacts were gained overnight. Intend getting closer to the 30 fathom line and see if there is any air activity as well as surface units.

1622 Land visual – the first we have seen for 50 days!

1745 The OOW called me to the control room as he had seen a helicopter through the periscope. I took the search periscope and quickly scanned the horizon and saw the helicopter tracking north to southwest at a range of 12000 yards. It looks like a lynx or a Puma from this distance and we also have I band radar but there is no certainty that it is the helicopter transmitting. It does not seem to have detected me and we will monitor until it is over the horizon. We may well be required to provide aircraft early warning in the next few days. I hand the periscope back to the OOW with instructions to watch the helicopter over the horizon but to keep a good lookout for anything else that might appear as he may not be alone.

1830 The OOW reported that the helicopter was now out of sight but decided to stay at periscope depth and continue an all sensor search. There is still no sign of any warships and I am beginning to wonder whether the sinking of the BELGRANO by HMS CONQUEROR has frightened the Argentine Navy back into port or at least inside their own twelve mile limit. 67497

We do have a very annoying defect as we have lost the ability to receive satellite communications on the search periscope as it appears that we transmitted through that AVS aerial by mistake and that has killed off the ability to receive as the UHF section of the AVS is now dead. It is unfortunate but investigation indicates that this was done in error. We will have to rely on the WT Wireless mast now.

2200 Receiving good information that the landings are going well although it would appear that the Royal Navy surface ships in the Falkland Sound around San Carlos are being hit quite hard. We do not have too many details yet but it looks as though HMS ARDENT has been hit and may be sinking. This is depressing news and it indicates that there is plenty of fight left in the Argentine Air Force even if their Navy does not seem to want to fight. This is a crucial part of the campaign and it may prove to be very difficult and we need to be braced for more casualties.

Saturday 22nd May 1982 – Day 52

Cup Final Day at Wembley Stadium in UK. It was between Tottenham Hotspur and Queens Park Rangers. Spurs were the holders of the Cup and hot favourites while QPR had just missed out on promotion from the Second Division.

After three and a half hours of football Spurs ran out as winners 1-0 in a replay with a Glen Hoddle penalty.

Tottenham's Argentinean player Ricky Villa refused to play in the final because of the ongoing Falklands War.

0700 I have been up most of the night doing a covert infiltration close to the Argentine Air base at Rio Grande and a bay close by where the Carrier was supposed to be operating but there was nothing there.

2215 Went deep for about 4 hours to do some minor repairs and continuing to move back towards RIO GRANDE to look for any sign of surface units.

0300 At periscope depth and detected several I band radars that were classified as AN/APN 59 which are usually fitted to C130 Hercules transport aircraft. Nothing in sight though.

0600 We can now see clearly lights on and around the approaches to Bahia San Sebastian and we have some sonar contacts but nothing of interest or suggesting warships. We will stay at periscope depth and continue to search just outside the twelve mile limit. This is another example of the patience required as a submarine captain waiting and looking hoping that something will come your way.

Now that the landings are underway there has been a reduction in the intelligence on Argentine naval units and, I suppose, the emphasis has changed to the land battle and trying to get the troops and their equipment ashore and then support them there.

1300 We now have firm instructions to get down to the Isle De Los Estados area and look for what is dubbed "the Argentine Rapid Launch Squadron." This is supposed to consist of INDOMITA and INTREPEDA, which are 280 ton fast attack craft with Exocet missiles and a gun but no real anti-submarine capability, and BOUCHARD. BOUCHARD was the ex- USS BORIE – an Allen M Sumner Class destroyer. [We found out later that she had been the escort to the GENERAL BELGRANO and had been hit by one of HMS CONQUEROR's torpedoes when she sank the GENERAL BELGRANO but it failed to detonate.]

I have suggested to Northwood that SPLENDID would be best employed so that the approaches from the west and southwest can be covered and with more water to the east I will be able to respond with speed in a faster manner. It is not often one "tells" one's Commander where one wishes to go. If you say "Intend" they know that you are going to do it and if they do not agree they will tell you. I prefer that option but with limited intelligence information, and I suspect they are in the same position, I thought that a suggestion from a "man on the ground" might be considered useful.

It is not clear what Northwood expects this Rapid Launch Squadron to do but there is obviously nervousness that they may close the Royal Navy Task Force and attack. I think that is unlikely but then we just do not know. I decide to stay at periscope depth although the visibility is only 8000 yards and the weather is dull overcast and raining.

HMS SHEFFIELD having been hit by an Exocet Missile. She later sunk

RFA Sir Galahad on fire

CHAPTER TWENTY-FIVE

BEING BOMBED!

Sunday 23rd May 1982 – Day 53

Falklands War Timeline: HMS ANTELOPE is hit by an Argentine bomb which fails to explode. One crewman dies and 10 Argentine aircraft are shot down.

After a night spending time searching both deep and at periscope depth there is still no contact on anything. We have had some low frequency noise to the east but no firm contact.

It is Sunday again although no one really seems to notice. That is until we have the usual church service and the congregation has swelled by 75%! There is something about sailors and religion that is difficult to understand. Many are religious but don't wish to show it outwardly but when times are difficult they seem to want be involved.

Having received a few more signals from Northwood there was no follow up on my change of area suggestion but by 1300 I had started to move north again away from the Isle De Los Estados area where there is no activity towards the likely transit routes from the west to the Falkland Islands. By 1700 after a quick dash I had set up patrol across the most likely transit routes.

1830 I was in my cabin when there were 4 VERY large explosions in a couple of seconds and I heard them on the Underwater Telephone sonar set which is on loudspeaker all the time in the control room. The boat shook and bounced and some alarms went off. "Bloody hell" I thought as I flew into the control room and tried to establish what on earth was going on. Was this a collision? Had we hit something?

We were at periscope depth and Chris Kalman the Doctor was on the periscope but yelled that he could see nothing. I demanded a bearing from the Sound Room but they did not have one. The OOW on ship control was Toby Spreckley and he was already asking all compartments to report. People started to appear in the Control

Room as though they were anticipating Actions Stations.

I took the periscope and scanned the surface – nothing and then the sky. And then I saw a Skyhawk fighter crossing my scope at a lateral range of about 1000 yards and clearly making for his home base. As he was in my scope and I was reporting to the rest of the control room what I was seeing I saw a large bomb drop from under the aircraft's belly and fall towards the sea. I waited for the splash and heard that on underwater telephone but there was no bang – that was one that would not have worked. There was very minor superficial damage to SPLENDID but it was a huge shock and we had not anticipated being on the track of Argentinean Skyhawks returning to base and more to the point dropping their unused bombs. They were clearly unhappy to land with them and I don't blame them.

After a few minutes discussing with Ian Richards we decided that we had better leave this area and we can monitor what is going on at Gallegos and Rio Grande without being in harm's way. Paul Slemon the Deputy Weapons Engineer Officer remembers that 'when the Argentine Air Force were jettisoning their bombs on the way back to base (to increase fuel consumption), thinking how ironic it would have been if they had accidently sunk a nuclear submarine which was on their flight path. Random, extremely loud explosions certainly gave our sonar operators a number of very frightening moments - in one case a very junior rating had to be relieved of his duties.'

Within an hour we were several miles off track of the returning Skyhawks and had been deep for most of that time moving off track.I came back to periscope depth and there was still nothing visual or on any other sensor but we did receive an intelligence signal which indicated that there was a possibility of trade for us from the west. Is this another wild goose chase or is it based on substantial intelligence. I suspect it could be both but I understand how difficult it is to make accurate assessments without first had knowledge from in theatre. That is why any report we make helps to build the overall picture. I do not know where or how this intelligence is being received or assessed and adequate weight put on it but I suspect we are groping in the dark at all levels.

Having searched our area north of Isle de los Estados and moved north to cover the most likely routes from the West and South towards the Southern entrance to the Falklands Sound we had detected nothing. The bomb ditching to the north caused some consternation but the reported possibility of some Argentine units moving east from the Rio Grande area has confirmed our assessment of the best area in which to patrol. We have also heard that the four loud explosions were also heard by VALIANT in an area to the north and west of us and they came to the same conclusion as we did. This may happen again.

Monday 24th May 1982 – Day 54

Falklands War Timeline: Frigate HMS Antelope abandoned after bomb detonates while being defused by disposal officer. 'Sir Lancelot' and 'Sir Galahad' hit but the bombs failed to explode.

The worst news today was the report that HMS ANTELOPE had been sunk. This was very distressing news but particularly so for Ian Richards who had served in that ship as the Navigating Officer and had a special affection for it. He also knew many of those who were still on board. There were no details of course but this hit him hard and it did the Ships' Company too as we had now lost two frigates in as many days.

This was really a hot war even if the heat did not seem to be in our area at the moment.

On a lighter note today is Lieutenant Jeff Thomas's 24th birthday and we are straddling the routes between Rio Grande and Ushuaia to the Falklands Sound.

The weather is clear and dry and visibility is 12000 yards so we have every chance of seeing anything within range.

1030 We have a couple of contacts which are at long range and are probably biological as they have no ship or submarine characteristics.

I decide to stay at 190 feet which seems to be the best depth for the sonar conditions.

At 1300 the Leading Seaman Nick Slide in the Sound Room reported 'Possible submarine contact Bearing 100. Plane noise and rythmic bio on the bearing.' I was in my cabin at my desk considering and reconsidering the intelligence, my assessments from the last 53 days and looking at my options. My one big fear was being detected by an Argentine diesel submarine before I detected him. The balance was in his favour as a well handled diesel boat is much quieter than a nuclear boat and has comparable sonar capability compared to the submarine's internal noise. By that I mean that a diesel boat makes very little noise at all on electric motors while a nuclear submarine has main engine turbines and turbo generators that will always make some noise.

I ordered the OOW in the Control room – Jimmy Fergusson – to go to the search quiet state and slow to 4 knots but he was already doing it when I was giving my order. I went along to the Sound Room and asked what they had on this contact. Ian Richards was right by my side and asked 'Any more characteristics?'

Nick Slide replied 'there is plenty of plane noise and it "sounds" like a submarine. Petty Officer Danny Fisher agreed saying 'it sounds just like a submarine.' A Commanding Officer who has such experienced and knowledgeable sonar operators will be wise to listen to their views and I always do – I may not like their answer but I have to believe it – after all they are the ones listening and analysing the waterfall displays.

Ian and I retreated back to the control room where Jimmy reported that the submarine was in the search quiet state. I looked at the Tactical displays and the bearing was drawing slowly left and the computer was doing bearings only analysis (after all that is all you really have – a bearing) and the target solution was computing as Bearing 089 Course 240° speed 4 knots.

This contact was showing all the characteristics seen previously and this time I will fire at it. The intelligence picture has indicated that an Argentine submarine may have been south east of the Falklands and another in South Falkland Sound.

1327 'OOW Go to Actions Stations remain in the search quiet state.'

Jimmy Fergusson made the pipe and I could hear the shuffling below me on 2 deck as people moved quickly but quietly to their posts. Within four minutes Jimmy reported to me that the 'Submarine is at

Action Stations.'

I sat in my Captain's chair in the control room and concentrated on the Tactical displays and listening to the verbal reports coming in from the Sound room. 'Any more classification details?' I asked and the reply came back 'Same as before – just plane noise and a background hum.'

The bowcap to 3 tube was open and I had a Tigerfish anti-submarine weapons loaded and ready. But the Tactical Display computers were giving me a range of over 25000 yards which was not good enough to fire and the characteristics were not strong enough or consistent. I had expected the classification to improve as we became quieter and more focused but this did not happen. I decided to go to periscope depth to see if I had any better luck there and went up slowly without changing speed. As expected there was nothing in sight and no rackets but the sonar conditions immediately resulted in the loss of the contact so I went deep again and turned towards the target to a course of 330° to produce a 90° track to the best computed course of 240°. But the contact was only intermittent and it became clear that if this was a submarine it was a long way away.

I went back to the Sound Room and Danny Fisher and Roger Crafts were going over the tapes again. I waited a minute and then Roger took off his headphones and said to me 'I am afraid there is not enough to classify this definitely as a submarine. Sorry Sir.'

'That's alright Danny' I replied and said 'Let's keep with it for a little longer and I will fall out Action Stations in 5 minutes time.'

1347 I waited 10 minutes and ordered the OOW to 'Fall Out Actions Stations, Remain in the Search Quiet State' The whole episode had taken no more than 20 minutes. We lost contact completely a few minutes later and after another 30 minutes went back to the Patrol Quiet State.

This was very frustrating again and I went back to my cabin very depressed that we did not seem to have any luck at all.

1510 We have been re-tasked again – this time back to investigate the Isle De Los Estados / Cabo San Diego areas and then up the coast looking for BOUCHARD and BUENA.

Did a 2-hour fast sprint deep and then returned to periscope depth. Having patrolled inside the TEZ looking for blockade runners or warships I am now south again and looking for any warship movement close to the coast or transiting between Ushuaia and Bahia San Sebastian. Faint contacts have been held at long range but I now think these were biological but the possible submarine could have been one.

This has been a bad day for the surface ships in Falkland Sound!

Tuesday 25th May 1982 – Day 55

HMS COVENTRY just prior to sinking

Falklands War Timeline: *HMS COVENTRY sunk by Argentine aircraft, killing 19. Twelve killed in Exocet missile attack on British Container ship ATLANTIC CONVEYOR. HMS BROADSWORD damaged.*

We are patrolling approximately 5 miles outside the Argentinian claimed twelve mile limit (TML). Our quarry are the Destroyers BUENO and BOUCHARD who are believed to be acting as radar pickets for the air base at Rio Grande but are supposedly inside the TML so we cannot attack them unless they stray outside the TML.

We are getting very conscious about stocks of food – better known in the Royal Navy as "Victualling" or in submarines as "Scran." In order to cover all eventualities and the likelihood that the boat may not depart for Devonport on or around 28th May which is what we are expecting it is necessary to eke out the victuals we have. At worst it could be 30th June before we get back to Devonport for a fast turnaround and back out again so some restrictions are necessary.

So, on the advice of the Supply Officer – Jimmy Fergusson – Ian Richards promulgated this to the Ships' Company.

1. Dinner and Supper will not change in quality, quantity or choice since we are reasonably well off for meat and vegetables.

2. However certain other items are in short supply. Economies will be as follows:

   Bread: Breakfast only and middle watch alternate nights
   Bacon/Sausage: Alternate days, but only one each
   Eggs: Every other day
   Coffee/Tea: Will be considerably reduced and monitored
   Milk: With the reduction in coffee/tea this should reduce

3. There is ample Marmite/Bovril, Cocoa, Rise and Shine and limers available so with careful thoughtful adjustments we can survive
4. Even with these restrictions each person on board will be getting approximately 2500 to 3000 calories per day as opposed to 3000 calories before – which is the same as taken by most athletes!
5. As soon as the future programme for our return to UK is clear and we are on our way home these restrictions may be relaxed.
6. The above is a small sacrifice to make when compared to the hard time the surface ships are having at the moment. As soon as we get a chance to even the balance I can assure you we will.

Having reached a position where we can monitor what is going on we have not detected any shipping of any sort around Isle De Los Estados or the approaches to Ushuaia so we will start our transit up the twelve mile limit towards Rio Grande. The weather is clear and the visibility around 12000 yards.

1100 have continued to remain at periscope depth and conducting an all sensor search for BOUCHARD.

1300 We have just been told that it is unlikely that we will see BOUCHARD as she has apparently suffered a complicated defect – but we don't know what it is – which probably means she is either in or close to Ushuaia. As she was apparently patrolling in our current area we will concentrate on moving north west so that the area north of Rio Grande towards San Sebastian can be covered before it gets dark. I will run deep and fast for 30-45 minute spells and then return to periscope depth for 20 minutes for a good look round before going deep again. This will greatly assist the area we can search and improve our speed of advance.

1530 Continuing with the "duck and up" technique. Visibility is quite good so any unit operating between 6 and 12 miles of the Argentine coast should be clearly seen.

There have been no sonar contacts or rackets but shore noise has been continuously present. I don't think the BOUCHARD is here unless he is at anchor or very close inshore.

1600 Three loud bangs heard – no bearing – aircraft dropping bombs before landing?

1700 At last – a sonar contact bearing 263° best solution Course 320° Speed 8 knots range 24000 yards. There is no good classification on this contact and it quickly started to fade in and out and then was lost.

2200 Having searched out from Cabo San Vincente along the twelve mile limit to Cabo San Sebastian there has been no sign of any warship, Carrier, or military activity. We had one faint sonar contact which held up for a couple of hours but there were no warship characteristics apparent. Visibility and twelve mile limit restrictions have made it difficult to discount the possibility of any vessel which may have been slow moving, stopped or at anchor close inshore.

2300 We have been directed to start our transit home with a view to conducting a quick turn round and returning to the South Atlantic. It is now Day 55 and by the time we return to Devonport around Saturday 12th June it will be 73 days since we left Faslane.

But we still have to withdraw carefully and be ready for anything.

CHAPTER TWENTY-SIX

WITHDRAWING

Wednesday 26th May 1982 – Day 56

Falklands War Timeline: The 2nd Battalion of the Parachute Regiment (2 Para) is ordered to set out for the neighbouring settlements of Goose Green and Darwin, which are held by Argentine forces.

We are now transiting north east past SPARTAN, VALIANT and CONQUEROR areas and still very much in the "war zone" and involved although we are withdrawing. The Rules of Engagement are in force until we are north of Latitude 5°South (around 2nd or 3rd June). On our transit we will continue to look for any Argentine warships and, if they are within the Rules of Engagement they will be attacked.

1230 We have received a signal which indicates that VALIANT may have detected me on a specific tonal frequency although none is apparent at that frequency from our regular self-monitoring. We are clearing the area anyway.

1430 Signalled VALIANT with positional information. VALIANT has been told to keep clear of my areas to ensure that there is no mutual interference – there should not be anyway if Northwood is doing their job.

2300 The transit from the western TEZ has continued without incident except the possible interaction with VALIANT but I do not consider his contact was me.

Commander Tom Le Marchand has not replied to me to confirm whether the positional information was relevant and his lack of response makes me consider that his contact was not me. WE have just received a signal slowing down our withdrawal as there is a strong belief that Argentinean "Surface Action Groups" [Groups of surface warships] may get under way tonight. I fully expected to be stopped at some stage during our withdrawal and to be honest I think we are being taken off too early notwithstanding the need to rotate the boats back to UK for maintenance etc and return to the theatre.

The news from the Falkland Islands has been dramatic and very worrying – the loss of COVENTRY and the attack on the ATLANTIC CONVEYOR – not only loss of life but the loss of 3 vital Chinook Helicopters will change things I have no doubt. It has been referred to as a "bad day for Royal Navy Air Defence" and I can't help thinking that successive government's penny pinching and cutting defence spending has been ill thought out and downright wrong.

Thursday 27th May 1982 – Day 57

Falklands War Timeline: *Battle for Goose Green and Darwin started. British forces are furious when the BBC World Service broadcasts that the men of 2 Para are advancing on Goose Green and Darwin, but the Argentine commander is convinced the report is deliberate misinformation.*

It is interesting to note that on this day in 1941 the German Battleship BISMARCK was sunk.

We are on the north-west edge of the TEZ and well placed to intercept any Argentine surface ship movement towards the islands. CONQUEROR is north east of us and SPARTAN to the north-west. WE have now circumnavigated the Falkland Islands and yet not seen them once!

1100. I intend to patrol in the northern part of my new allocated areas and we seem to have been deployed and positioned to deal with any units heading towards the Falklands from Deseado but a gap exists between us and CONQUEROR on the route from Puerto Belgrano to the Falkland Sound. We do not have any good location data on Royal Navy Surface ship positions so it is difficult to assess the best place to be to offer them the best protection.

2300. Today has been spent loitering in the northwestern TEZ looking for any surface or air activity. There has been none and we have been ordered to resume our northerly transit.

Friday 28th May 1982 – Day 58

<u>Falklands War Timeline</u>: *2 Para attack Goose Green and Darwin. After fierce fighting, the Argentines surrender. Seventeen British servicemen die during the battle, including commanding officer Lt Col "H" Jones. Although initial reports speak of 250 Argentine dead, the figure is now thought to have been much lower - possibly below 50. British troops, who are vastly outnumbered, take more than 1,000 prisoners of war. ATLANTIC CONVEYOR eventually sinks today.*

Atlantic Conveyor just prior to sinking

Continued transit from the TEZ clear of the operational areas.

Saturday 29th May 1982 – Day 59

We have continued our passage north and have crossed latitude 38° 30' South. It looks as though we are scheduled to arrive in Devonport on Saturday 12th June and we may be getting a mail drop on 3rd June – my birthday!

Sunday 30th May 1982 – Day 60

Falklands War Timeline: *3 Para and 45 Commando Royal Marines reach Estancia House and Teal Inlet. Mount Kent captured by 42 Commando Royal Marines and SAS.*

Continued transit out of area and now north of latitude 32° 45 South' – still a very long way to go!

We have started to receive some admin signals now and it is clear that some ratings drafts have been changed and I think we can expect some considerable turbulence when we return. We must make sure if we are to have a quick turn round that we do not allow the drafting authorities to reduce our capability.

There is a lot to do but we all can't help thinking that we have been pulled off too early – particularly as we enter a crucial stage of the re-invasion. But we have to accept it and of course there is also great relief amongst many of the Ship's Company. We left Devonport on 6th February and it has been a long time to be away from our home port.

We have been told that Paul Raymond's Revue Bar will let servicemen in for £1 only on production of a Royal Navy ID Card (Normal entry fee is £7!)

Monday 31st May 1982 – Day 61

Falklands War Timeline: *British forces advance towards the capital Port Stanley from San Carlos, taking the Argentine positions on Mount Kent and Mount Challenger.*

0800 We are now at Latitude 29 South and making good progress north. When we are normally at sea we operate under Standard Operating Procedures [SOPs] and Emergency Operating Procedures [EOPs] and at night the Captain writes his "Night Orders" which are instructions for the OOW for the night. During the transit down to the Falklands I had written my "Captain's War Orders" which itemised the areas of SOPs and EOPs that were in abeyance or changed as a result of a war situation. For example I ordered that the OOW no longer had authority to use Emergency Blows – I reserved that decision for myself as it may not be a good thing to automatically rush up to surface for an emergency if the enemy was above. It had been extremely interesting to write them and discuss items with the Heads of Department and they had added an extra focus to how we did what we would see as normal things. In reality I changed very little which shows that we do operate nuclear submarines on a war footing all the time.

Tuesday 1st June 1982 – Day 62

Falklands War Timeline: *5 Brigade reinforcements arrive at San Carlos Water.*

0800 We are now across latitude 19 °30' South and north of Argentina. As we continue our transit north we have received a signal form CINCFLEET and FOSM.
From Admiral Sir John Fieldhouse, Commander in Chief Fleet:

"As a (founder member of) the UK forces spearhead you have completed a vital albeit occasionally frustrating task most competently. Your presence has caused Galtieri much heartache and the Argentine Fleet a bad case of the yellows. Well done."

From Vice Admiral Sir Peter Herbert, Flag Officer Submarines:

"Without being pompous it has been a splendid SPLENDID job. Continued sea and air attacks could have severely jeopardised the landing. The very presence of you and your chums has made the Argentine Fleet scared to go to sea and that has kept the course of this war in our favour. I was particularly impressed by the way you mended yourself in difficult circumstances. Safe journey home and look forward to seeing you all on return. Bet you wish you were here (Dolphin 79)"

The Dolphin Code is a method of encrypted communications designed to enable submarines, submariners, ship captains, helicopter pilots, anti-submarine aircraft to speak to each other in areas of submarine operations or in many cases, social and domestic activities surrounding people of "The Trade". So all you had to say in a signal or on the radio was to use the word Dolphin and the appropriate number. The message would be clear and sometimes less that flattering. The details of all the meanings are included later.

Wednesday 2nd June 1982 – Day 63

Falklands War Timeline: *2 Para airlifted to Fitzroy.*

Another uneventful day of transit but there is much excitement as it looks as though we are going to get a mail drop by a Nimrod from Ascension Island tomorrow. That will be a big morale booster – I just hope the weather is okay.
2000 We have crossed latitude 12° South.

Thursday 3rd June 1982 – Day 64

Falklands War Timeline: *2 Para advance and capture Fitzroy and Bluff Cove.*

Today is my 37th Birthday and I did not expect to be spending it like this – still I have managed to pack a great deal into those years and reflect that I will be seeing my family soon. I think everyone is tired although they are not showing it.

1200 Surfaced for the mail drop. The wind was windy and dry but there was a 10-15 foot swell. Recovery conditions were marginal and although we had tethered divers it was quite dangerous on the casing. Four out of nine canisters were dropped but unfortunately we could not get to the 3rd canister before it sunk which was very distressing.

We took the opportunity to run the diesel and ventilate the boat – fresh air! Thankfully there was plenty of private mail but little official. [I found out later that the 3rd canister contained my new passport!]

1645 After trying to do some repairs on the AVS stub on the search periscope we dived again and are now 60 miles astern of the centre of our subnote box so will need to catch up over the next few hours.

There is plenty of preparation for the Crossing the Line Ceremony planned for tomorrow.

I had a pleasant birthday with an excellent chocolate cake made by Barny Barnard and although there were plenty of other ways I could have celebrated my birthday – still being in the fray or with my family it was good to be with this fantastic set of submariners.

Friday 4th June 1982 – Day 65

1327 Crossed the Equator and King Neptune graced us with his favour this afternoon and came to initiate all those who had not crossed the Equator before. This involved 44 new recruits to his kingdom and we had a jolly time.

Saturday 5th June 1982 – Day 66

We surfaced this morning to try to repair the AVS aerial on the search periscope.

We spent an hour on the surface and then dived again to continue our passage. Sadly the repair to the AVS aerial has not worked.

2000 Passed 10° North.

Sunday 6th June 1982 – Day 67

A quiet day on transit with Evensong as a change which was well

attended.
A nasty problem with the Sewage Pump required some difficult and unpleasant work for the outside staff today but they fixed and so well done to them.

Monday 7th June 1982 – Day 68

0800 Passed latitude 21° North.
 A quiet day on passage although there is plenty going on to ensure we are looking good – both boat and people before our arrival in Devonport. Hair is getting long but we do not have a barber on board and we will have to have an amnesty over this issue until a few days after our return.
 I will be doing Captain's Rounds before arrival and the time-honoured scrubbing out of every nook and cranny is ongoing.

Tuesday 8th June 1982 – Day 69

<u>Falklands War Timeline</u>: *Landing craft RFA Sir Galahad and RFA Sir Tristram, with units of the Welsh Guards on board, are bombed by Argentine aircraft off Fitzroy. More than 50 men die.*

Another day on passage although the news of the bombing of the two RFAs has made all realise that this is not over yet.

Wednesday 9th June 1982 – Day 70

Another day on passage with preparations for arrival continuing. 0800 Now passing 36° North.

Thursday 10th June 1982 – Day 71

Sub Lieutenant Toby Spreckley's birthday. He is far too junior to have a cake made for him!

I conducted Captain's Rounds today going round the after machinery compartments in the morning and the forward compartments in the afternoon.

Captain's Rounds are a time honoured Royal Navy tradition and are designed to provide an opportunity for the Captain to visit very part of his ship, inspect the state of readiness and cleanliness of the machinery, the mess decks and bathrooms, give the chance for those reporting each compartment to identify shortcomings and give praise when it is due. The Captain is preceded by the Master at Arms, announcing the Captain's presence with shrill from a bosun's call, but in a submarine's case this is the Coxswain and the train of people behind include the First Lieutenant, Head of Department and others. Each compartment is reported to the Captain by the Junior Rate in charge of cleaning and preparing that compartment. The Captain is armed with a torch at least and it is important to try to get to inaccessible places – not only because you are unlikely to have seen them recently but also as you know that someone has spent a considerable amount of time cleaning them out.

This process took 2 and ½ hours at each end of the submarine and, as expected, I was amazed at how clean everywhere was bearing in mind the amount of time we had been at sea. In many cases it is easier to keep a submarine clean and well maintained at sea than in harbour as you have the Ship's Company's undivided attention throughout.

On completion I made a pipe on the main intercom and told everyone how well they had done and how well the boat looked.

We are certainly low on the food side on certain things and we are now very much on a mixture of tinned and dry victuals. The shortages have brought out a number of responses. At auction the last tea bag went for £50 and was used around 10 times before it died! And the last sausage went for £60. Such is the way of sailors when anything is for charity and it was wonderful to see such generosity.

2300 Passed Latitude 45° 35' North which means we are now west of the Bay of Biscay and very much close to home waters.

Friday 11th June 1982 – Day 72

Falklands War Timeline: British troops take the key objectives of Mount Longdon, Two Sisters and Mount Harriet from the Argentines after bloody hand-to-hand fighting. British destroyer HMS Glamorgan is badly damaged by a shore-launched Exocet missile. Three Falklands civilians, all women, are killed during a British naval bombardment of Stanley.

While we are approaching our home port it is difficult to take in what is still going on in the Falklands and how our troops on the ground are having to operate and fight. I think most people are still reeling from the reports of the loss of the Welsh Guards in RFA Sir Galahad and Sir Tristram.

Suddenly as we approach the south west approaches the number of sonar contacts exploded and the sonar operators and Tactical systems operators were very busy reporting, analysing and evaluating each contact. After so much time with little contact in the South Atlantic is was very strange to be dealing with so many contacts.

1700 We were travelling at 200 feet approaching the southwest approaches of the UK and Lieutenant Jeff Thomas was the OOW. One of the things I had been doing for a number of months was initiating the younger seaman officers into bringing the submarine up from deep to periscope depth. This had first been done by Captain John Speller in HMS SWIFTSURE and numerous officers including me had benefitted from this important training.

Anyway, Jeff Thomas was the OOW and I asked him to have the responsibility of bringing the boat up for the last time before we surfaced at the end of the patrol and did the last few miles into Devonport on the surface. So Jeff duly cleared the sonar picture and worked out where everything was. This took about 20 minutes and involved clearing stern arcs – there were around 20 contacts on the plot. I was watching him throughout and when he turned to me and said 'Ready to return to periscope depth' I told him it was his decision and he should carry on when he was ready.

Anyway, he started to come up ordering '10 degree up Speed 8 knots Keep 65 feet.'

The boat moved to his command and he went to the attack periscope and as we passed 80 feet he said 'Up attack' and met the periscope as it reached deck level. He trained it right ahead and as the periscope broke and he could see shouted loudly 'Full dive on the planes 15 down Revolutions 70 Keep 200 feet Down attack.'

The boat settled at 65 feet for a few seconds before reversing and starting back down again as the planes and speed took effect.

'What is it?' I said to a startled Jeff Thomas who stammered out 'Supertanker right ahead at 2000 yards, fine on his bow' clearly unnerved.

We were now at 120 feet going down at 15 degrees of pitch and the speed was up to 15 knots and rising. 'Let's slow down then and level off' I said and he ordered '5 down speed 6 knots keep 180 feet.'

The planesman had control of the situation and we settled at 180 feet. Jeff and I both went to the Tactical screens and there was no indication that there had been anything there. But he had seen a supertanker and it was clear that because we were so fine on his bow that we were blanketed from his screws and sonar had not picked him up. We were certainly back in UK waters with a bang and within a minute we heard the supertanker going over the top.

We let it go by and I said to Jeff 'Well done, now you can clear again and bring the boat back to periscope depth. It took another 20 minutes and Jeff brought the boat back up again although he looked slightly alarmed until he had done his first all- round look and seen the stern of the supertanker going away at 5000 yards. There was nothing close but it was another good lesson for us all. Bringing a boat up from deep to periscope depth is essentially the most dangerous maneuver that a submarine can conduct as you go from the only reasonably known to the visual known.

Jeff was showing visible signs of relief and I told him that it was a good lesson and he had reacted very well. You must always be prepared for that every time you return to periscope depth from deep.

1800 Surfaced and continued passage to Devonport.

On a lighter note we had the Grand Draw this evening and the winner would receive the keys to a brand new Mini when we returned. We had sent various signals on the way home to organize this as the amount that was being deposited in the fund was substantial and with 104 people on board the odds were pretty good. It is amazing how much has been raised for charity.

Having supper on the surface was a novel experience and we spent a very enjoyable couple of hours reminding ourselves what we had gone through. We were also every aware that the war was still ongoing and there was plenty of action for the troops ashore.

Saturday 12th June 1982 – Day 73

We went to Harbour Stations and Special Sea Dutymen at 0530 and went through the breakwater at Plymouth at 0600 and were attached to C buoy by 0645.

We had come her to clear customs and receive a visit from Flag Officer Submarines [Vice Admiral Sir Peter Herbert] and the Captain Second Submarine Squadron [Captain Mike Ortmans].

FOSM and SM2 arrived by boat at 0730 and we received a great reception from them and the other members of staff who came out. We gave them coffee and it was ironic that the fresh milk they brought out was sour and we had to use what was left of ours!

After a quick walk around the boat to welcome SPLENDID Ships' Company back they left and we waited for the customs officials to complete their work – all a bit of a waste of time really as we hadn't been anywhere! However by 0900 they had gone and we slipped from the buoy and started up to our berth at 9 berth bows West at the Submarine Base. As we came alongside there was a great reception with plenty of families waiting excitedly on the jetty.

1030 We were stopped and tied up alongside and were shutting down the reactor. The boat was full of families which was great.

It was all over for the time being as the boat would be going back down after some leave and maintenance but for me personally it was all over as I left the boat a week later having handed over to Commander Tony Smith and prepared to go to the United States to spend a year at the Naval War College at Newport Rhode Island.

Sunday 13th June 1982 – Day 74

Falklands War Timeline: British forces take Argentine positions on mountains overlooking Port Stanley on Mount Tumbledown, Wireless Ridge and Mount William amid further fierce fighting.

But the war went on despite the fact that SPLENDID was in harbour in UK. When I got home to my house in Bristol my wife, Roisin had kept all the newspapers for me. As I slowly worked my way through them over the next few days I was amazed that what they were reporting was complete anathema to me and they were certainly in a different place with a different approach to me and my Ship's Company.

Ever since I have had a healthy scepticism about what is written in the press and how much you should actually believe. I can't help thinking that, for much of the time, you really can't believe what you read.

Monday 14th June 1982 – Day 75

Falklands War Timeline: White flags are seen flying over Port Stanley, and by noon British forces have advanced to the outskirts of the Falklands capital. General Mario Menendez surrenders to Major General Jeremy Moore, and 9,800 Argentine troops put down their arms. British troops march into Stanley.

The UK Defence Minister Peter Blaker announces that the official count of British war dead is 255, with approximately 300 wounded.

The following day, Argentine President Leopoldo Galtieri resigns as leader of the country's military junta.

HMS INVINCIBLE returns to Portsmouth

ARCHITECTS OF THE FALKLANDS WAR VICTORY

Margaret Thatcher
– Prime Minister

Sir Henry Leach
- First Sea Lord

Sir John Fieldhouse
– CinC Fleet

Sir Sandy Woodward
– Task Force Commander

Falklands War Commanders at Northwood
Far Left: Vice Admiral Sir Peter Herbert – Flag Officer
Submarines

Margaret Thatcher and Admiral Sir John Fieldhouse with British troops in the Falklands

Re-raising the flag above Government House in the Falkland Islands

CHAPTER TWENTY-SEVEN
REFLECTIONS FROM ME

So, two days after returning to Devonport, the Argentine forces have surrendered and the Falkland Islands have been liberated. In reflecting, I am clear that I was fortunate to have a settled crew, despite some key changes before going to sea, and they all performed extraordinarily well indeed.

It was difficult to change one's mind set from obsession with the Soviet Submarine Force to dealing with a tin-pot dictator many miles away from home and, in some ways, we were fortunate to be able to have the long passage south to get our act together. It was a crazy venture for General Galtieri and the Junta to do, but then dictators do stupid things and he was probably looking for a diversion from problems at home.

The question of whether it was all worthwhile is one I have been asked many times over the years. The invasion was unprovoked, although I am in no doubt that the British Government and the FCO in particular had taken their eye off the ball over a number of years, and it is not as though there were not sufficient warning signs.

In 1977, a group of Argentinean sailors had landed on Morrell, in the South Sandwich Islands, for supposedly scientific research. The new Labour Government under Prime Minister James Callaghan launched new talks, led by Foreign Minister Ivor Richard, with sovereignty again under discussion. I had been in CTF 311 at Northwood when, in 1977, Jim Callaghan sent HMS DREADNOUGHT and two frigates to the Falklands as there was increasing tension. The communication line was tenuous as there was no satellite communications then. We had to transmit HF to HMS ENDURANCE – the Antarctic Patrol Ship in the South Atlantic who then flies its helicopter to pass the messages via UHF to HMS DREADNOUGHT!

There is no doubt in my mind that we had to react in 1982, and I am very proud of the fact that the First Sea Lord, Admiral Sir Henry

Leach, told Margaret Thatcher that not only could we raise a task force to re-take the islands but that we should. How right he was, although there is no doubt that it was a close run thing with many mistakes made and a certain amount of luck on our side. I am clear that it was a just cause and my Ship's Company agreed.

So, it was worthwhile and it was right to respond to such behaviour against a dictator who had invaded UK sovereign territory. The cost was heavy on both sides. We should not forget the 255 who died or the 300 who were wounded some very badly. The Argentine casualties were high too.

We lost two destroyers HMS SHEFFIELD and HMS COVENTRY [I was later to command the new HMS COVENTRY and had HMS SHEFFIELD as one of my ships as Captain, First Frigate Squadron]; two frigates [HMS ARDENT and HMS ANTELOPE]; a large container ship, ATLANTIC CONVEYOR; an LSL [SIR GALAHAD]; 24 assorted helicopters and 10 Harriers.

We were very well led by Admiral Sir John Fieldhouse as Commander in Chief; Vice Admiral Sir Peter Herbert, as Flag Officer Submarines and Rear Admiral Sandy Woodward as the Task Force Commander.

But my main praise goes for my Officers and Ship's Company. I am still extremely proud of every one of them and I could not have been better supported. The fact that we are meeting up for dinner 30 years later – and most of them are coming along - suggests that they also felt it was a special time. This book is in tribute to them all, as this account is about them too.

Naturally we were all "up for it" and contemplated successful attacks, so it was disappointing not to have been allowed to sink something.

At the time I was professionally envious of Chris Wreford-Brown's success in HMS CONQUEROR but admired the classic submarine attack he conducted. It is interesting to note that today I am glad that it was not me.

REFLECTIONS FROM JIM KNIGHT – TG TIFF – HMS SPLENDID – 1980 to 1983

I have often wondered if you were aware, at the time [I was not!], of the fact that I was the brother of Radio Electrical Artificer Keith Knight. As I was a "back-aftie" Keith and I rarely saw each other, but

I can vividly recall the occasion, sitting down to dinner together as the boat headed south, when someone pointed out that one of us shouldn't be there. At first Keith and I were bemused. Then it hit home. We were off to war and the assumed protocol was that one of us should have been left behind on 5th Watch. I think that in the rush to get the boat stored for war, repaired and ready in all respects, the technicalities of such matters were easily overlooked. After all, when we sailed the invasion hadn't even taken place so it wasn't considered that serious at the time. For us it wasn't a problem, although our mother (not officially informed of the boat's tasking) was beside herself with worry. Every time it was announced that a ship had been sunk her heart momentarily stopped, particularly when a report began "HMS S...." Our mother was a formidable lady so you can consider yourself lucky you brought us both back safe and sound! In retrospect if one of us had been left behind for the patrol it would have been unbearable to live with.

I served 30 years in the Submarine Service and can honestly say that the 3 years on SPLENDID were the happiest of the lot. There was sense of everything being "right"; a sound boat with a good crew and, if I may make so bold, the right man in command. I have never been so impressed, before or since, by the manner in which a crew strove to keep a boat fully operational, particularly during Operation Corporate. To a man we seemed determined, whatever the mission, to keep the SPLENDID on station and play our part in full. In most respects these were halcyon days to be a submariner in the Royal Navy. With larger than life Commanding Officers such as "Beasty Biggs" and some very competent men, such as Barry Carr (who I had the pleasure to serve under on SCEPTRE) we felt part of a very special organisation.

I probably speak for all the crew when I say that respect for the Commanding Officer was integral in our motivation for making SPLENDID such a good boat to serve on; basically we were very secure and confident of success under your command.

Of course the bread and butter of our existence were the Cold War patrols. Nobody in their right mind would want to return to those dangerous days but strangely I miss them. Our work had a real sense of purpose and it generated an atmosphere of camaraderie sadly lacking today.

HMS HERMES returns to Portsmouth

HMS CONQUEROR returns to Faslane

Left to right: Admiral Sir Sandy Woodward (Task Force Commander) Commander Chris Wreford-Brown (HMS CONQUEROR) Commander Roger Lane-Nott (HMS SPLENDID) Commander Rupert Best (HMS COURAGEOUS) Commander James Taylor (HMS SPARTAN) Admiral Sir Hugo White (HMS AVENGER)

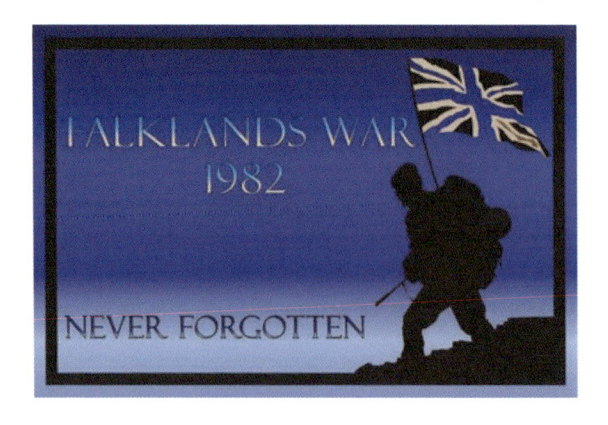

A splendid effort has to go unsung

By MICHAEL CHARLESTON

THE first Royal Navy warship to return from the Falklands has sailed into Plymouth.

But the exploits of the nuclear submarine Splendid must remain officially untold.

For the Ministry of Defence public relations men have missed the boat again.

The submariners are the only branch of the Services who can still claim 100 per cent success in the battle for the islands.

The decision by Whitehall to gag Commander Roger Lane-Nott and his 97 crew is a chance lost to tell the world about one of Britain's most amazing wartime successes.

Argentine navy chief Admiral Jorge Anaja has never dared to order his ships out for battle.

They include destroyers as modern as any in the Task Force and they are armed with the deadly Exocet missile. But his officers know too much about the capabilities of Britain's hunter-killer submarines.

Press Cutting written by Michael Charleston

This was the only press cutting of HMS SPLENDID returning from the Falklands

EPILOGUE

VISIT TO RUSSIA IN 1992

Ten years after the Falkland War and I had left HMS SPLENDID I was fortunate to find myself given the opportunity to visit Russia. Remember this was some three years after the fall of the Soviet Union and I was the Chief of Staff to Flag Officer Submarines. I am not sure how this came about but we had accepted an invitation to send a diesel boat to Severomorsk for a visit. This was our oldest diesel submarine and it was unthinkable that we would send a nuclear boat. Anyway I was asked to support the visit and I started by flying to Moscow and being hosted by the Naval Attaché Captain John Dobson. I was accompanied by Captain Paul Branscombe – Captain of the First Submarine Squadron to which HMS OPOSSUM belonged and also with Robert Avery a MOD interpreter who was to prove an outstanding addition to the team and ensured that proper translation and interpretation was happening at all times. After a couple of days in Moscow where I met the Ambassador visited the Kremlin and Red Square and went to the circus I still felt very uncomfortable. It was strange to be in Moscow and I did feel as though there were eyes on me the whole time. I don't think there were but then one does not know!

We flew by Aeroflot from Moscow to Murmansk late one afternoon. The cabin staff were indifferent and all the aisles were crammed full of cases and bags and any evacuation if required was likely to be very difficult. We arrived in Murmansk in the late evening and the crew – all of them – shut down the plane turned off all the lights and walked off. We were left to our own devices. A taxi took us to the Hotel Arctica in the central square of Murmansk. It has since been developed and is still there today although significantly different to my time. We checked in and were told that it was $72 for the night and $75 if we wanted water! It was late and very humid and we had a busy day ahead of us so we all decided to retire for the night. There was no night bar so there was little option.

The room was bizarre. The carpet was threadbare and I suspect that the bed was full of bugs. It was very warm and there was no air conditioning. There was a dirty window with no curtain overlooking the square. And the water in the tap was a trickle. I repaired to bed hoping that the next day would be really interesting.

I awoke the next morning having had a disturbed night – too hot. I got up and went to shave and have a shower but ... No water! After a call to reception which resulted in nothing as the person answering did not speak English I tried for 10 minutes to get some water out. I failed so had to resort to shaving with cold tonic water a bottle of which I happened to have in my bag. That was strange and just about worked but I could not wash my hair or shower before getting into my uniform. Breakfast consisted of coffee of sorts and some bread and jam – nothing else was offered.

We were collected at the hotel by a Soviet liaison officer which had been arranged by the British Embassy in Moscow. So with the Naval Attaché Captain John Dobson, Captain Paul Branscombe and Robert Avery we set off to drive to Severomorsk to be there prior to the arrival of HMS OPOSSUM.

Severomorsk Russia

The journey was interrupted by the car overheating but we went through the controlled gates of Severomorsk and down the hill to this important Soviet Navy town. The site from the top of the hill above the town was extraordinary. There were ships everywhere all moored alongside with an ancient Kashin class destroyer moving off the jetty and belching out smoke. But the striking memory is that it was looking like turning the pages of Jane's Fiighting Ships.

On arrival at the jetty we could see HMS OPOSSUM in the distance and we were met by Admiral Oleg Yerofeyev the Commander of the Northern Fleet and his deputy Vice Admiral Suchkov. They were very welcoming and with the help of Robert Avery we soon had a rapport – particularly with Vice Admiral Suchkov.

Awaiting the arrival of HMS OPOSSUM at Severomorsk

When HMS OPOSSUM came alongside and was tied up to the jetty the whole of the Ship's Company came up in No 1 uniform and lined the casing before the Captain, Lieutenant Commander John Drummond came ashore to meet the two Admirals. We then invited Admiral Yerofeyev down HMS OPOSSUM for a tour and he presented the Long Service and Good Conduct medal to the Leading Cook. The Admiral was in good form and talked to many of the Ship's Company.

The next few days consisted of a cocktail party in HMS OPOSSUM, a tour and dinner in a Victor class Soviet submarine, toured a Slava class cruiser which included a sauna, a visit to the Mayor of Severomorsk, a band concert and a visit to the local museum.

The first time the Royal Navy came to the Kola peninsula was in 1918, as part of a joint expeditionary force with the French and Americans. To this day arguments continue over why they came – was it to stiffen the Bolsheviks against the Germans or overthrow

Lenin? The next visit was during the Second World War, when two Royal Navy submarines patrolled the water around Severomorsk and many British sailors and airman lost their lives delivering supplies to Russia. Of course British and American submarines have been active around the Northern Fleet for decades.

Admiral Yerofeyev – Commander of the Russian Northern Fleet and Commodore Roger Lane-Nott on HMS OPOSSUM in Severomorsk 1992

Commodore Roger Lane-Nott and Vice Admiral Suchkov on board a Soviet Slava Class Cruiser in Severomorsk 1992

Meeting the locals in Severomorsk

Meeting with the Mayor of Severomorsk

Vice Admiral Suchkov and Commodore Lane-Nott at the war memorial in Severomorsk

Commodore Lane-Nott and Vice Admiral Suchkov
in Severomorsk

Vice Admiral Suchkov and Commodore Lane-Nott swopping caps on the Slava in Sevoromorsk

Commodore Roger Lane-Nott, Lieutenant Commander Drummond and Captain Paul Branscombe outside Soviet Northern Fleet Headquarters Severomorsk

Meeting with Russian Officers in Severomorsk 1992
Russians on the right: Vice Admiral Suchkov, Admiral
Yerofeyev, Captain Priladyshev   Royal Navy on the left:
Captain Paul Branscombe, Mr Robert Avery, Commodore
Lane-Nott, Lieutenant Commander Russell

We had formal bilateral discussions with Admiral Yerofeyev, Vice Admiral Suchkov Rear Admiral Titerenko and two Commanders (Priladshev and Abramov) who were clearly KGB. These discussions were cordial but Admiral Yerofeyev started by asking how far we had come into the Barents Sea and remained undetected. He complained that there were too many incursions into Soviet areas and wanted to know what we were doing. This was a difficult question to answer but I replied that we were aware that Soviet submarines were also coming into our waters. After pushing hard about this Yerofeyev admitted that there had been incursions but was quick to point out that the Americans and British were always coming into the Barents Sea and they knew – although they did not elaborate – that we were doing this on a regular basis. I responded that these were international waters whereas the Clyde was territorial waters.

They continued to say that our actions were irresponsible and had resulted in several collisions and unnecessary incidents. This was true and apart from the US incidents we had had several over the years including HMS WARSPITE, HMS SCEPTRE and HMS SPLENDID (after my time).We asked about changes in the Soviet

Union and what this would do for the Navy and they admitted that things were changing although they were not sure where it would take them. They were very guarded about the changes in the Soviet Union, but were much happier talking about how we could work together on submarine escape and rescue.

Roger Lane-Nott on HMS OPOSSUM periscope (top) and
WWII Russian periscope in Severomorsk (bottom)

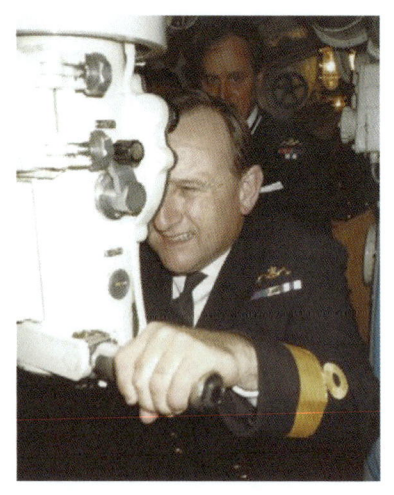

Roger Lane-Nott on HMS OPOSSUM periscope

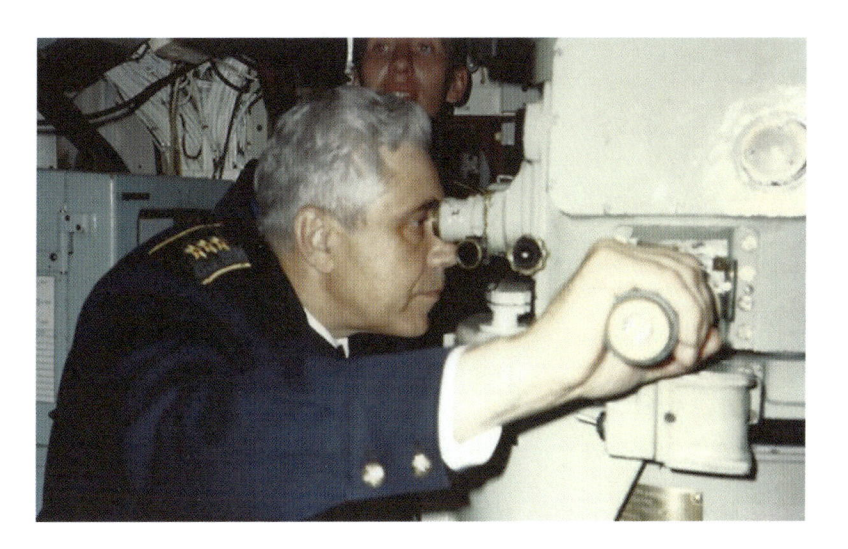

Admiral Yerofeyev on HMS OPOSSUM periscope

They were very supportive of closer links on this subject but when it came to the KURSK several years later they ignored all offers for assistance until it was too late. Incidently Suchkov was Commander of the Northern Fleet when this happened and was dismissed afterwards. I suspect that Suchkov wanted the help but was stopped by Putin and the Russian Defence Ministry. A disgrace as there was a good chance that both the US and UK Deep Sea Rescue Vehicles [DSRV] could have made a significant difference to saving the lives of some of the casualties particularly in the after end of the Kursk. There was much to discuss and fear of saying too much was clearly evident on the Soviet side.

The night before we left I held a dinner for those who had helped us including the Russian team. The dinner for 20 was held in the only private restaurant in Severomorsk and we dined on a meat stew of sorts, vodka and Russian champagne. The total cost was US $120!

My overall perception was that Russia was struggling to find the right way forward and it was staggering to see so many ships and submarines tied up with little going on. I was impressed with Yerofeyev and Suchkov. They were very hospitable, very friendly and very respectful. The whole of Severomorsk had little to recommend it and the lack of decent fresh food – particularly vegetables – was acute. There was one Government shop with little in apart from the basics and it was clear that people lived a hard life. There was considerable optimism that things would change but it all went backwards when Putin came to power and although there is much more money being spent on the Navy today I suspect that morale and training is still poor amongst the conscripts.

So should we be afraid? Russia under Putin is pushing hard to re-arm and this is particularly noticeable in the fact that Russian warships and submarines are venturing further apart. They are competing with China as much as the US but the real worry is that after annexing Crimea and invading Ukraine they will continue their empire building ambitions. Despite sanctions they have considerable resources including gas and oil that we all in Europe need and they will continue to play hard ball. The threat to the Baltic States is real but I think Putin is more interested in the former Soviet States to the East. Any threat to Latvia, Estonia, Lithuania or Poland will inevitably bring a NATO response but based on the NATO response to Ukraine I doubt whether the same response will be forthcoming despite the rhetoric!

So what should the UK and the Royal Navy do? We are supposedly committed to the NATO 2% of GDP but this is not enough. The Navy is modern but too small and has too few people to make it as professional as it should be. We absolutely have to replace the Trident submarine hulls and we are still very late in doing this. IT should have been done in the last parliament and needs to be done now. Trident is our ultimate safeguard – particularly against the Russians and we need it. The record of the submarine service over 46 years of Continuous At Sea Deterrence is stunning and we must ensure that we do everything we can to keep this going. We need more frigates and destroyer and need to bring back our expertise in Anti-Submarine Warfare where we were a world leader. Skills and equipment have lagged behind in the stupid view that the submarine threat has gone. It has not! And never will. The two new carriers are a clear statement but how and where are we going to operate them when the aircraft eventually arrive? And do we have enough manpower?

So these are difficult time for the Royal Navy and retired Admirals in particular. At a recent retired Admiral briefing at the Ministry of Defence there was lots of talk about political and economic credibility but none about the Threat and what we are going to do about it. Worrying times indeed!

War Memorial in Severomorsk

APPENDICES

APPENDIX 1
NAVAL CAREER SUMMARY

It was 1954 and I was a nine year old staying with my grandfather at Almondsbury near Bristol when he took me to see an S class diesel submarine that was on a port visit to Bristol and was moored in the centre of the city for a few days. Although I did not know it at the time this was a WW II relic and not very sophisticated but as I was taken below I was fascinated and intrigued by the size, the compactness, the pipes and valves and of course the periscopes.

The periscopes intrigued me. What a view I could see all around me and I could change the magnification and elevation at will. This visit of no more than ¾ of an hour had a profound effect on me and I kept the visions of what I could remember with me.

As a 12 year old for some unexplained reason I had told my father that I wanted to go to sea. I have no recollection as to why except for having an uncle as a Captain in the Watts Watts Line of tramps and general cargo ships. I did visit him on one of his ships when it visited Avonmouth but I have distant memories and I don't think this was the underlying reason. In the early days of television there was series called "Victory at Sea" and I consumed the images and stories eagerly.

My father acted with considerable speed and verve and, despite the fact that I had been enrolled for Clifton College pretty much from birth, he found me a place at the Nautical College Pangbourne, although I still had to pass the Common Entrance Exam from my prep school Tockington Manor. That was about the time that the 13 year old entry to the Britannia Royal Naval College at Dartmouth had been stopped and entry to the Royal Navy had been changed to 18 years of age and 2 A levels. So Pangbourne became an obvious choice for parents whose sons would have gone to Dartmouth at 13.

Cadet Roger Lane-Nott RNR
On joining Pangbourne College September 1958

I started at Pangbourne in September 1958 and immediately loved it. We were gazetted as Cadets Royal Navy Reserve and I wore naval uniform at all times. My father was appalled at the price of my best uniform which had to be bought from the official outfitters – Gieves [not with Hawkes at that time] of Savill Row – for 7 guineas!

I was an average student but loved sport and played everything on offer. Rugby, hockey, cricket, boxing and even cross country running. Pangbourne was essentially a college set up by the Devitt and Moore shipping company in 1917 to educate and train their young officers for their shipping line. The aim was to produce resilient, resourceful and confident young men with excellent leadership qualities.

I think at the time I went to Pangbourne I was interested in going to one of the romantic shipping lines like P & O or Shaw Savill or even Union Castle but somewhere along the line the Royal Navy crept up on me. I don't know whether it was my father trying to persuade me or what but by the time I was 15 I was in front of a Royal Navy Interview Board going for a naval scholarship. This involved a series of tests both practical and academic and although I did not get a scholarship I did get a reserved Cadetship in the Royal Navy. That meant that the Navy would keep a place for me.

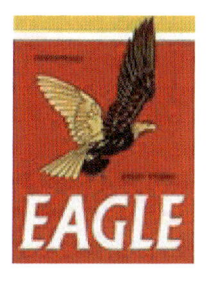

I was also an avid reader of the 'Eagle' comic for boys which each week had a cutaway in the centre pages of some new vehicle or craft. The picture above shows HMS DEVONSHIRE. I had also become intrigued by motor sport and had been taken to Castle Combe to see Stirling Moss, Mike Hawthorn and Tommy Sopwith racing in 500cc racing cars and Jaguar saloons. I had on my bedroom wall two cutaways of particular interest. One was of Stirling Moss's Vanwall Formula One car and the other was of HMS DREADNOUGHT the

Royal Navy's first nuclear submarine. Although I have had a lifelong love of motor sport I don't think that the Vanwall was ever going to win over Dreadnought.

At Pangbourne I was Captain of Rugby in 1962 when we had an unbeaten season. I was Captain of Hockey in 1963 and wicketkeeper for the 1st XI cricket team. In 1963 I had my last year at Pangbourne where I was Chief Cadet Captain of the College and won Her Majesty the Queen's Gold Medal. This was presented to me at Founders Day by Lord Carrington who was First Lord of the Admiralty at the time.

I joined the Royal Navy in September 1963 and went to Dartmouth as a Supplementary List Seaman Officer [I had only got one A level – too much cricket!] and this was the best way in as there would be chances to transfer to the General List if I did well enough.] I did alright at Dartmouth and hooked for the 1st XV and as there was little new to me after being at Pangbourne which gave me a big advantage. But I did come under the influence of my Assistant Divisional Officer Bob Worlidge who was a submarine engineer and who frequently indicated that the future lay in nuclear submarines – how right he was!

I went to sea as a Midshipman initially to the Far East in HMS BULWARK which was a helicopter carrier being used to transport Royal Marines and Army personnel in and out of Borneo during the Malaysian/Indonesian Confrontation. This was a great time where one had the chance to learn everything at the sharp end and the Midshipman's programme made sure that we were seconded to every department for sufficient time that we could understand what made a warship tick.

I was lucky enough to be on the bridge as second officer of the watch when the Commander Air asked the Captain if he could have a Midshipman to run the air net at Nanga Gaat in Borneo. The Captain turned round, say me and said "there's a Midshipman – he will do" 24 hours later I was in Nanga Gaat.

This was a fascinating experience and we lived in huts on stilts over the river, were guarded by Gurkhas and the evening rig was grass skirts flip flops and beads. We were close to Iban settlements and we worked closely with them. Low level fog meant that there was no flying before around 1000 and the air net was not difficult to run with only about 5 helicopters around at any one time. It was a memorable time.

The Royal Navy's Fleet Air Arm Commando helicopter squadrons, 845 and 848 were known as "Junglies" because of their long deployments in the Borneo jungle between 1964 and 1966, combatting Indonesian guerillas.

Nanga Gaat Borneo

After about 9 months BULWARK went into a long docking period in Singapore and the Midshipman's Training Officer – Lieutenant Commander Shaun Glennie who was also the Ship's Navigator offered me the chance to go to a submarine for 6 weeks.

So it was that I joined HMS ANDREW under the command of Lieutenant Commander Bill Swinley. This was a magic time as I found myself fully integrated into the running of a WWII diesel submarine [which even had a 4" gun] although I was still effectively under training. The whole team of officers – Norman Dingemans the First Lieutenant, Oliver Windle the Third Hand, Bill Taylor the Engineer, and Chris Walters the Fourth Hand – they all were so helpful and full of interesting stories but above all they taught and I learned quickly. It was hot and sticky in a diesel submarine in the South China Sea but when my time had ended and I went back to BULWARK I had made up my mind that submarines were for me.

In mid-1964 I was transferred to HMS CHAWTON, a ton class minesweeper which was being used as a patrol boat in the Singapore Straits at night. We spent two weeks at a time patrolling from 1800 until 0700 then anchoring in the commercial harbour for the day. It was an interesting and enjoyable time and again I learnt a great deal from those around me.

My two great friends Toby Elliott and Mike O'Driscoll were in similar ships and we spend the nights chasing saboteurs in sampans trying to get from Indonesia to Singapore. The ships were not really suited for this task but we did a reasonable job but at the loss of Mike O'Driscoll who was killed by a booby trapped sampan when he had gone into it to inspect it. He is buried in the Singapore War Cemetery and I have been to see his grave since then and I am pleased to say that it is looked after well.

By the end of 1964 CHAWTON was given a good maintenance period and all the officers changed except me. We went to the Persian Gulf and were stationed at Bahrain as the lead ship of the 7th Minesweeping Squadron.

Midshipmen Toby Elliott, Mike O'Driscoll and Roger Lane-Nott in the Officers Club at HMS TERROR in Singapore 1965

Midshipman Toby Elliott and Roger Lane-Nott in Singapore 1965

By mid-1966 I was back in UK, 21 years old, able to watch England win the World Cup and reported for submarine training at HMS DOLPHIN at Fort Blockhouse Gosport in September 1966.

So that is how I ended up in submarines and I wanted to write this book because so many books about submarines fail to explain what it is like to be in a submarine yet alone in command. All but one of the stories in this book are about my time as Commanding Officer of HMS SPLENDID, then the Royal Navy's latest nuclear submarine.

Before I took command in 1979 I had served in HMS OPOSSUM, HMS OTUS both based in Gosport, the new Polaris submarine HMS REVENGE(Starboard crew) as part of the building crew at Cammell Lairds in Birkenhead followed by 3 patrols, HMS CONQUEROR as Navigating Officer, and HMS AENEAS as First Lieutenant.

HMS OTUS in 1967

I completed the Commanding Officer's Qualifying Course (The Perisher) in 1974 and was appointed as Commanding Officer of HMS WALRUS for the next three years.

HMS WALRUS – 1975

Lieutenant Commander Roger Lane-Nott in Gosport 1976

Left to Right: Lt Neil Yockney, Lt David Kingham, Lt Tom Scully, Lt Roger Lane-Nott, Lt Pat Chapman, Lt Richard Peck, Lt Mike Browning

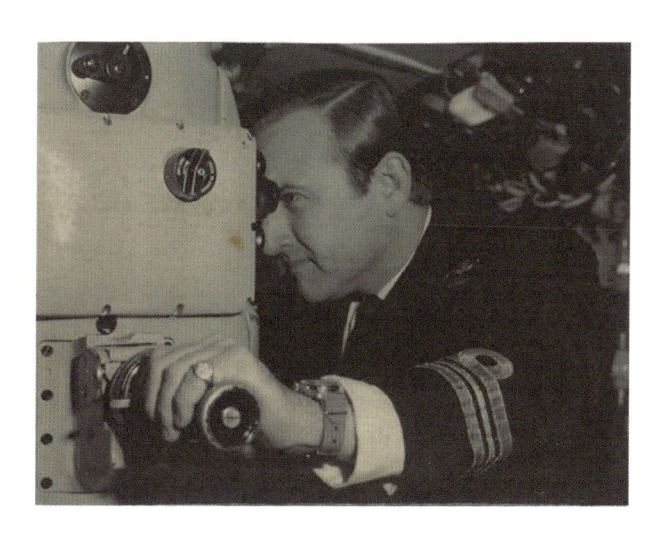

Lieutenant Commander Roger Lane-Nott at the periscope in HMS WALRUS

Commander Roger Lane-Nott on promotion in 1978

Two exciting years at Northwood HQ followed when I was in at the outset of the centralization of submarine Command and Control. Planning, running and controlling covert submarine operations at a time when the Soviets were being very adventurous. Flag Officer Submarine (Rear Admiral John Fieldhouse) moved his HQ from Gosport to Northwood in January 1978 and has controlled submarine operations from Northwood to this day. I was promoted in January 1979 and spent 10 months as Commanding Officer of SWIFTSURE before being appointed as the Commanding Officer of the latest nuclear submarine HMS SPLENDID which was building at Vickers in Barrow in Furness.

Launch of HMS SPLENDID 1979

Launch of HMS SPLENDID in Barrow in Furness 1979

Signing the Visitors Book at Barrow in Furness Town Hall after the Commissioning of HMS SPLENDID in 1981. Mrs. Roisin Lane-Nott is on the left.

Commissioning Ceremony March 1981

Mrs. Roisin Lane-Nott cutting the Commissioning Cake with the youngest sailor

HMS SPLENDID Officers in Faslane during workup 1981
Top row left to right: Lieutenant Jim Fergusson, Lieutenant Commander David Crothers, Commander Roger Lane-Nott, Lieutenant Commander Gavin Lane, Lieutenant Graham Holmes, Bottom Row left to right: Lieutenant Jeff Thomas, Sub Lieutenant Paul Slemon, Sub Lieutenant Toby Spreckley, Lieutenant Nick Harris, Lieutenant Frank Burton

After 3 years in HMS SPLENDID, including service in the Falklands War, and a year at the US Navy War College in Newport Rhode Island I spent 2 years as the Submarine Flotilla Warfare Officer in Northwood before promotion to Captain and appointment as Captain of the Third Submarine Squadron in Faslane.

Captain SM 3

Third Submarine Commanding Officers in Faslane in 1986 Left to Right: Commander Jeff Tall, Commander John Chadwick – Squadron Weapons Officer, Lieutenant Commander Malcom Avery, Commander E, Lieutenant Commander Paul Boissier, Commander Steve Ramm, Commander Mike Gilbert, Lieutenant Commander Chris Munns, Commander Dan Conley

With Her Royal Highness the Princess Royal at the Submarine
Attack Teacher in Faslane in 1986

After that I spent 2 years in the Ministry of Defence as Assistant Director Defence Concepts before attending the Royal College of Defence Studies in London for a year.

Captain Chris Wreford-Brown and Captain Roger Lane-Nott
do their bit to knock down the Berlin Wall during the Royal
College of Defence Studies visit to Berlin in 1989 about a week
before the demise of the Soviet Union

Following that I was appointed as Captain of HMS COVENTRY and Captain of the First Frigate Squadron based in Devonport. Apart from Command of HMS COVENTRY I was also responsible for the other five frigates in the First Frigate Squadron [HMS BRAVE, HMS BEAVER, HMS BOXER, HMS LONDON, HMS SHEFFIELD]. Apart from several towed array patrols, hosting the first Sea King helicopter to operate from a Type 22 frigate I commanded Group ZULU [HMS SCYLLA, HMS BRAVE, RFA ORANGELEAF] in the Gulf This included the latter stages of the First Gulf War and I was also the Senior Officer Middle East at this time.

HMS COVENTRY entering Plymouth 1991

HMS COVENTRY in Devonport

HMS COVENTRY with the US Battleship USS IOWA

HMS COVENTRY alongside HMS BELFAST at the Pool of London 1991

Talking to The Minister of Defence Mr. Tom King on the flight deck of HMS COVENTRY in Singapore in 1991

After 18 months at Northwood as Chief of Staff to Flag Officer Submarines I was promoted to Rear Admiral and appointed as Flag Officer Submarines and Commander Submarine eastern Atlantic in succession to Vice Admiral Sir Toby Frere who had been my "Teacher" during Perisher. So I was now the Head of the Submarine Service.

Flag Officer Submarines and Commander Submarines Eastern Atlantic 1993 – 1996

Accepting HMS VANGUARD, the Royal Navy's first Trident submarine into service in 1996
Left to Right: Captain John Boyd (CO Starboard Crew) Rear Admiral Roger Lane-Nott, Rear Admiral Richard Irwin (Chief Strategic Systems Executive) Captain David Russell (CO Port Crew)

HMS VANGUARD

On the bridge of HMS VANGUARD during the first Trident missile firings in Florida

On Board German Submarine U25 in 1995

Leaving the Royal Navy in a McLaren F1 Car in February 1996

After 32 years in the Royal Navy I retired in February 1996. The last 20 years are another story and not part of this book!

Launch of Cold War book – "We Come Unseen" 2001
Left to Right: Commander Jeff Tall, Commodore James Taylor, Commodore Martin MacPherson, Jim Ring (author) Captain Chris Wreford-Brown, Commodore Toby Elliott, Rear Admiral Roger Lane-Nott

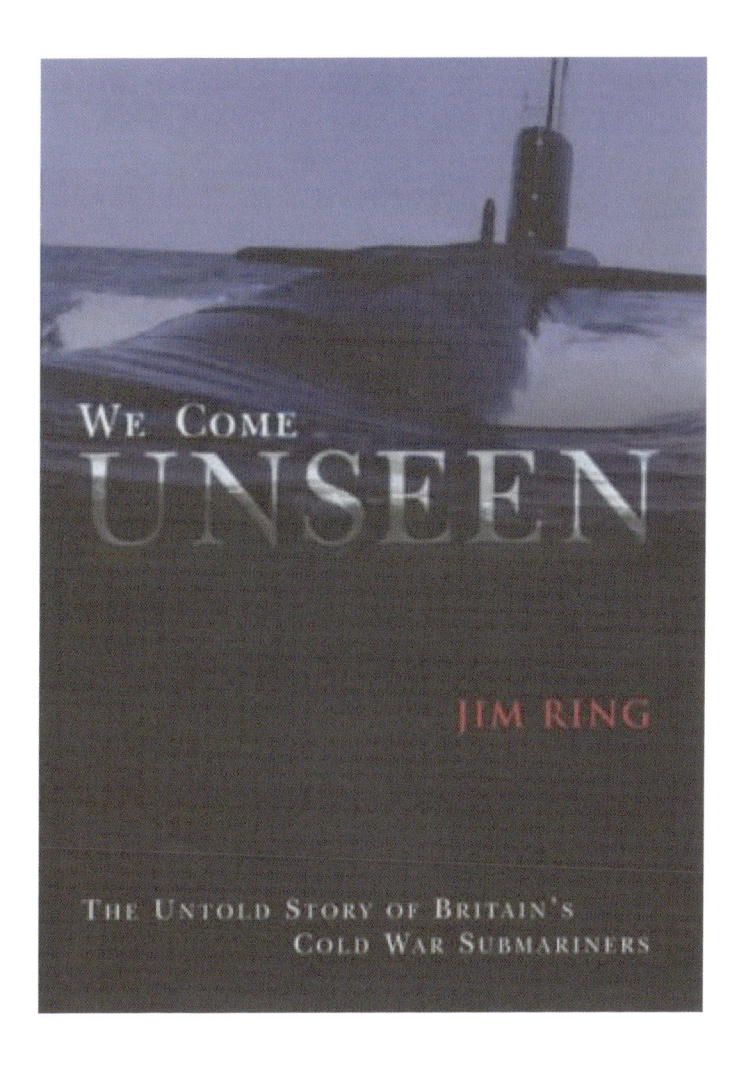

We Come UNSEEN

JIM RING

THE UNTOLD STORY OF BRITAIN'S COLD WAR SUBMARINERS

HMS SPLENDID Commanding Officers

Left to right:
Commander Bill Beatty, Captain Mark Stanhope (later First Sea Lord) Roger Lane-Nott, Vice Admiral Sir Ian McGeoch – Commanding Officer HMS SPLENDID in 1942, Captain Chris Roddis, Commander Nigel Hibbert

APPENDIX 2

HISTORY OF HMS SPLENDID

HMS SPLENDID was a Royal Navy nuclear powered fleet submarine of the Swiftsure class and much of this book recounts my time as its first Captain.

HMS SPLENDID was launched at Barrow on 5 October 1979, by Lady Ann Eberle, wife of Admiral Sir James Eberle, then Commander-in-Chief Fleet. The boat was built by Vickers Shipbuilding and Engineering Limited in Barrow in Furness in Lancashire, and between 1979 and 1982 was under the command of Commander Roger Charles Lane-Nott, Royal Navy. I had the privilege to be its first Commanding Officer.

Launched	5th October 1979
Commissioned	21st March 1981
Displacement	4900 tonnes (dived)
Length	82.9 m (272 feet)
Beam	9m (32ft 2")
Draught	8.5 m (27ft 11 in)
Propulsion	Rolls Royce Pressurised Water Nuclear Reactor (PWR 1)

Two WH Allen turbo generators
One Paxman diesel alternator
One emergency drive motor

HMS SPLENDID is capable of speeds underwater in excess of 30 knots. Her basic equipment includes a Kelvin Hughes Type 1006 navigational radar, a Type 2001 bow sonar array, a Plessey Type 2020 sonar array, a Marconi/Plessey Type 2074 sonar, a BAC Type 2007 flank array and a Ferranti Type 2046 towed array.

She is fitted with five [21inch] bow torpedo tubes. Armament can include the McDonnell Douglas UGM-84 Sub Harpoon Subsurface to Surface missiles, WW II diesel powered Mk 8 torpedoes which were still on board when I was in command, Mk 24 electric, wire guided Tigerfish torpedoes. Spearfish torpedoes and Tomahawk Cruise missiles were after my time.

She was very active during the Cold War and did several patrols against Soviet submarines. Her first major conflict came in 1982 during the Falklands War when Argentinian forces invaded the British-held Falkland Islands. Splendid was one of the first submarines to reach the islands, arriving mid-April, after sailing from Faslane.

Unlike HMS Conqueror, Splendid did not directly engage Argentinian forces, however she shadowed the Argentine carrier 25 de Mayo, the Splendid running within a mile outside of the Argentinian territorial line, 12 miles off its Atlantic coast.

The Captain of HMS Splendid made the bold and disputable claim, that running on the edge of the exclusion zone around the Falklands, declared by the UK government, he had the right in international law and approval from the British PM, to fire at the 25 de Mayo, a couple of miles away within Argentine waters, and would have fired MK 8 torpedoes at the 25 de Mayo, if he had confirmed his precise position. But just at the moment, he lost sight through the periscope of the carrier due to fog and was not immediately able to regain contact.

The Naval Commander of the task force, Admiral Sandy Woodward, does not appear to be entirely clear that HMS Splendid had the right to fire, but says he established, against his prior view, that the SPLENDID had orders to engage and approval of the PM. SPLENDID did however provide valuable reconnaissance to the Task Force on Argentine aircraft movements. Splendid's presence along with HMS Conqueror effectively restricted the freedom of action of the Argentine Navy, which spent most of the war confined to port.

In November 1998, the Royal Navy attained initial operational capability for the American-built Tomahawk Cruise Missiles with the missile's deployment aboard Splendid. In March 1999, Splendid fired Tomahawks in battle against Serbian targets during the Kosovo War, becoming the first British submarine in the conflict to do so; she would fire 20 Tomahawks throughout the war. She again fired these weapons against Iraqi targets in the 2003 invasion of Iraq.

In July 2003 HMS SPLENDID returned to her home at Faslane. The youngest of the Swiftsure class, she was decommissioned in Faslane in 2004.

HMS SPLENDID was present, along with the US Navy submarines the USS Memphis and USS Toledo at the Russian war games during which the Russian submarine Kursk exploded and sank, resulting in the loss of that submarine and all 118 sailors and officers on board.

Despite the conclusions of independent forensic inquiries and the eventual corroborating admission by the Russian navy that the explosion was triggered by a faulty torpedo on board the Kursk, various conspiracy theories posit that Kursk was actually sunk by one of the US or British submarines. This may partly stem from the Russian Navy's initial attempts to shunt away criticism of its failed efforts to rescue the surviving crew members from the ocean floor and of the generally poor condition of its own equipment, which was eventually found to be the cause of both the sinking and the failure of the Russian rescue attempts.

In the days immediately after the explosion, Russia suggested that the cause of the disaster was a collision with one of the US or British submarines present. Though the accusation proved to be unfounded, conspiracy theorists have inevitably picked up on and elaborated it in various directions over time.

After 23 years' service HMS SPLENDID was decommissioned in Devonport in 2004.

HMS SPLENDID flying 'paying off' pennant in 2004

Rear Admiral Roger Lane-Nott in Flag Officer Submarines HQ at Northwood with his Chief of Staff Commodore Martin MacPherson

APPENDIX 3

HMS SPLENDID SHIP'S COMPANY – 1982

Commander Roger Lane-Nott	Commanding Officer [CO]
Lieutenant Commander Ian Richards	Executive Officer/ First Lieutenant /No 1 [XO]
Commander John Davis	Marine Engineer Officer [MEO]
Lieutenant Commander David Crothers	Weapon Engineer Officer [WEO]
Lieutenant Commander Chris Gillooly	Deputy Marine Engineer Officer [DMEO]
Lieutenant Commander Mike Potter	Assistant Marine Engineer Officer [AMEO]
Lieutenant Ian Mackenzie	Navigating Officer [NO]
Lieutenant Tiny Holmes	Torpedo and Sonar Officer [TASO]
Lieutenant Commander Jim Fergusson	Supply Officer [SO]
Lieutenant Jeff Thomas	Communications Officer [SCO]
Lieutenant Paul Slemon	Deputy Weapons Engineer Officer [DWEO]
Lieutenant Tony Rowe	Assistant Marine Engineer Officer [AMEO]
Sub-Lieutenant Toby Spreckley	Casing Officer & Captain's Secretary Surgeon
Lieutenant Commander Chris Kalman	Medical Officer
Chief Petty Officer Roger Colborne	The Coxswain

Sonar Department

Chief Petty Officer (Sonar)	Jeff Thomas CPO (Ops) (Sonar)
Petty Officer Roger Crafts	PO Sonar
Petty Officer Danny Fisher	PO Sonar and Second Coxswain
Leading Seaman Nick Slide	Sonar Operator
Leading Seaman Mick Chandler	Sonar Operator Leading
Seaman Ian 'bomber' Wells	Sonar Operator Leading
Seaman Mick Kettleton	Sonar Operator
Leading Seaman Andy Rainey	Sonar Operator
Able Seaman 'jelly belly' Elliot	Sonar Operator
Able Seaman Andy Sims	Sonar Operator

Able Seaman 'Oily' Rigg   Sonar Operator
Able Seaman Pete Curran   Sonar Operator

Tactical Systems (TS)
Chief Petty Officer (TS) Ken Douglas   CPO (Ops) (TS)
Petty Officer (TS) Sean Runham   PO (TS)
Petty Officer (TS) Collin   TS Operator
Leading Seaman Pip Cox   TS Operator
Leading Seaman John Boddy   TS Operator
Able Seaman Smallwood   TS Operator
Able Seaman Scott   TS Operator
Able Seaman Berry   TS Operator
Able Seaman Padgett   TS Operator
Able Seaman Few   TS Operator

Communications Department
Chief Radio Supervisor 'Pincher' Martin   Chief Radio Supervisor
Leading Radio Operator Kenyon   Radio Operator
Radio Operator Whitehouse   Radio Operator
Radio Operator Mortel   Radio Operator

Supply & Secretariat Department
Chief Petty Officer Stores Accountant Turner   Stores Accountant
Leading Stores Accountant Weaver   Stores Accountant
Petty Officer Cook Barny Barnard   Petty Officer Cook
Leading Cook Pete Preston   Leading Cook
Cook Jones   Cook
Cook Sturman   Cook
Petty Officer Steward Eddie McCabe   PO Steward
Steward Savage   Steward
Steward Brumbley   Steward
Leading Writer Max Wall   Leading Writer

Forward Mechanical Department
Marine Engineering Mechanic 1   George Elward – Outside Wrecker
Chief Marine Engineering Mechanic McLaughlin
                                                 Chief Stoker
MEMN Buster Brown   Outside Staff

LMEM Chunky Evans   Outside Staff
MEMN Conway   Outside Staff
Leading MEMN Holmes   Outside Staff
MEM Phil Potterton   Outside Staff
MEM Turner   Outside Staff
MEM Duval   Outside Staff

Forward Weapons Department
WEMN Soapy Watson   Weapons
Weapons Artificer Neil French   Weapons
WEMN Mac Blenkinsop   Weapons
WEMN Hancock   Weapons
WEMN 1 Steve Hogg   Ordnance Artificer
Chief Petty Officer Geoff Matthews Torpedo Instructor
WEA Peter Harris   Weapons
WEA Keith Knight   Radio Artificer
PO Sutherland   POLTO
LWEM Nick Addison   Weapons
LWEM Chris Shone   Weapons
LWEM Briggs   Weapons
WEM Taff Simons   Weapons
LWEM Andy Trewin   Weapons

Propulsion Engineering Department
Nuclear Chiefs of the Watch [NCOOW]
Fleet Chief MEA Turner   Nuclear Chief of the Watch
MEA Grove   Nuclear Chief of the Watch
CMEMN McCarthy   Nuclear Chief of the Watch
CMEMN Godfrey   Nuclear Chief of the Watch

Reactor Panel Operators
MEA Gardner   Reactor Panel Operator
MEA Lomax   Reactor Panel Operator
MEA Tose   Reactor Panel Operator

Electrical Panel Operators
MEA Paddy Porter   Electrical Panel Operator
POMEM Jarvis   Electrical Panel Operator
POMEM Jacobs   Electrical Panel Operator

MEAOW
MEA Jim Knight   MEA of the Watch & TG Tiff
MEMN Western   MEA of the Watch & PPO
MEA Stoker   MEA of the Watch

Main Machinery Space Senior Rates
MEA Reynolds   Main Machinery
MEA Harding   Main Machinery
POMEM Jackson   Main Machinery

Diesel Generator Room
LMEM Carter   Diesel Generator
LMEM Frank Grinnall   Diesel Generator
MEM Smith   Diesel Generator

Main Machinery Space Junior Rates
MEM Buxton   Engine Room Lower Level
LMEM Brown   Engine Room Lower Level
MEM Johnson   Engine Room Lower Level

Medical Department
Chief Petty Officer "Doc" Fraser
Leading Medical Assistant Thorpe
Medical Assistant Smith

ACKNOWLEDGEMENTS

I would like to thank the following for their support and photos in the writing of this book:

Commander Ian Richards
Lieutenant Commander David Crothers
Lieutenant Jim Fergusson
Sub Lieutenant Paul Slemon
Leading Seaman Nick Slide
MEA Jim Knight
OA Steve Hogg
and the Officers and Ship's Company of HMS SPLENDID who were the best and supported me so well.

Thank you to Toby Vintcent for 'publishing' the book in this form.

And, of course, to my wife Roisin for putting up with me!

Printed in Great Britain
by Amazon